IMAGES
of America

CARSON

ON THE COVER: This 1908 photograph depicts dairy operations on the Carson estate. (Courtesy Special Collections and Archives, California State University, Dominguez Hills.)

IMAGES
of America

CARSON

Cindy Tino-Sandoval

ARCADIA
PUBLISHING

ISBN 978-0-7385-3104-5

Published by Arcadia Publishing
Charleston, South Carolina

Printed in the United States of America

Library of Congress Catalog Card Number: 2005936978

For all general information contact Arcadia Publishing at:
Telephone 843-853-2070
Fax 843-853-0044
E-mail sales@arcadiapublishing.com
For customer service and orders:
Toll-Free 1-888-313-2665

Visit us on the Internet at www.arcadiapublishing.com

Contents

ACKNOWLEDGMENTS

This book is intended to provide an enjoyably visual look at the history of Carson, California, where I reside and gratefully own a home. As such, it was important to me, as it is to Arcadia Publishing, to group together a substantial number of images that, cumulatively, would be nearly otherwise inaccessible to the interested public. It has been my humble pleasure to be allowed to glean photographs and other historic documents that are pertinent to the Rancho San Pedro, of which Carson was the cultural and geographic center, from the Special Collections and Archives of California State University, Dominguez Hills. Thanks are due to archives director Gregory Williams and his staff for their patience and hospitality. Of course, images mean little apart from their context, and for this I must give credit to those works that are truly scholarly, which are included in the bibliography at the back of the book. Smiling thanks are also due to Gil Smith, former mayor and councilman, for his generous contribution of both images and firsthand lore, and for introducing me to many people for whom dedication to this city is a true mission. Thanks also to Ms. Iva Voldase for her photographs and commentary, and to Carson High School, especially Sandy Jiles in the student store. At city hall, Sherri Repp and Nate Williams provided access to photographs with enthusiastic support from Carole Keen. I would also like to thank the Apollo West Players, director/commissioner Marvin Clayton, and Marilyn Dorlac. Joe Merton provided images from the Filipino community, and Jim Bono allowed my nose (and camera) into his kitchen at Rosario's. My husband Ed Sandoval's old friends, Steve Macera, Skip Babbit, and the Veek family, also generously shared their stories and images. Kellogg Garden Products has indeed been keepers of community history throughout their 80 years in Carson, and its contributions have been graciously shared by the lovely Jan Kellogg. Very special thanks also go to the Claretian Brothers at the Dominguez Seminary for providing the historic Rancho Adobe to the community as a museum, and to Donna Harris, its tireless curator, for welcoming others and myself into its fold of docents. And last, but not least, thanks to the Dominguez family descendants for keeping history alive by continuing to foster a family legacy of community enrichment.

INTRODUCTION

The city known today as Carson, California, was a long time in the making, and it is deeply rooted in early California history. The earliest human history of the area is that of the local Native Americans, the Suanga Indians, whose original village site has been commemorated as a state landmark in the Watson Industrial Center. The land was then barren, grassy plains and low, rolling hills that were subject to seasonal flooding and droughts, but they were rich with grazing and agricultural possibilities. As with several other California communities, the 1769 expedition of Gaspar de Portola first brought this land to the attention of Spanish explorers and missionaries. Juan José Dominguez, a member of the volunteer guard known as the "leatherjackets," accompanied de Portola's mission northward from San Diego to establish a colony in Monterey, primarily to keep the area from falling into Russian hands. Ultimately, this expedition failed to "find" Monterey, although it camped on its beach without recognizing it.

Juan José Dominguez, however, had taken note of the land's vast richness along the way and toward the end of a lengthy military career petitioned for, and was awarded, a 76,000-acre land grant by the king of Spain in 1784. This land was located strategically between the port at San Pedro and the Pueblo de Los Angeles and was well watered by rivers and channels. Don José, however, spent most of his retirement at the presidio in San Diego and accomplished little for the rancho's development, leaving his large herds of cattle and horses (5,000 horses, according to the 1805 census) to roam the hills unmanaged and unbranded, much to the frustration of his neighbors. A few years after Don José's death, his nephew Cristobal Dominguez struggled for many years to free the rancho from its "administrator," Manuel Gutierrez, who refused to give up possession. Yet, under Gutierrez's management, the Rancho San Pedro had begun to prosper. Cristobal died in 1825. In 1834, the rancho was legally returned to Dominguez heirs, although Palos Verdes was deeded to the Sepulvedas in the process.

Of Cristobal's three sons, Manuel Dominguez took the greatest interest in his family's hard-won legacy. He built his adobe home on Dominguez Hill in 1826, where it still stands on unincorporated Los Angeles County territory at the northeast end of Carson. Don Manuel, just 22 when he took over rancho operations, was studious, articulate, well read, spoke English fluently, and was a devout Catholic. Significant works on the early history of California are filled with narratives on his business and political careers, as well as the importance of his home as a social center and stopover between Los Angeles and San Pedro. Manuel, who had married Maria Engracia Cota in 1827, had 10 children; two died in infancy and two in young adulthood. Their six surviving daughters were born between 1829 and 1847. For extended accounts of the fascinating lives of the Dominguez family, there are recommend works in the bibliography.

Many people don't know it, but the Carson area was the site of a skirmish during the Mexican-American War known as the Battle of Rancho Dominguez, which took place on October 8, 1846, as American troops were advancing toward Los Angeles. On the American side, the more than 300 foot soldiers were armed with muskets; the mounted Mexican force of 100 had only bladed lances and one very small cannon on wheels. Lasting only hours, the battle ended with the retreat of the Americans, whose limited accuracy with the muskets could not repel the swift horsemen. Manuel and his family were not involved in the conflict, although they were compelled to house and feed the Americans who had camped on their land.

In 1855, Manuel and Maria's middle daughter, Dolores Simona, married lawyer James Alexander Watson. In 1857, another daughter, Maria Victoria, married George Henry Carson. These unions were significant to the history of Carson, in that the city was named after John Manuel Carson, George's son, who brought farming operations into the 20th century under the Carson Estate Company. James A. Watson died suddenly in 1869 before the age of 50, and eventually his widow Dolores Simona returned to the rancho to live out her years. Her four sons established homesteads of their own near and around the ranch. Their activities led to the formation of the Watson Estate Company, which managed family lands.

During the early 1900s, many aspiring farm families moved into the area, and the Dominguez Estate Company began to sell and lease some of its lands. The first real subdivision of land into plots was called Nestoria, later known as Keystone, which was located approximately between Figueroa Street and Avalon Boulevard, from around 213th Street to 228th Street. Oil operations owned by the Dominguez family still occupied much of the northeastern territory.

The area's population grew substantially after the Great Depression, and in addition to farming and oil, commercial and industrial businesses located here. Carson experienced the same postwar housing boom as other Southern California suburbs and struggled to make sure the growing community was supported by shopping venues and other necessary commercial amenities.

As unincorporated county territory, Carson had long been the repository for the garbage, waste, and automotive junk of the established South Bay cities, which provided considerable blight to challenge the growing community. As part and parcel of this challenge, it became necessary to unite the scattered residential areas under a single entity, and ultimately city hood.

Eventually the name "Carson" was chosen, with "Dominguez" coming in a close second. For a detailed account of these early days and the struggle for incorporation, see Jack Jerrills's book, *The History of a City: Carson California.* Carson was finally incorporated as a city on February 20, 1968, at Carson High School before a crowd of more than 600 residents. Several of those far-sighted individuals involved are still active in Carson politics and community service.

Today Carson is a thriving city with many attractive, sparkling commercial and residential developments. Along with its population, which numbered nearly 90,000 at the turn of the 21st century, Carson's ethnic diversity includes more than 30 percent Latinos and more than 20 percent each of African Americans, Asian/Pacific Islander (mostly Filipinos, but also Samoans), and Caucasians, with many other ethnicities represented in smaller numbers. As a community, it is this diversity that is a unique strength among the cities of the South Bay. Carson is a city whose slogan "future unlimited" continues to be proven true.

One

Rancho San Pedro

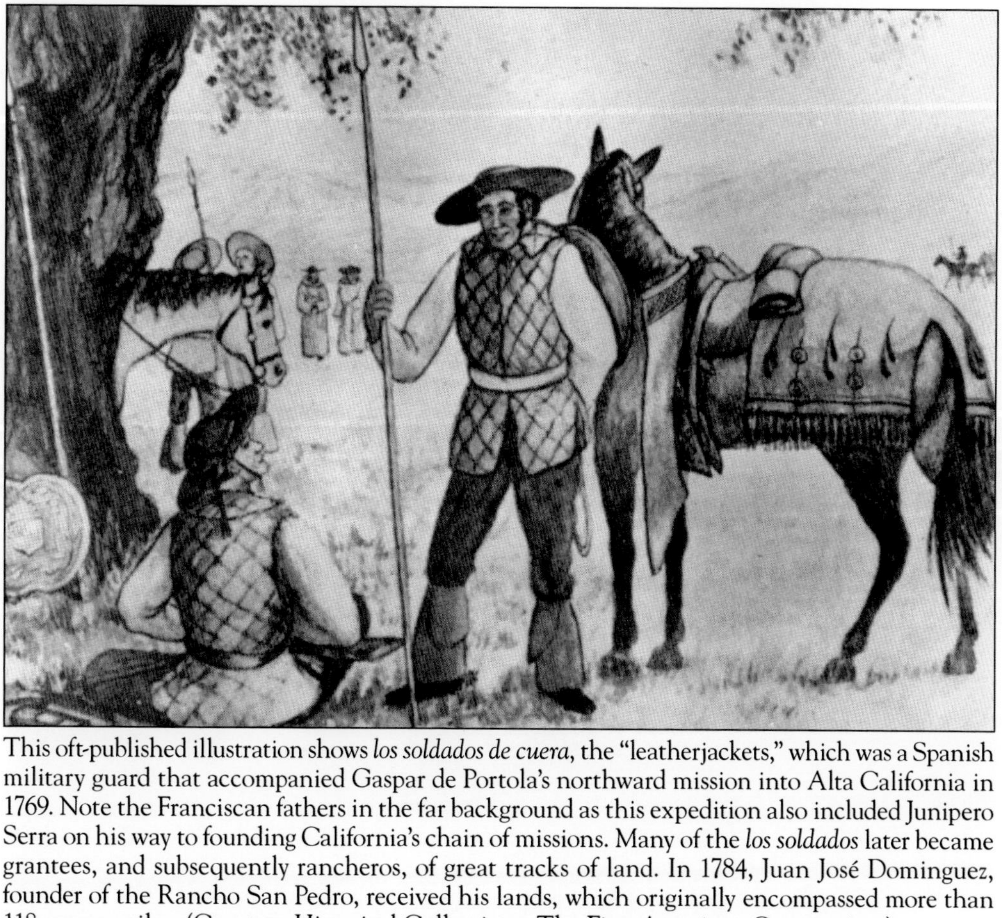

This oft-published illustration shows *los soldados de cuera*, the "leatherjackets," which was a Spanish military guard that accompanied Gaspar de Portola's northward mission into Alta California in 1769. Note the Franciscan fathers in the far background as this expedition also included Junipero Serra on his way to founding California's chain of missions. Many of the *los soldados* later became grantees, and subsequently rancheros, of great tracks of land. In 1784, Juan José Dominguez, founder of the Rancho San Pedro, received his lands, which originally encompassed more than 118 square miles. (Courtesy Historical Collections, The First American Corporation.)

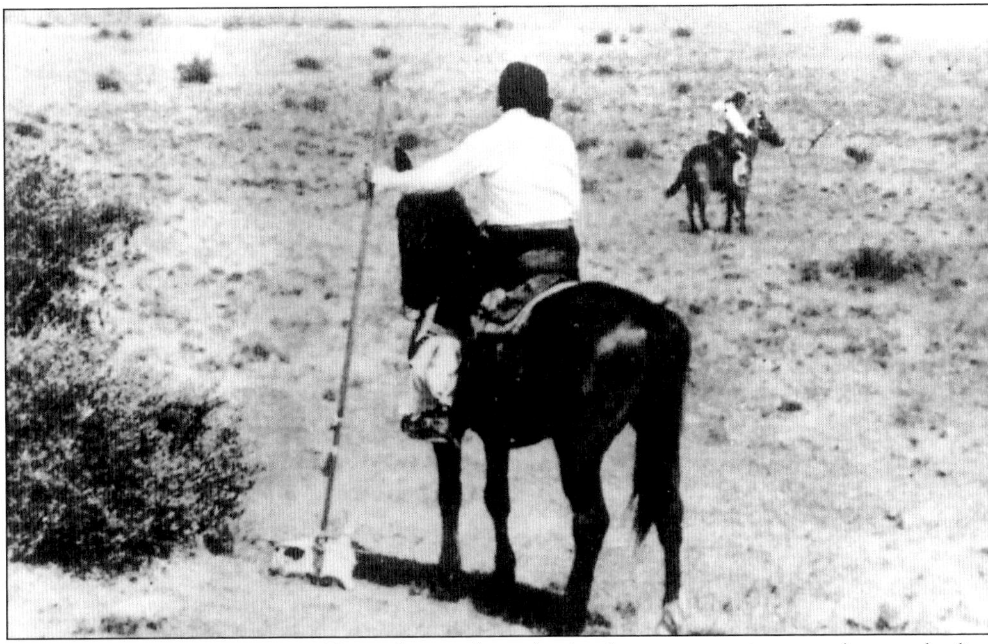

The earliest measurements and boundaries of rancho land were approximate at best and relied on landmarks such as cattle skulls, trees, gullies, and rocks. As more properties became occupied, more accurate measurements became necessary. Advanced measurement methods included surveys made on horseback, using a 50-*vara reata* (approximately 50 yards), and placing boundary markers at every 20-such intervals. This c.1870 photograph shows surveyors on unidentified rancho lands. (Courtesy Historical Collections, The First American Corporation.)

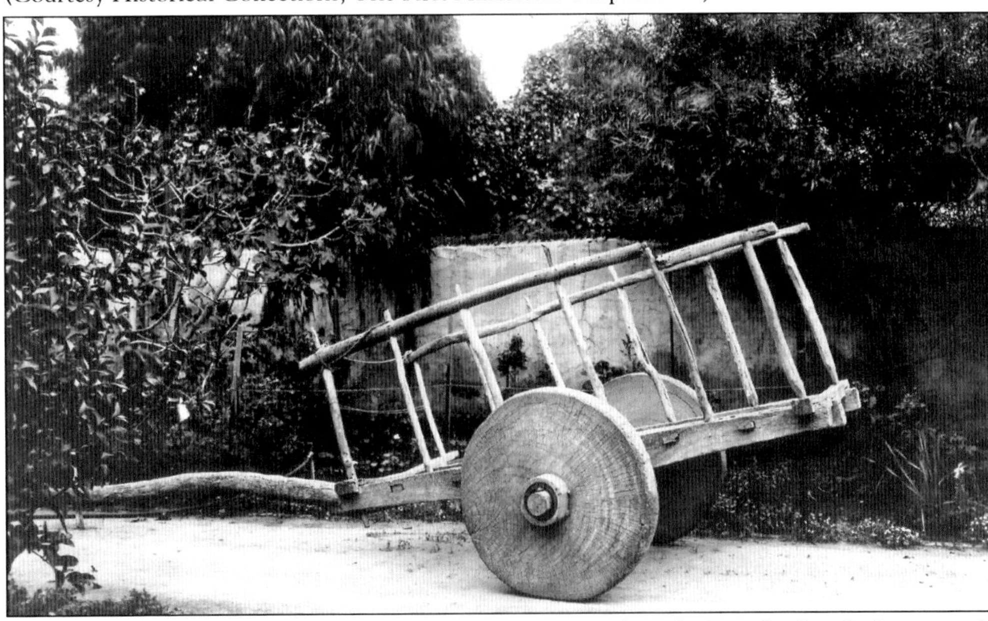

Primitive *carretas*, or carts, such as the one above, were used on the Rancho San Pedro not only as practical farm implements, but also for land measurement by means of flagging a wheel and counting its rotations. Four-wheeled wagons were not used for hauling until after 1850. (Courtesy Special Collections and Archives, California State University, Dominguez Hills.)

This corroded iron stake was used as a boundary marker in the late 1800s. (Courtesy Historical Collections, The First American Corporation.)

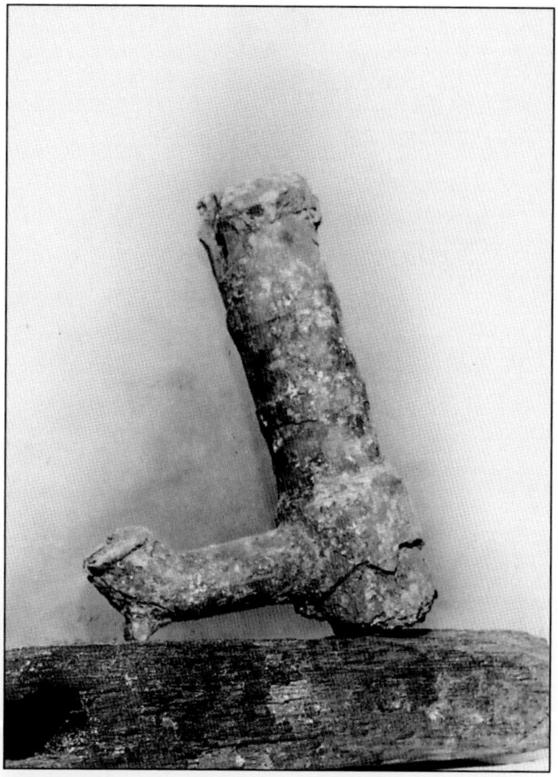

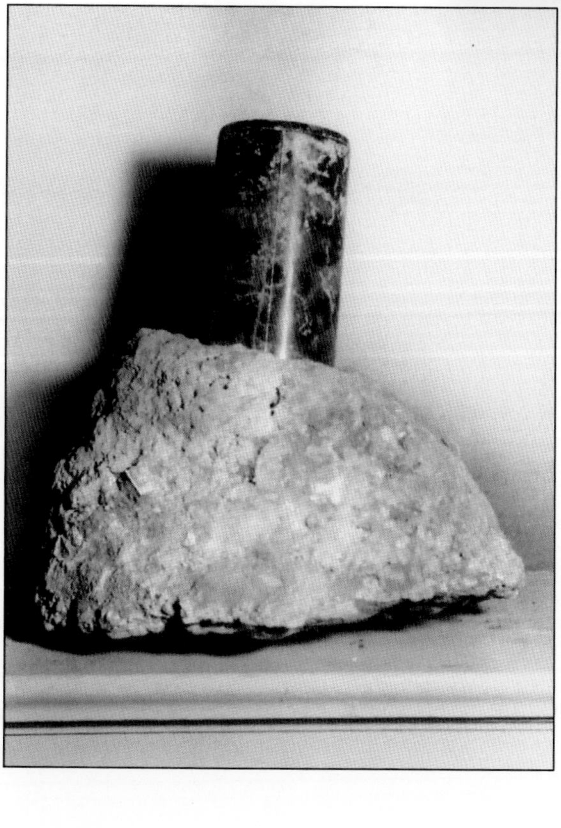

Pictured here is a slightly more modern version of the above boundary marker, embedded in concrete. (Courtesy Historical Collections, The First American Corporation.)

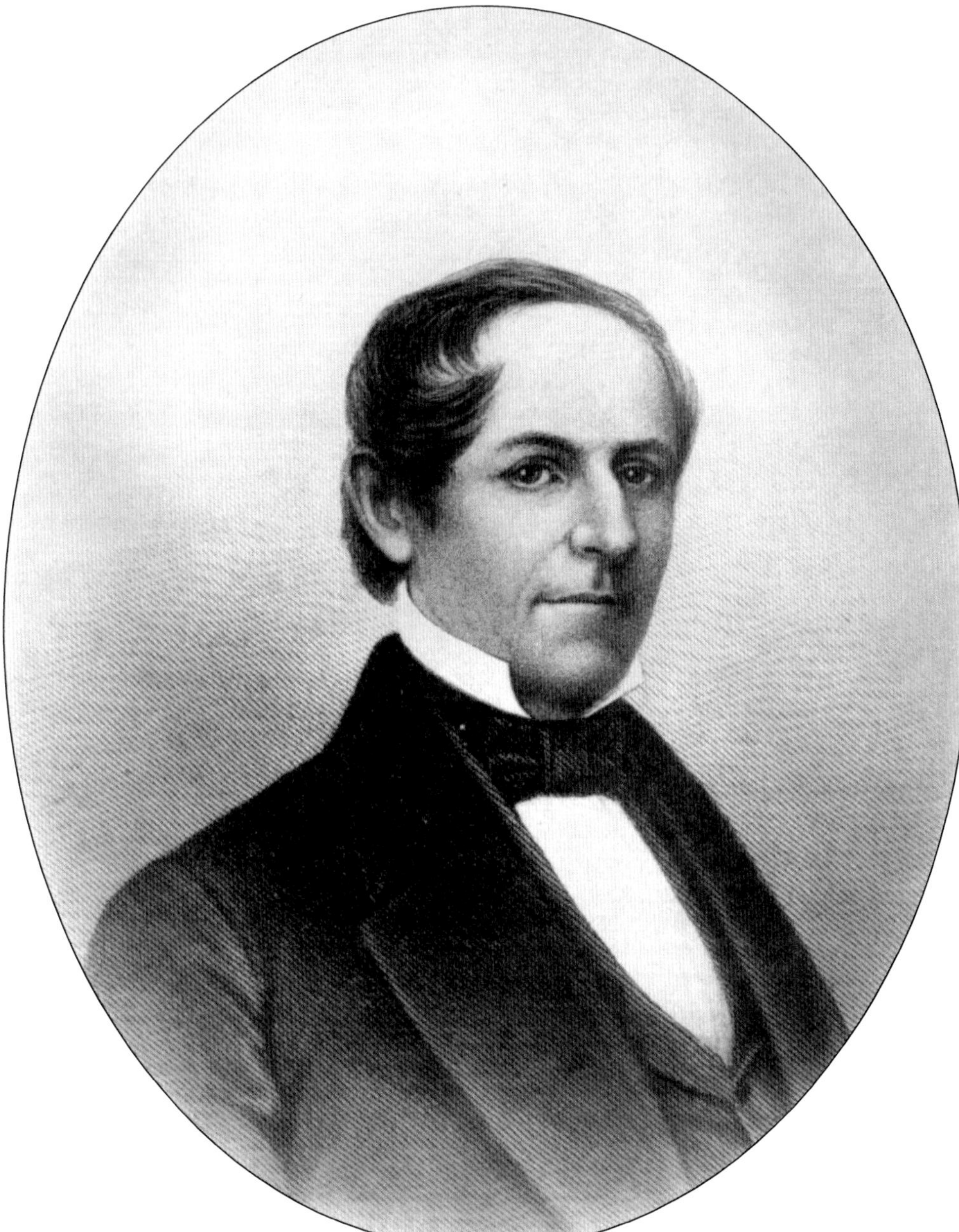

This is a portrait of Manuel Dominguez (born in 1803) around 1854. Don Manuel, grandnephew of Juan José Dominguez, was the son of Cristobal Dominguez, Juan José's nephew, and heir to the rancho. After Cristobal Dominguez's death, Manuel actively took over rancho operations and completed construction of his own home close to, but much larger than, that occupied by Juan José. (Courtesy Special Collections and Archives, California State University, Dominguez Hills.)

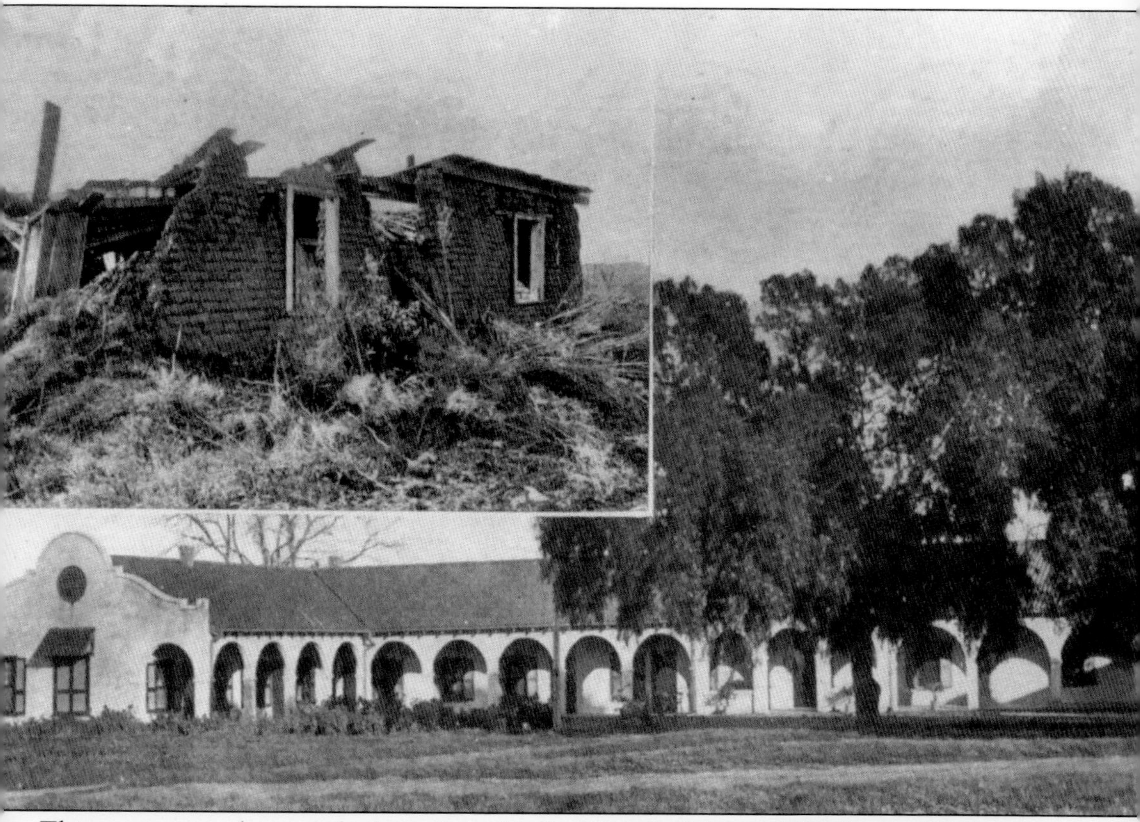

This composite photograph shows Juan José's original adobe and the home of Manuel Dominguez, built in 1826. (Courtesy Special Collections and Archives, California State University, Dominguez Hills.)

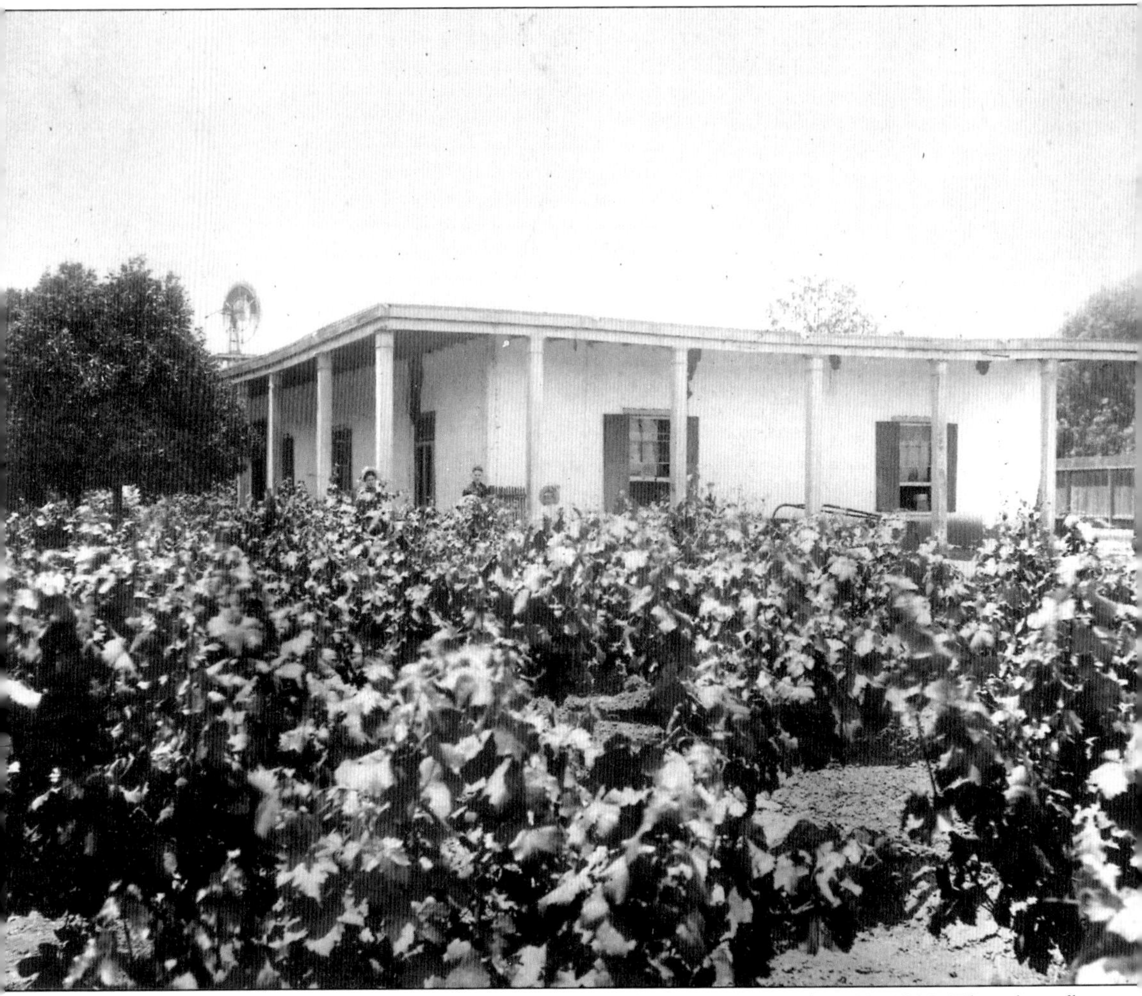

This image shows the north end of Don Manuel's home on December 28, 1888. The plain flat roof was later sloped and covered with red tile. A close look reveals three faces, two women and a child, next to the building. Under magnification, the woman in the middle looks like Maria Victoria Dominguez. (Courtesy Special Collections and Archives, California State University, Dominguez Hills.)

A *reata*, or braided leather rope, had many uses on the rancho. (Courtesy Historical Collections, The First American Corporation.)

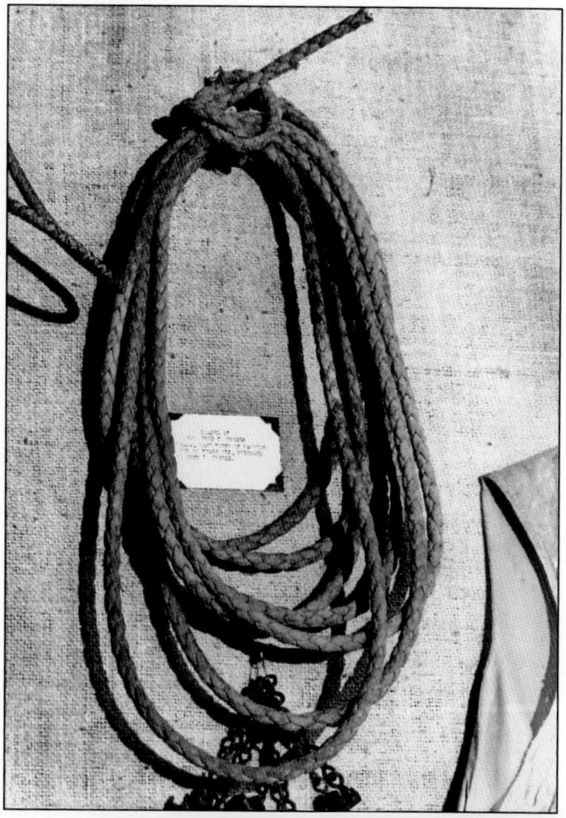

Dueling pistols such as these could be used to resolve more serious matters among the landed gentry. (Courtesy Historical Collections, The First American Corporation.)

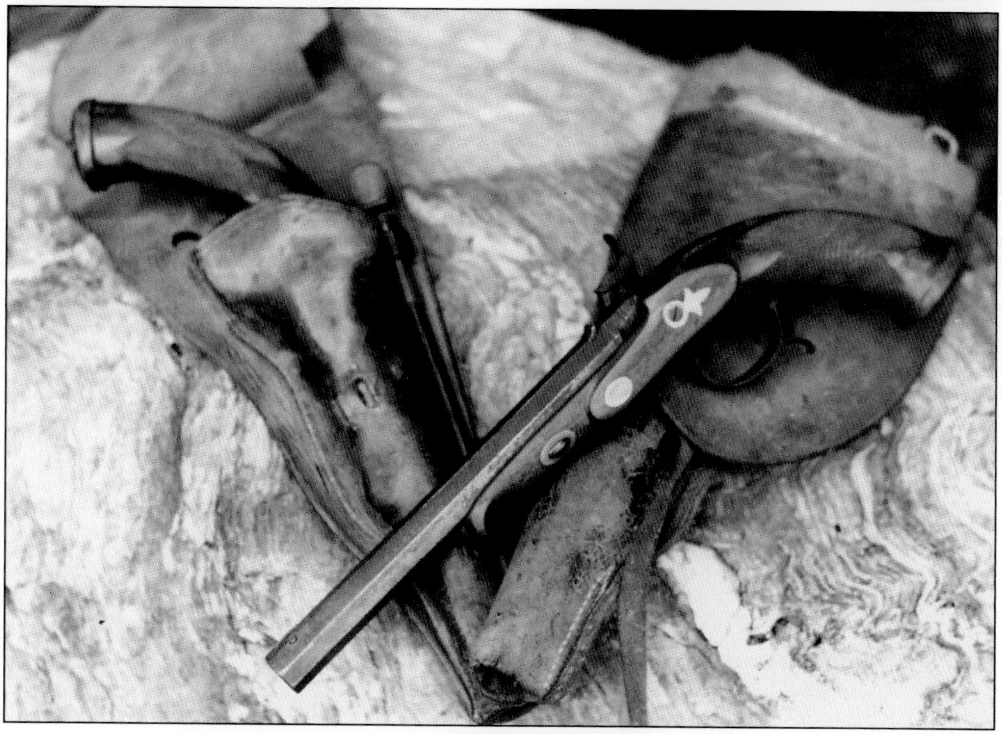

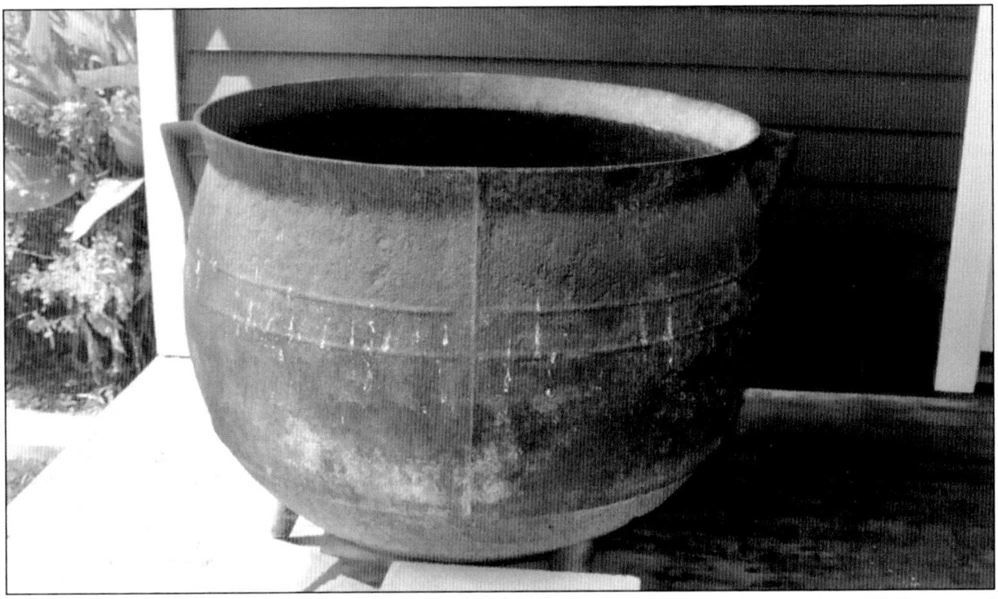

This large iron cauldron was used for boiling beef fat to make tallow on the ranchos. Tallow, used for candles and soap, was worth more than twice as much as the meat, which was often thrown away, although later there was a market for dried beef (*carne seca*) after the gold rush began. This particular cauldron was used on the Rancho Cañon de Santa Ana, owned by Bernardo Yorba. His father, José Antonio Yorba, was a contemporary of Juan José Dominguez, who was also part of the de Portola expedition. Yorba received his own 62,516-acre land grant in Southern California around the same time Dominguez received his.

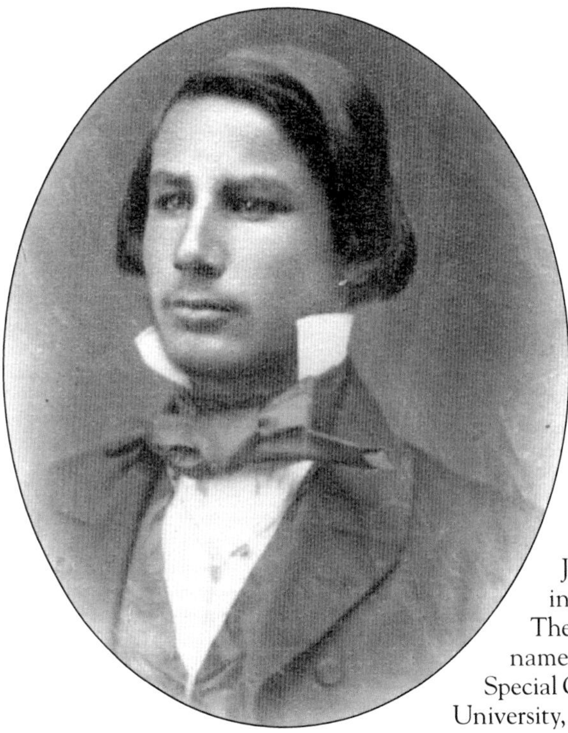

Manuel Antonio Dominguez, the eldest son of Manuel Dominguez, died in Los Angeles of tuberculosis in 1858 at the age of 20. Don Manuel's only other son, José Antonio, died from injuries sustained in a riding accident in 1863 at the age of 23. These sons never married, and the Dominguez name was not directly carried on. (Courtesy Special Collections and Archives, California State University, Dominguez Hills.)

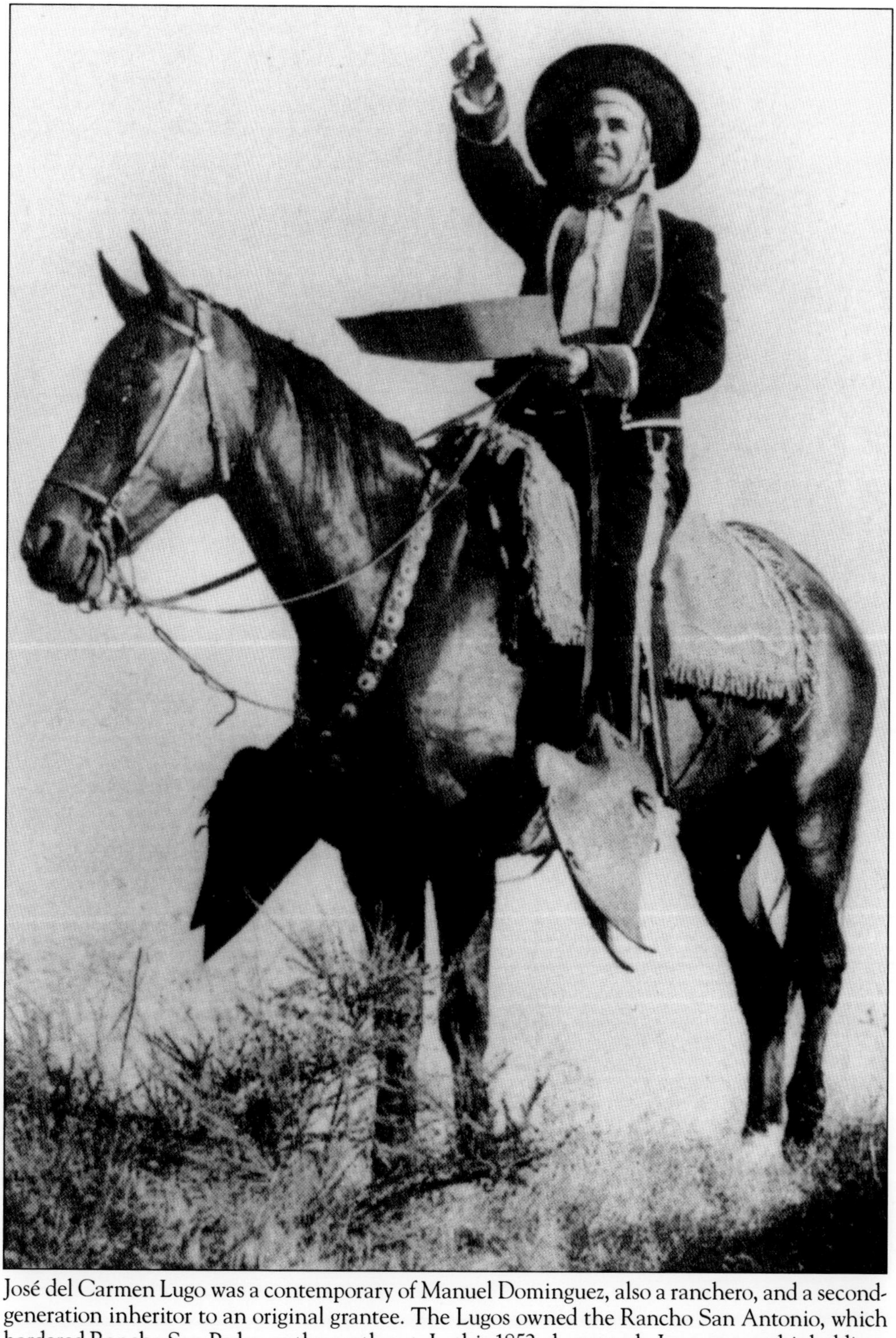

José del Carmen Lugo was a contemporary of Manuel Dominguez, also a ranchero, and a second-generation inheritor to an original grantee. The Lugos owned the Rancho San Antonio, which bordered Rancho San Pedro on the northeast. In this 1852 photograph, Lugo surveys his holdings "as far as the eye can see." (Courtesy Historical Collections, The First American Corporation.)

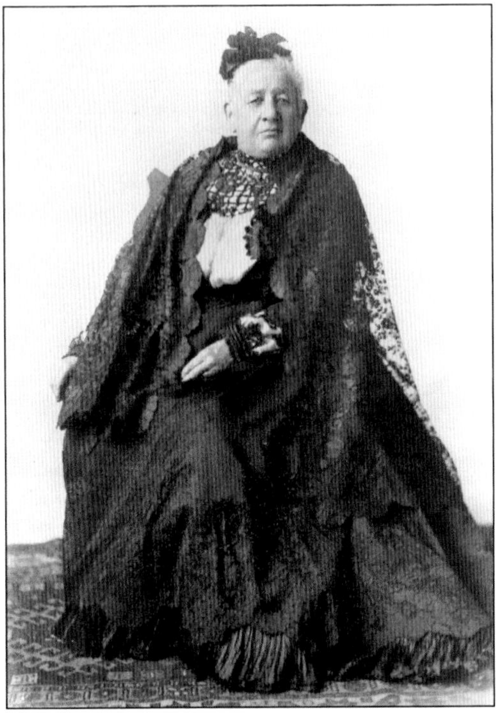

Ana Josepha Juliana Dominguez de Guyer (1829–1907) was the eldest of Manuel and Maria Dominguez's 10 children, two of whom died in infancy. She was the only one to have been born on the rancho and among the six surviving daughters was, by all accounts, one of the most attractive Spanish belles of her day. Along with her mother, Ana Josepha helped to manage the household and was over 40 when she married Judge William G. Dryden. She was widowed one year later when the judge died of a heart attack at the age of 70. In 1884, she married Charles Guyer, whose interests included real estate, banking, and horses. By mutual agreement, Guyer inherited no rancho lands upon her death in 1907. (Courtesy Special Collections and Archives, California State University, Dominguez Hills.)

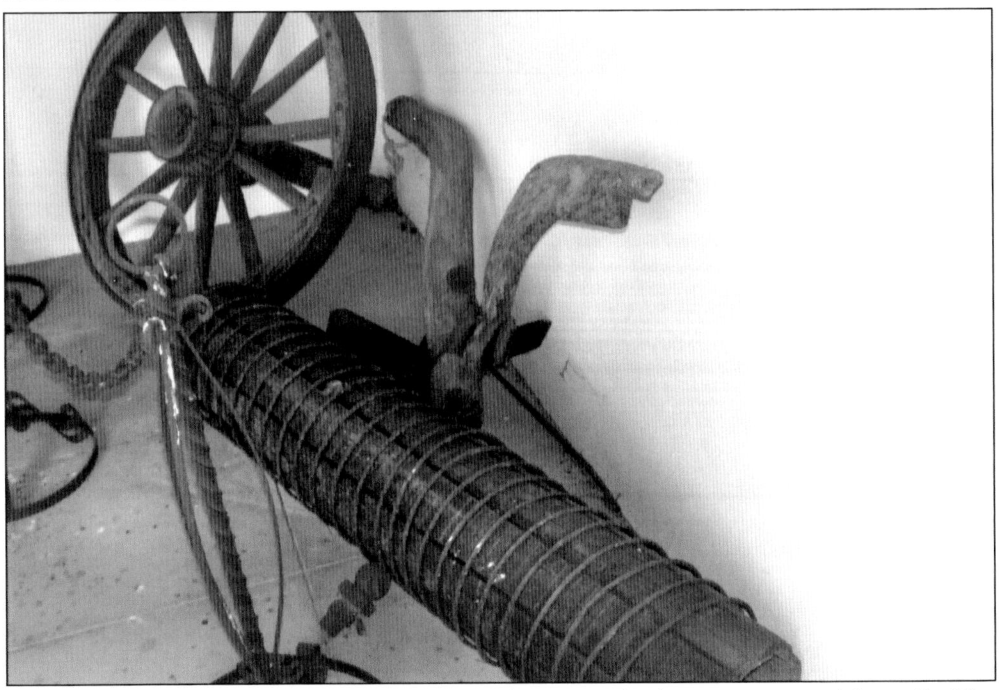

Farm implements from different eras of the Rancho San Pedro lean against its adobe walls. The primitive wooden harness yoke was probably used for a single ox to pull a *carreta* (cart) while the iron-and-wood wagon wheel with hubs was from closer to the beginning of the 20th century. The water pipe is made of redwood slats, which expanded when wet and were held together by iron strapping.

Judge William Dryden, Ana Josepha's first husband, is pictured here around 1868. They resided in Los Angeles at Fifth and Los Angeles Streets. (Courtesy Special Collections and Archives, California State University, Dominguez Hills.)

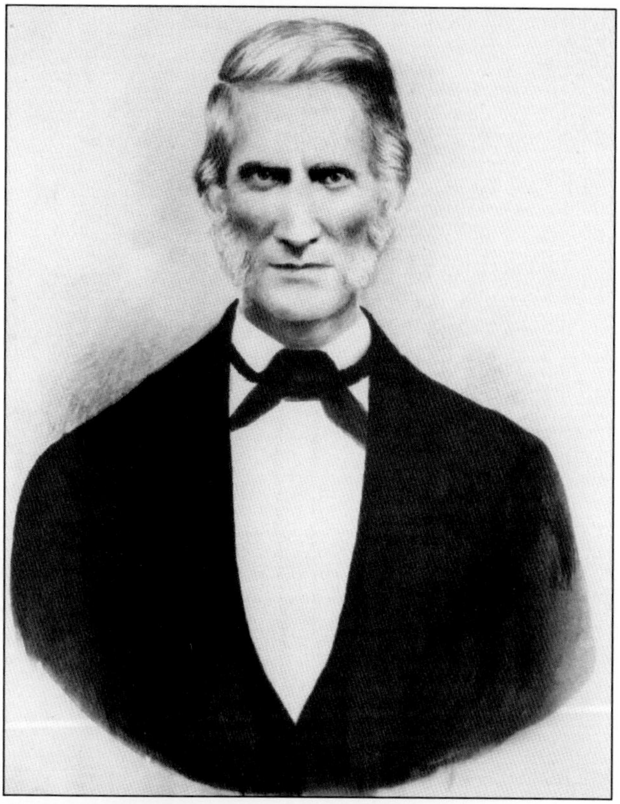

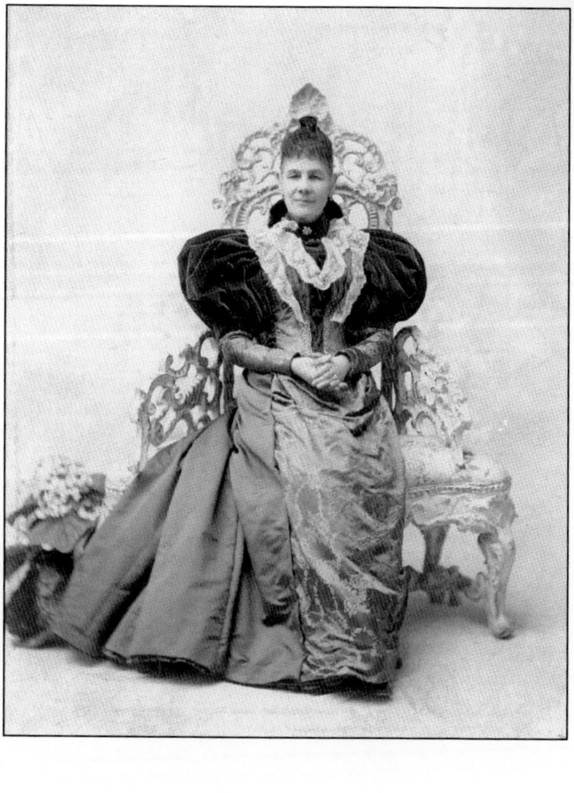

Another of Don Manuel's daughters, Guadalupe Marcelina Dominguez, is seen here around 1885. The only daughter who never married, Guadalupe cared for her parents in their later years and was described as reserved and formal. She was a major contributor to the Catholic Diocese of Los Angeles and dedicated a memorial window to her parents in St. Vibiana's Cathedral in downtown Los Angeles. (Courtesy Special Collections and Archives, California State University, Dominguez Hills.)

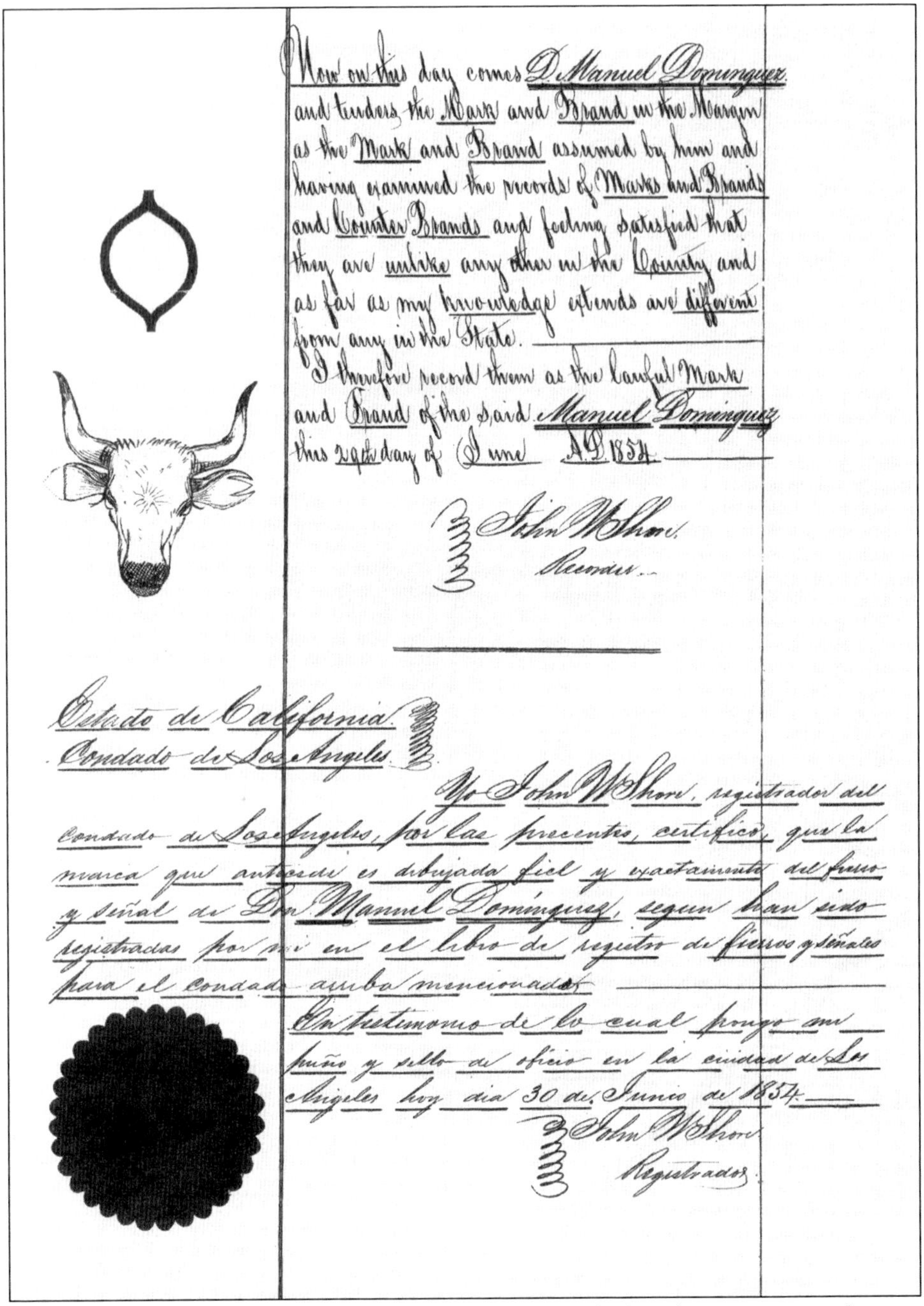

Now on this day comes D. Manuel Dominguez and tenders the Mark and Brand in the Margin as the Mark and Brand assumed by him and having examined the records of Marks and Brands and Counter Brands and feeling satisfied that they are unlike any other in the County and as far as my knowledge extends are different from any in the State.

I therefore record them as the lawful Mark and Brand of the said Manuel Dominguez this 29th day of June A.D. 1854.

John W. Shore.
Recorder.

Estado de California.
Condado de Los Angeles.

Yo John W. Shore, registrador del condado de Los Angeles, por las presentes, certifico, que la marca que antecede es dibujada fiel y exactamente del fierro y señal de Don Manuel Dominguez, segun han sido registradas por mi en el libro de registro de fierros y señales para el condado arriba mencionado.

En testimonio de lo cual pongo mi puño y sello de oficio en la ciudad de Los Angeles hoy dia 30 de Junio de 1854.

John W. Shore
Registrador.

Reproduced here is Don Manuel's brand registration. Previously thought to represent a lemon, the brand has recently been reinterpreted as an oxen yoke after an observation by a family descendent, who was "disappointed" by the mistake. In fact, lemons were never cultivated as crops by Manuel Dominguez. After 1900, George Henry Carson did plant about 200 acres of lemons and oranges, but they were never very profitable and were removed by 1932. Cattle were also notched at the ears for identification from the front and upon sale were branded at the shoulder to indicate release by the former owner. (Courtesy Special Collections and Archives, California State University, Dominguez Hills.)

Manuel and Maria's fifth daughter, Maria Dolores, married James Alexander Watson when she was 17. They took their vows at the old Plaza Church in downtown Los Angeles on October 13, 1855, and she was henceforth Maria Dolores Simona de Watson. Her husband had been a U.S. army colonel and lawyer and served as a California state assemblyman for five years. After he died suddenly in 1869, she was left with four sons under the age of 10. She remained at their home in Los Angeles until 1887, when she returned to the rancho where her sons began farming the family lands. (Courtesy Special Collections and Archives, California State University, Dominguez Hills.)

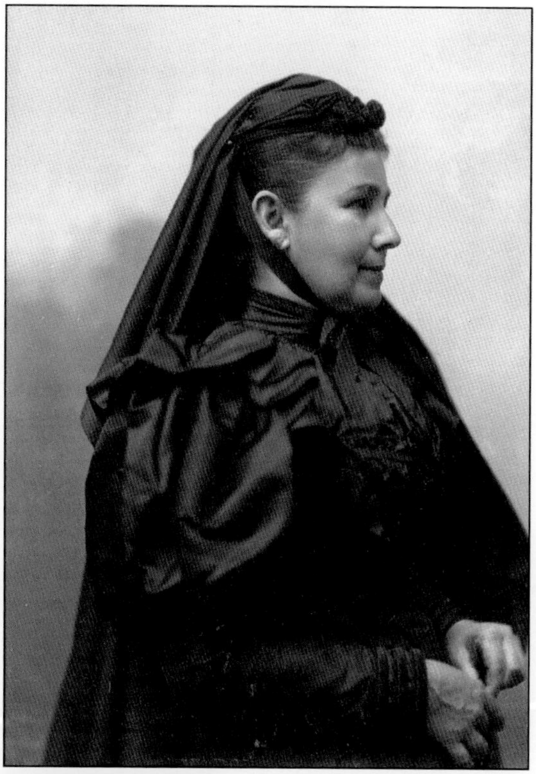

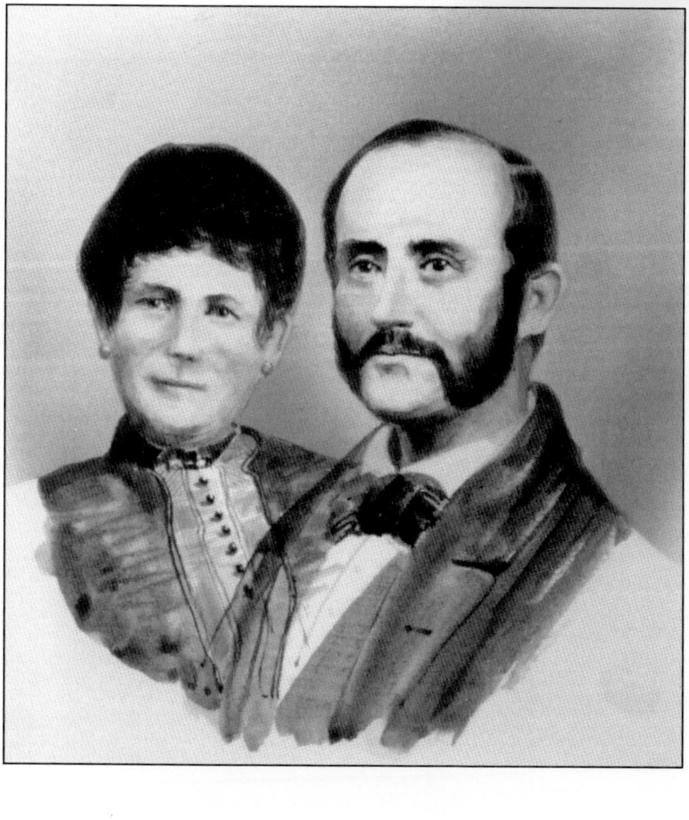

This composite portrait of Maria Dolores Simona and James Alexander Watson is from around 1865, 10 years after their marriage. (Courtesy Special Collections and Archives, California State University, Dominguez Hills.)

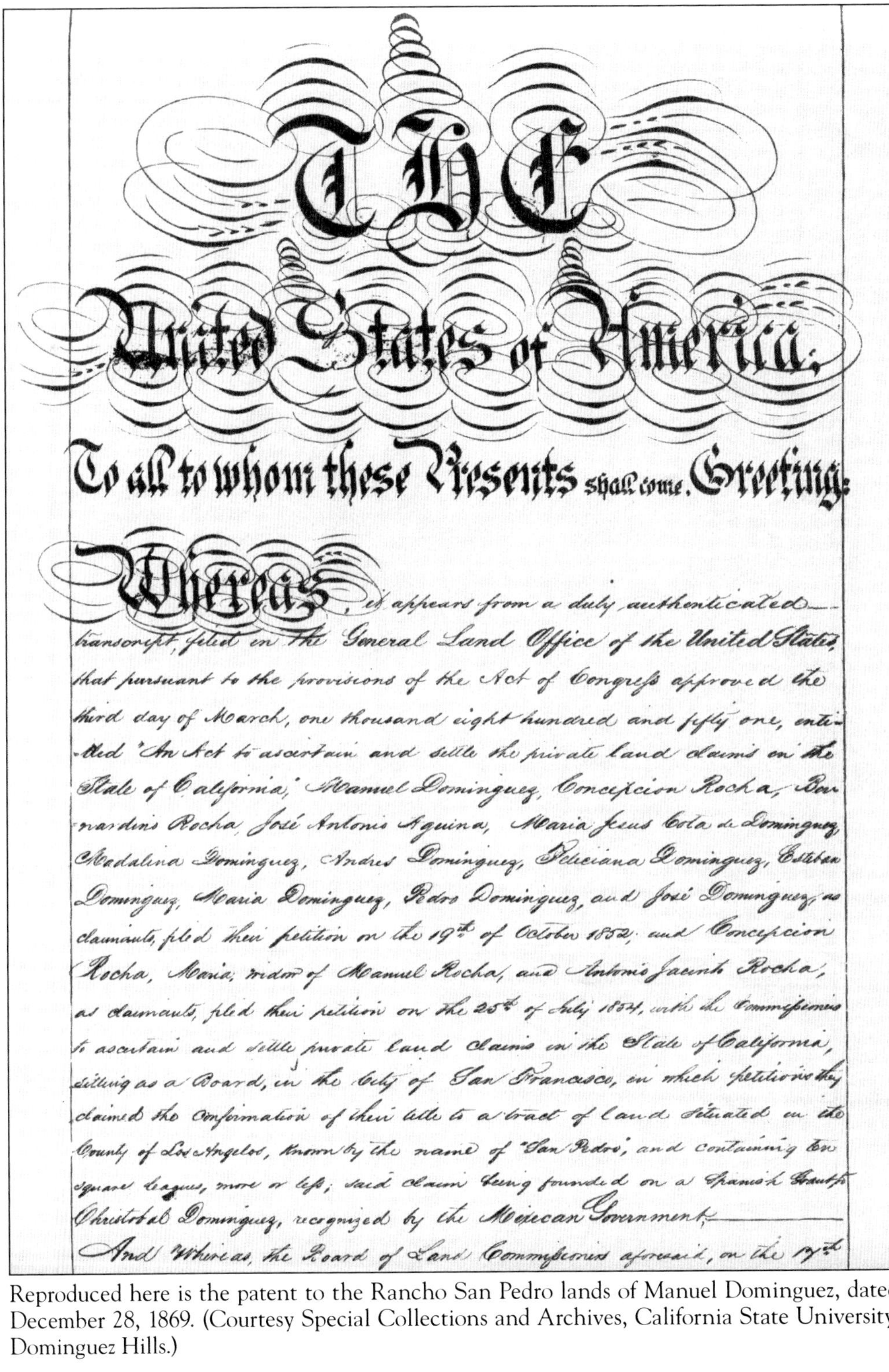
The
United States of America,
To all to whom these Presents shall come, Greeting:

Whereas, it appears from a duly authenticated transcript, filed in the General Land Office of the United States, that pursuant to the provisions of the Act of Congress approved the third day of March, one thousand eight hundred and fifty one, entitled "An Act to ascertain and settle the private land claims in the State of California," Manuel Dominguez, Concepcion Rocha, Bernardino Rocha, José Antonio Aguina, Maria Jesus Cota de Dominguez, Madalena Dominguez, Andres Dominguez, Feliciana Dominguez, Esteban Dominguez, Maria Dominguez, Pedro Dominguez, and José Dominguez, as claimants, filed their petition on the 19th of October 1852; and Concepcion Rocha, Maria, widow of Manuel Rocha, and Antonio Jacinto Rocha, as claimants, filed their petition on the 25th of July 1854, with the Commissioners to ascertain and settle private land claims in the State of California, sitting as a Board, in the City of San Francisco, in which petitions they claimed the confirmation of their title to a tract of land situated in the County of Los Angeles, known by the name of "San Pedro," and containing ten square leagues, more or less; said claim being founded on a Spanish Grant to Christobal Dominguez, recognized by the Mexican Government;

And Whereas, the Board of Land Commissioners aforesaid, on the 17th

Reproduced here is the patent to the Rancho San Pedro lands of Manuel Dominguez, dated December 28, 1869. (Courtesy Special Collections and Archives, California State University, Dominguez Hills.)

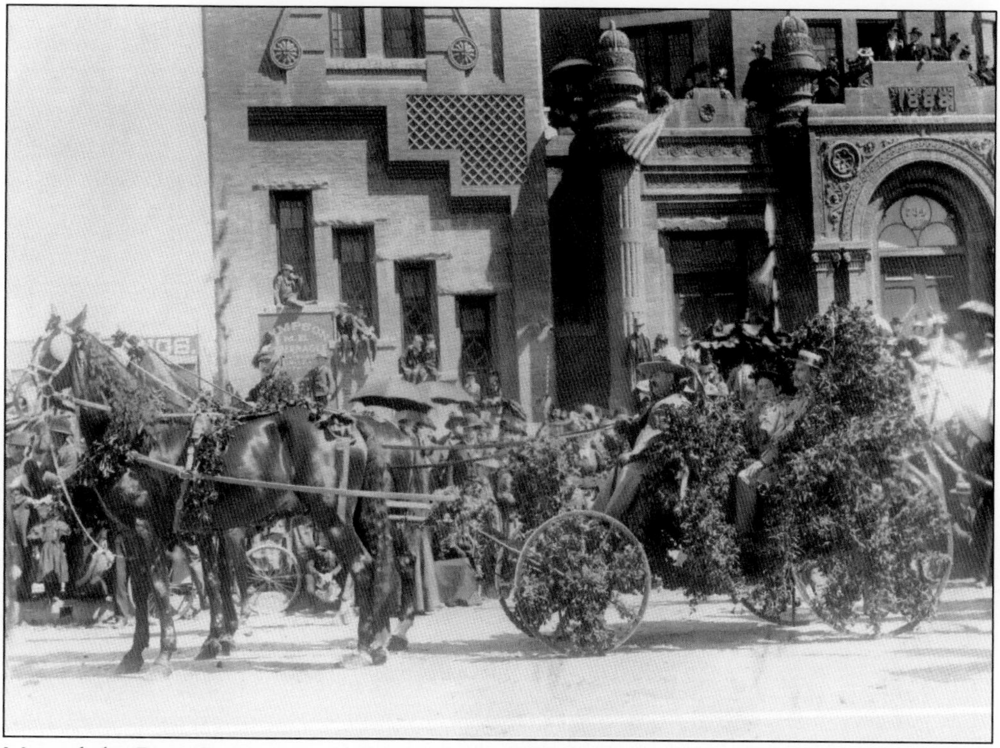

Maria de los Reyes Dominguez de Francis (1847–1933), the youngest of Don Manuel's daughters, and her husband, John Francis, participate in Los Angeles's Fiesta Parade in front of the Simpson Methodist Episcopal Tabernacle. La Fiesta, as the annual event was called, was an effort by Los Angeles and its merchants to create local pageantry, similar to Mardi Gras, for promotion of the city and its wares. The event, later criticized widely for its blatantly racist caricatures, is examined in-depth by William Deverell in his 2004 book *Whitewashed Adobe*. This photograph was taken in 1895, the second year of La Fiesta. (Courtesy Special Collections and Archives, California State University, Dominguez Hills.)

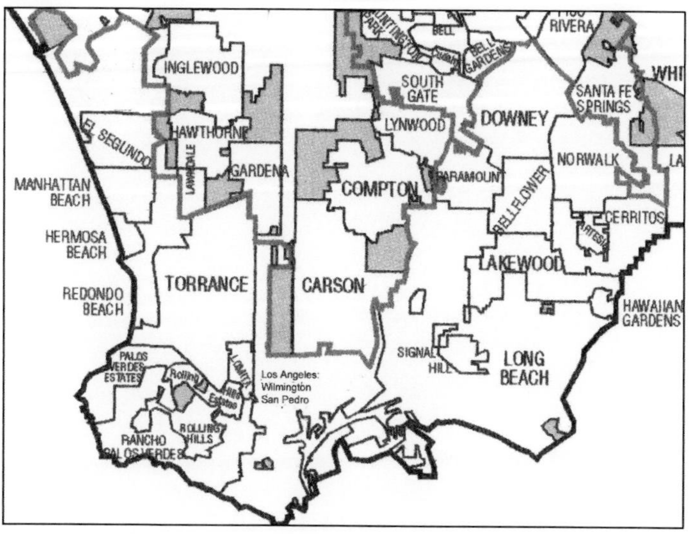

This map shows Carson's location in the present-day South Bay. Shaded areas represent unincorporated county territory. The narrower "point" of the old map (on pages 24 and 25) indicates the slice of the Palos Verdes Peninsula lost to the Sepulveda family. This slice subsequently became Rancho Palos Verdes.

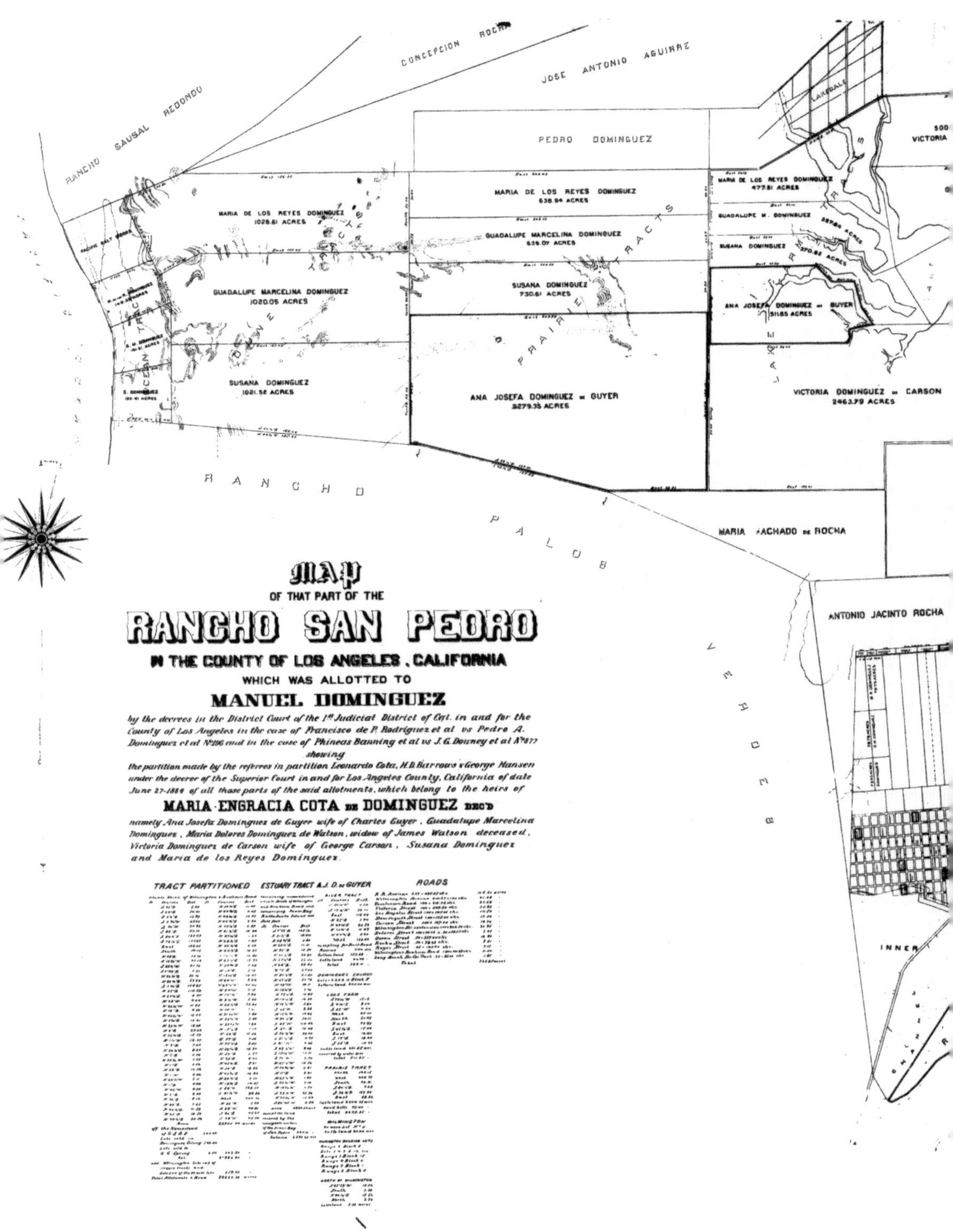

CONCEPCION ROCHA
JOSE ANTONIO AGUIRRE
RANCHO SAUSAL REDONDO
PEDRO DOMINGUEZ
LAKEDALE
VICTORIA
MARIA DE LOS REYES DOMINGUEZ
1028.61 ACRES
MARIA DE LOS REYES DOMINGUEZ
638.94 ACRES
MARIA DE LOS REYES DOMINGUEZ
477.81 ACRES
GUADALUPE MARCELINA DOMINGUEZ
639.07 ACRES
GUADALUPE M. DOMINGUEZ
SUSANA DOMINGUEZ
370.82 ACRES
GUADALUPE MARCELINA DOMINGUEZ
1020.05 ACRES
SUSANA DOMINGUEZ
730.61 ACRES
ANA JOSEFA DOMINGUEZ DE GUYER
511.65 ACRES
PRAIRIE TRACTS
DUNE TRACTS
OCEAN TRACT
SUSANA DOMINGUEZ
1021.52 ACRES
ANA JOSEFA DOMINGUEZ DE GUYER
3279.35 ACRES
VICTORIA DOMINGUEZ DE CARSON
2463.79 ACRES
RANCHO PALOS VERDES
MARIA MACHADO DE ROCHA
ANTONIO JACINTO ROCHA
INNER
MAP
OF THAT PART OF THE
RANCHO SAN PEDRO
IN THE COUNTY OF LOS ANGELES, CALIFORNIA
WHICH WAS ALLOTTED TO
MANUEL DOMINGUEZ
by the decrees in the District Court of the 1st Judicial District of Cal. in and for the County of Los Angeles in the case of Francisco de P. Rodriguez et al vs Pedro A. Dominguez et al No 196 and in the case of Phineas Banning et al vs J. G. Downey et al No 877
showing
the partition made by the referees in partition Leonardo Cota, H. D. Barrows & George Hansen under the decree of the Superior Court in and for Los Angeles County, California of date June 27-1884 of all those parts of the said allotments, which belong to the heirs of
MARIA ENGRACIA COTA DE DOMINGUEZ DEC'D
namely Ana Josefa Dominguez de Guyer wife of Charles Guyer, Guadalupe Marcelina Dominguez, Maria Dolores Dominguez de Watson, widow of James Watson deceased, Victoria Dominguez de Carson wife of George Carson, Susana Dominguez and Maria de los Reyes Dominguez.
TRACT PARTITIONED
ESTUARY TRACT A.J. D. DE GUYER
ROADS

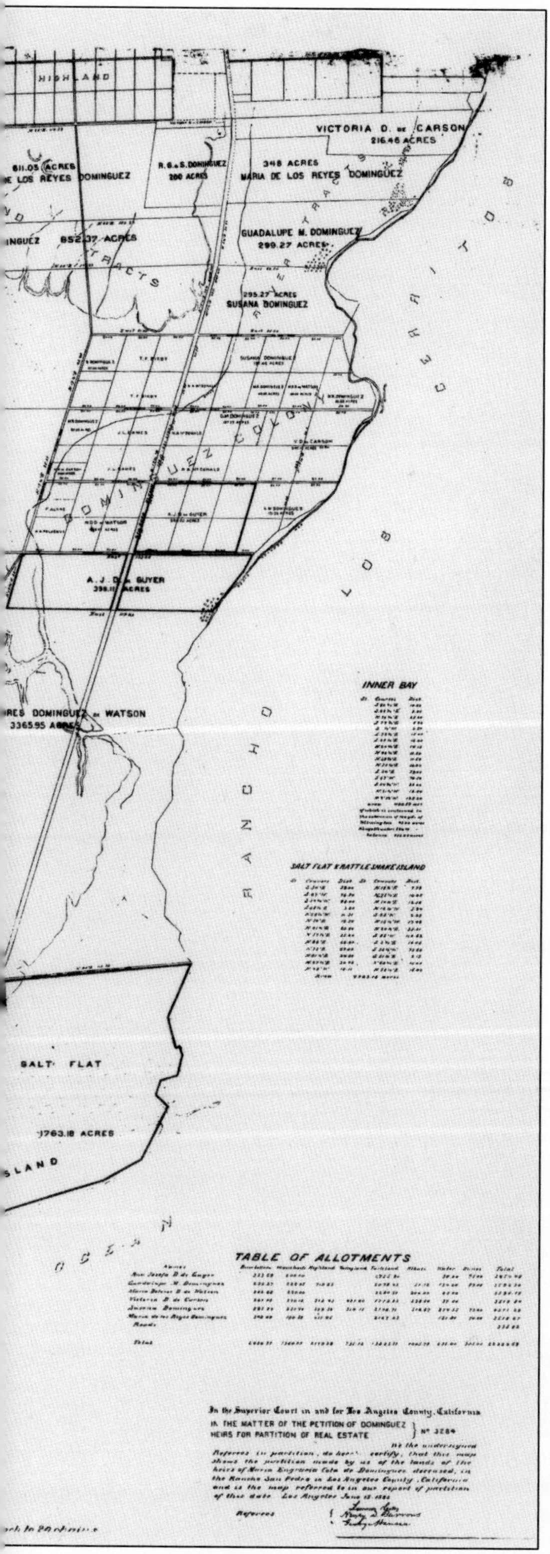

This map depicts the Rancho San Pedro as it was in 1885 when partitioned after Don Manuel's death in 1882. (Courtesy Special Collections and Archives, California State University, Dominguez Hills.)

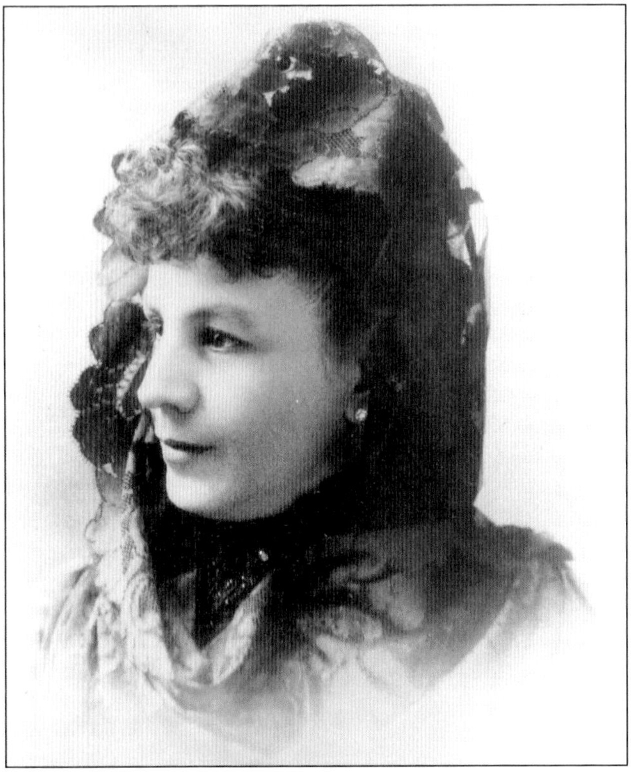

Susana Delfina Dominguez, Don Manuel's fifth surviving daughter, married Dr. Gregorio Del Amo y Gonzalez, a Spanish aristocrat who became a consul for Spain in San Francisco. They married in 1890, when Susana was 46. (Courtesy Special Collections and Archives, California State University, Dominguez Hills.)

This family gathering at the rancho took place in 1894. (Courtesy Special Collections and Archives, California State University, Dominguez Hills.)

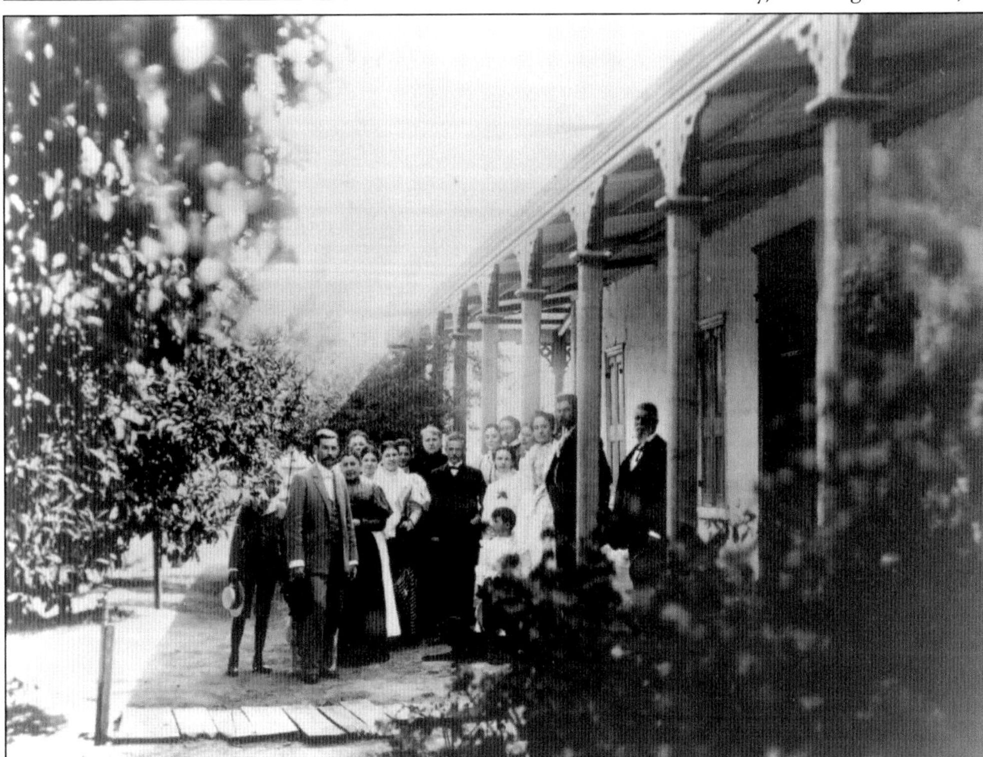

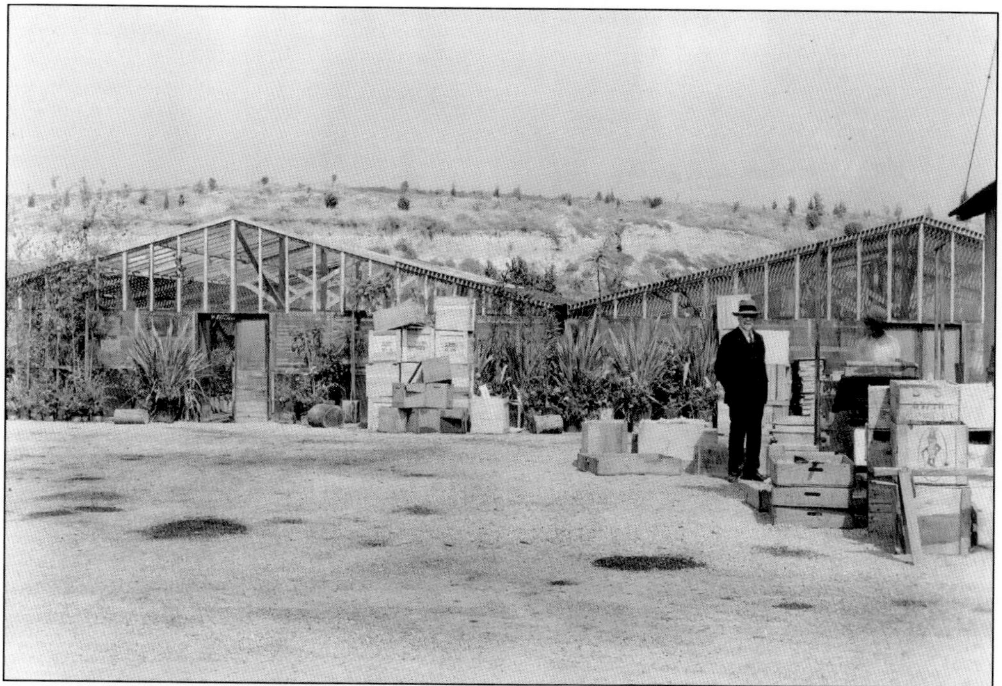

Dr. Gregorio del Amo established the Del Amo Nurseries, which originally included lands that, non-contiguously, covered around 100 acres in the areas located where the east/west-running Del Amo Boulevard crosses Wilmington Avenue and Alameda Street today. Dr. Del Amo is pictured here in 1935, six years before his death. His and Susana's remains were encrypted beneath the chapel at the Claretian Seminary on the Rancho San Pedro site. (Courtesy Special Collections and Archives, California State University, Dominguez Hills.)

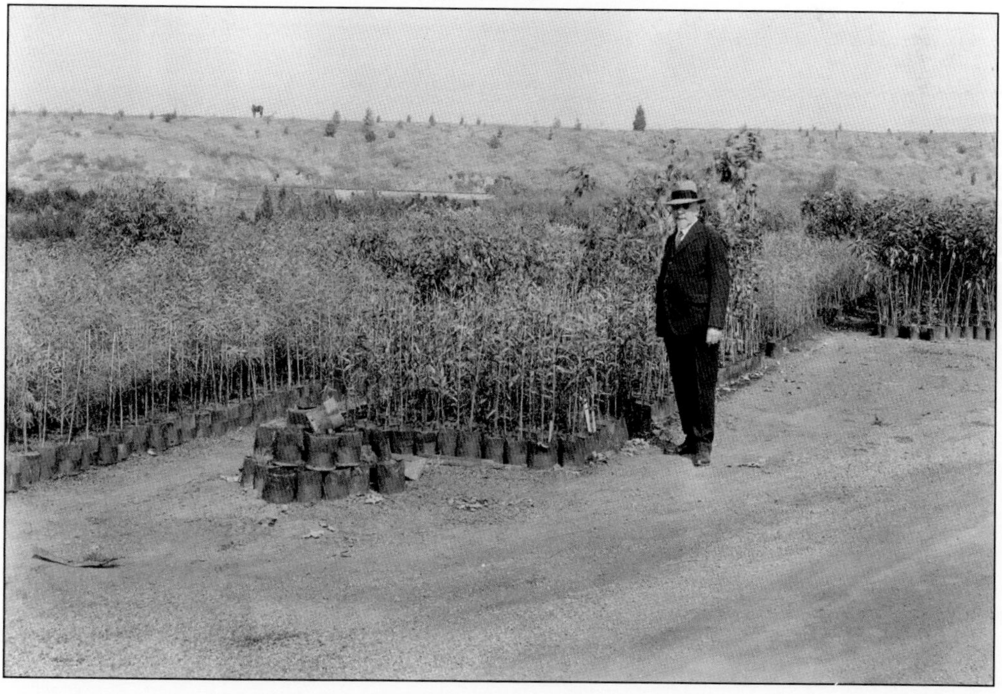

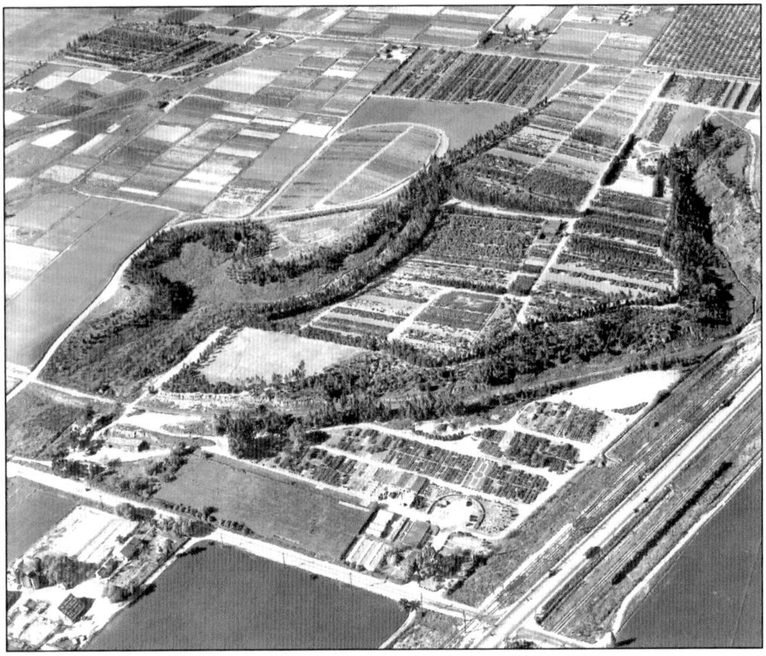

This aerial view of Del Amo Nurseries was taken on February 25, 1938. In the right foreground are railroad tracks and Alameda Street. The entrance to the nursery was located at the corner of Del Amo Boulevard and Alameda Street; Rancho Way is the curved street at far left. (Courtesy Special Collections and Archives, California State University, Dominguez Hills.)

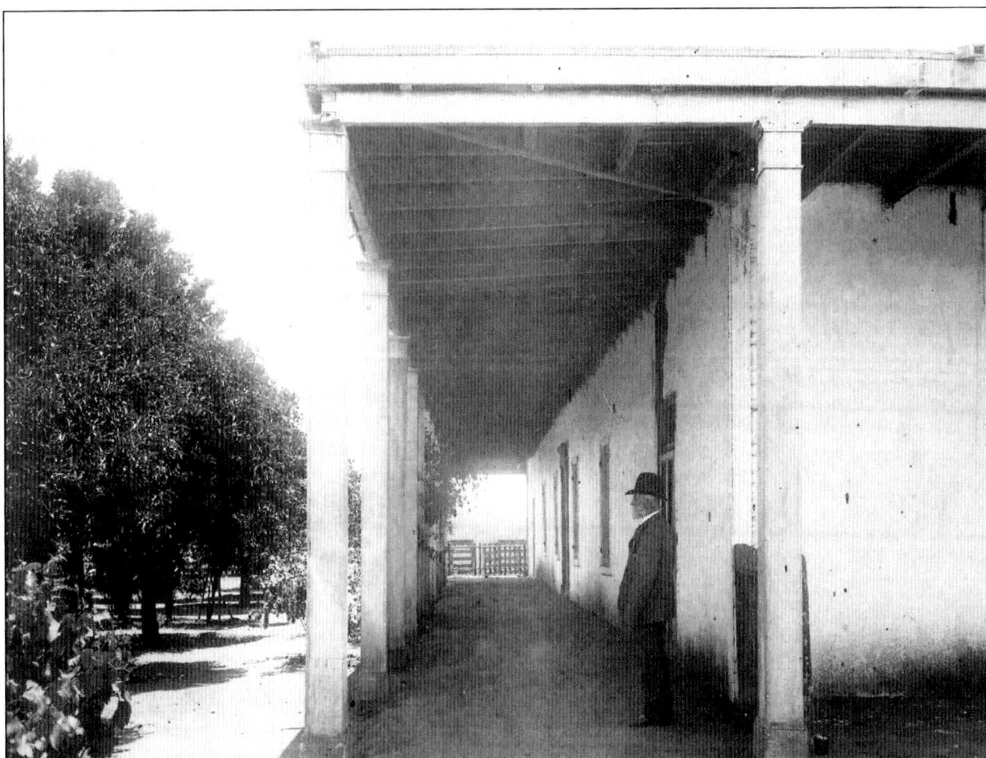

This 1888 photograph shows the house in its earlier state. The gentleman is facing north into the courtyard, which was planted with fruit trees for the family's use. (Courtesy Special Collections and Archives, California State University, Dominguez Hills.)

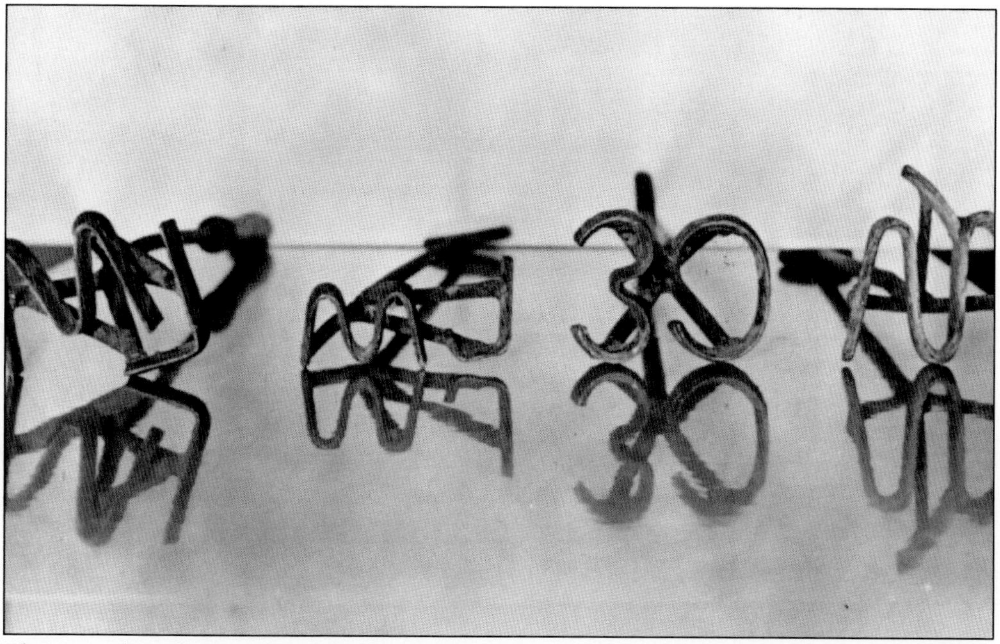

These iron brands are some of those actually used on local ranchos. Cattle roamed the Rancho San Pedro lands up through the 1960s when the city of Carson was founded. (Courtesy Historical Collections, The First American Corporation.)

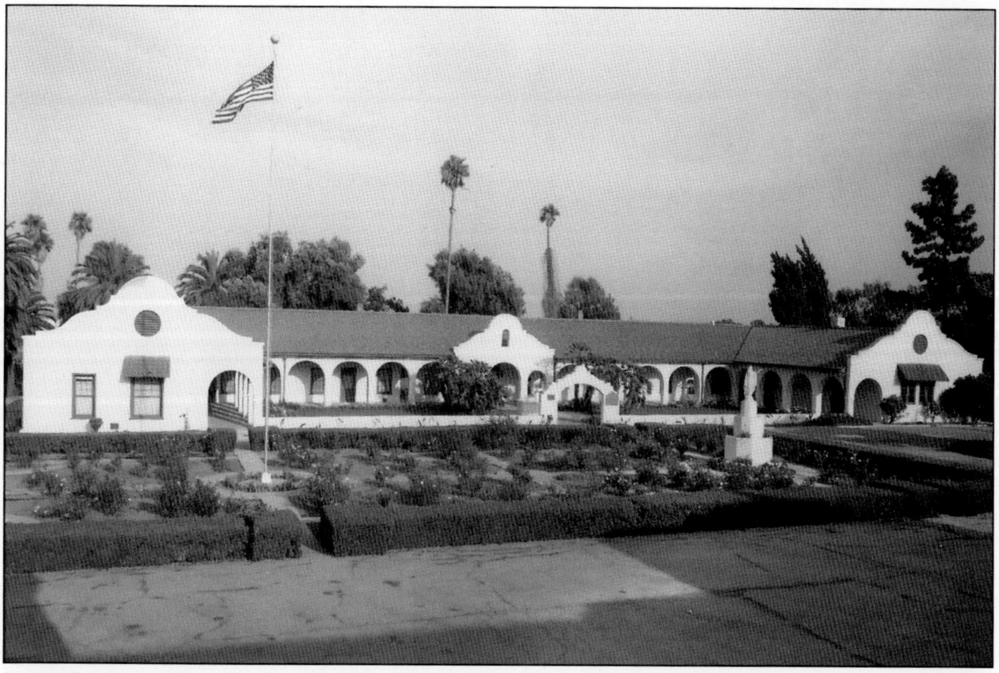

In 1905, Maria Victoria moved back to the rancho. Two years later, she had the house modernized in the Mission Revival style, replacing the old flat roof with a pitched red-tile one and adding the rancho's now signature white arches. It was at this time that the house was enlarged from its original "L" shape to the "U" of its present configuration. (Courtesy Special Collections and Archives, California State University, Dominguez Hills.)

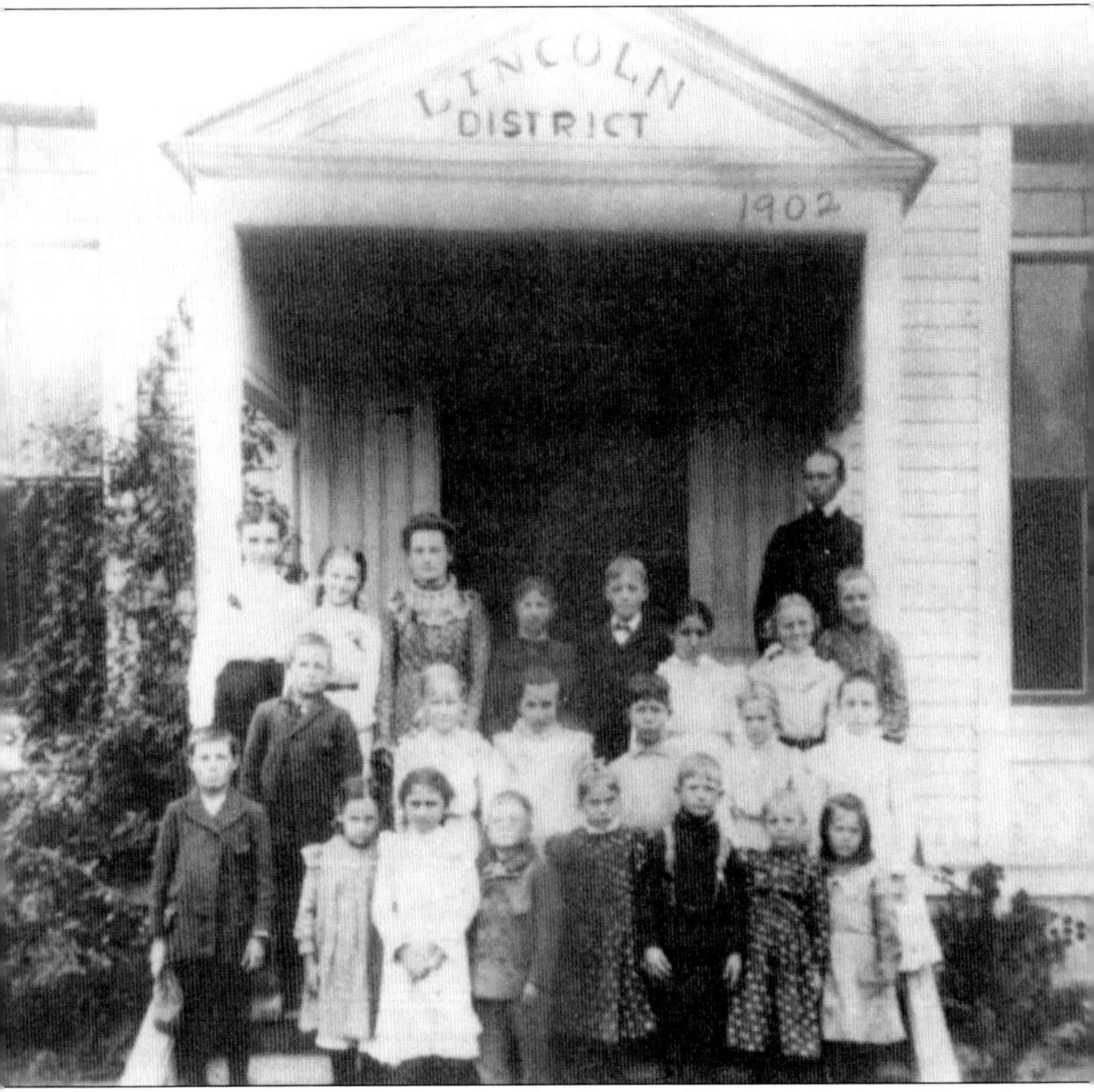

Lincoln District School No. 3 stood at Main Street and Sepulveda Boulevard. It was later known as the Rocha School. Next the American Can Company stood for many years at the site but became part of the growing city's blight after several years of abandonment. Today the sparkling new Home Depot/Albertson's shopping center anchors dozens of other businesses at the intersection's southeastern corner.

Two

Dominguez and Carson

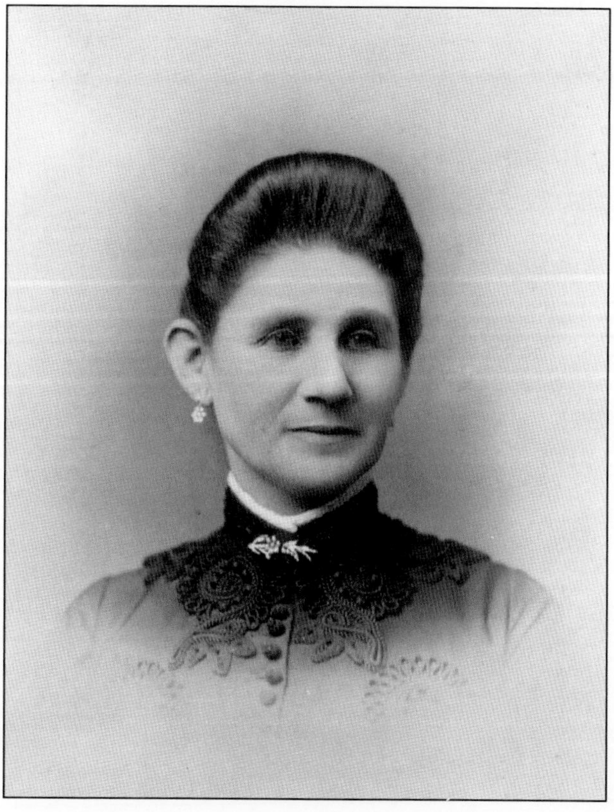

Where did Carson get its name? Maria Victoria Dominguez (1842–1916) married George Henry Carson in 1857 when she was 15. They built their grand home next to the Rancho San Pedro five years later and engaged in various farming and dairy activities. The Carsons had 15 children, one of whom was John Manuel Carson, father of Victor Carson, who became a family historian. This portrait is from around 1885. (Courtesy Special Collections and Archives, California State University, Dominguez Hills.)

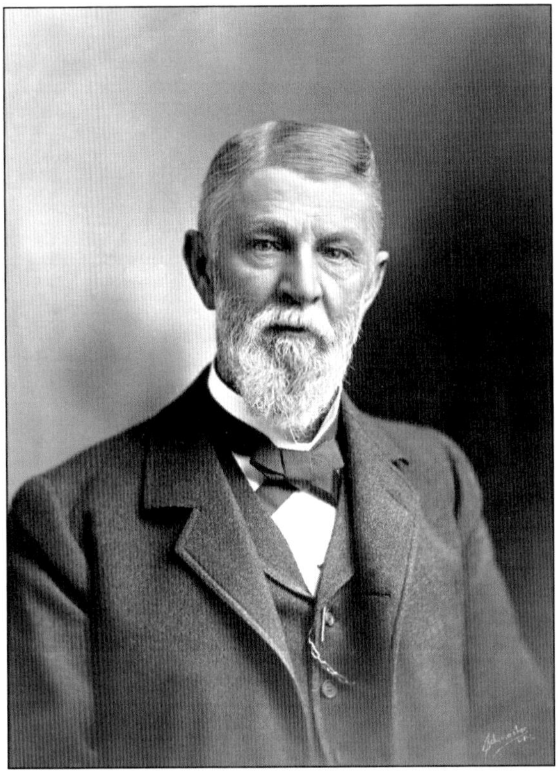

Pictured here is George Carson, c. 1890. A merchant born in New York, he led a colorful and successful life in the West as a soldier, Chapman Ranger, trader, and livestock dealer. He was eventually involved in Los Angeles politics and became a city council member and Los Angeles County public administrator. (Courtesy Special Collections and Archives, California State University, Dominguez Hills.)

The George Carson home, seen here around 1920, stood just north of the Rancho San Pedro and was demolished in 1970. It was a hub of business and social interaction due to its strategic location halfway between the Port of Los Angeles at San Pedro to the south and the main portion of the city of Los Angeles to the north and was a stop along the railroad built by Phineas Banning. (Courtesy Special Collections and Archives, California State University, Dominguez Hills.)

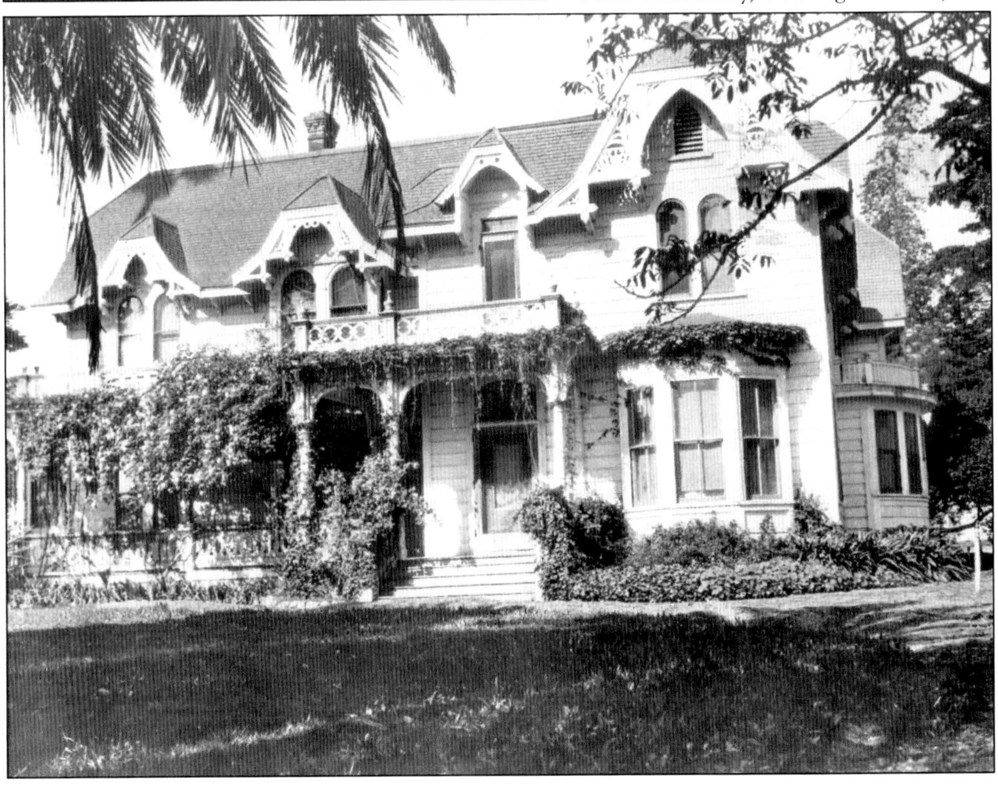

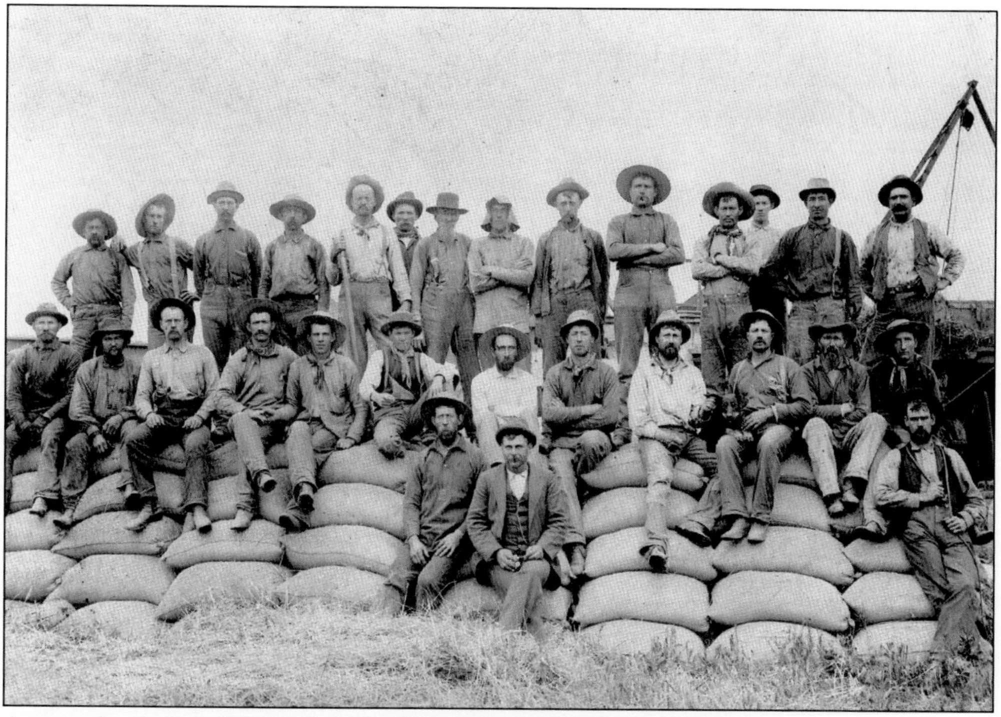

A grain-threshing crew poses for this photograph on the Carson estate in 1897. (Courtesy Special Collections and Archives, California State University, Dominguez Hills.)

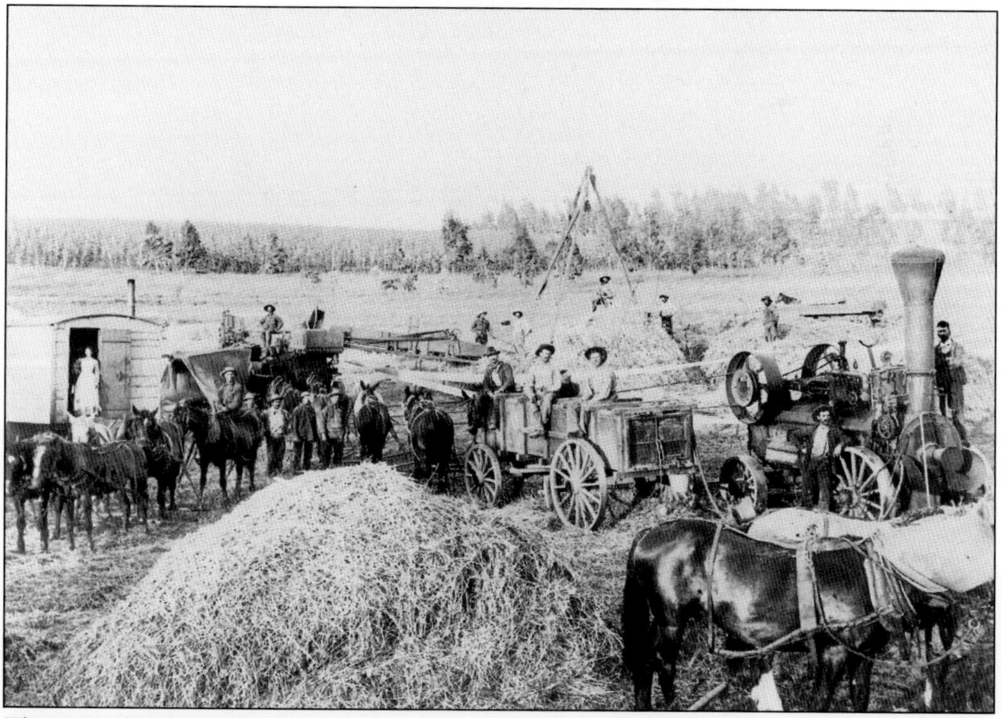

The grain-threshing crew is hard at work in 1897. (Courtesy Special Collections and Archives, California State University, Dominguez Hills.)

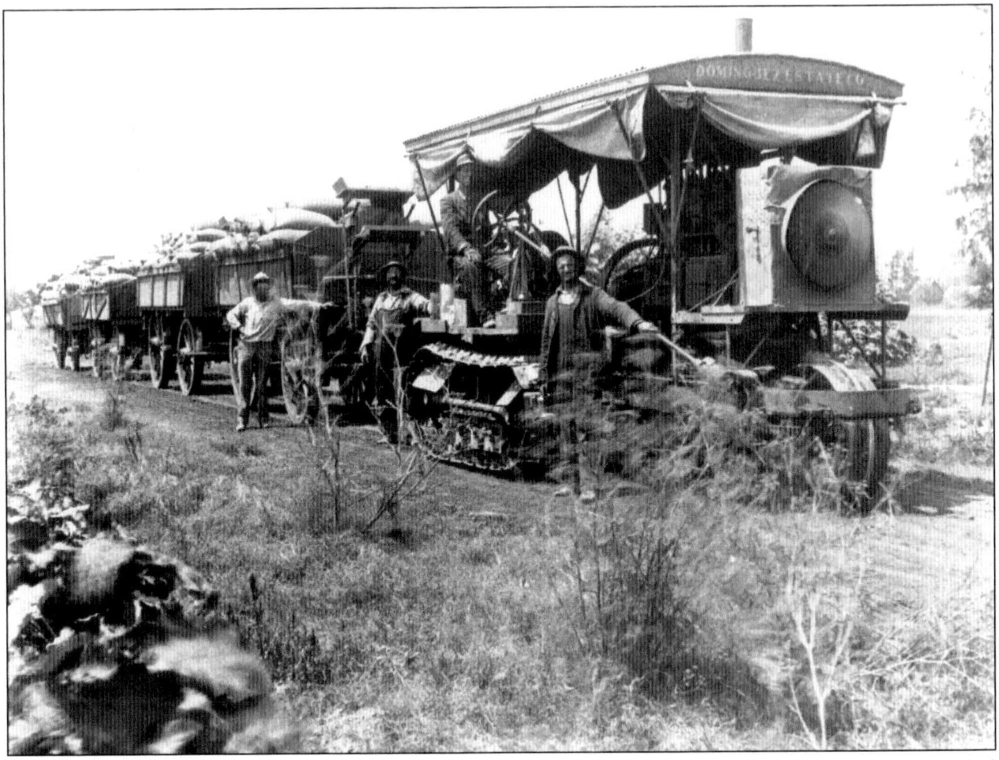

A mere half-century after the use of the two-wheeled *carreta*, or cart, the then highly mechanized Rancho San Pedro used tractor rigs to haul grain in 1912. (Courtesy Special Collections and Archives, California State University, Dominguez Hills.)

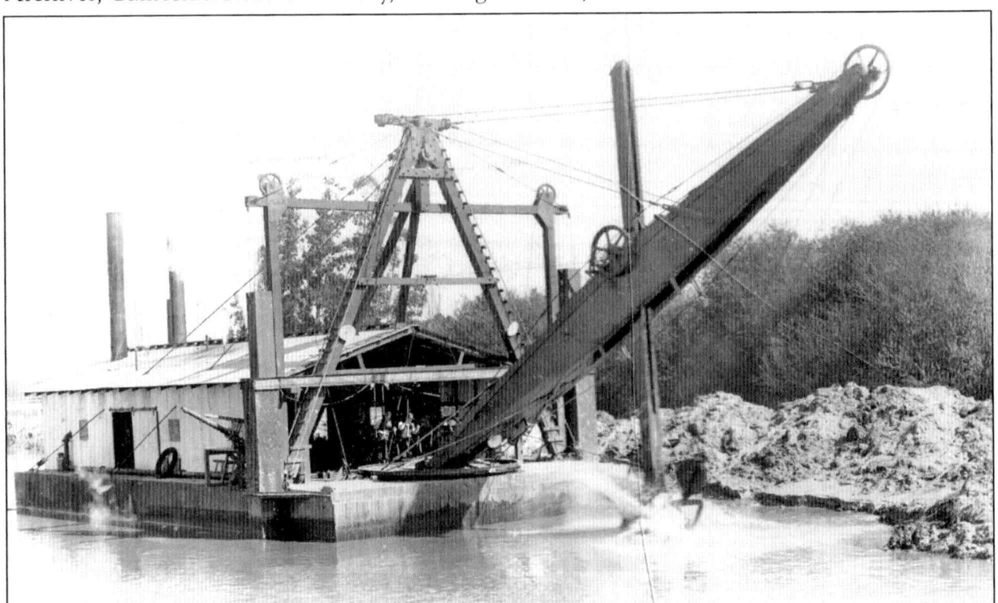

Carson lands were mostly low-lying and subject to frequent flooding. Seen here is a channel-dredging operation in 1914. The steam-powered dredge was later washed out to sea and lost forever. (Courtesy Special Collections and Archives, California State University, Dominguez Hills.)

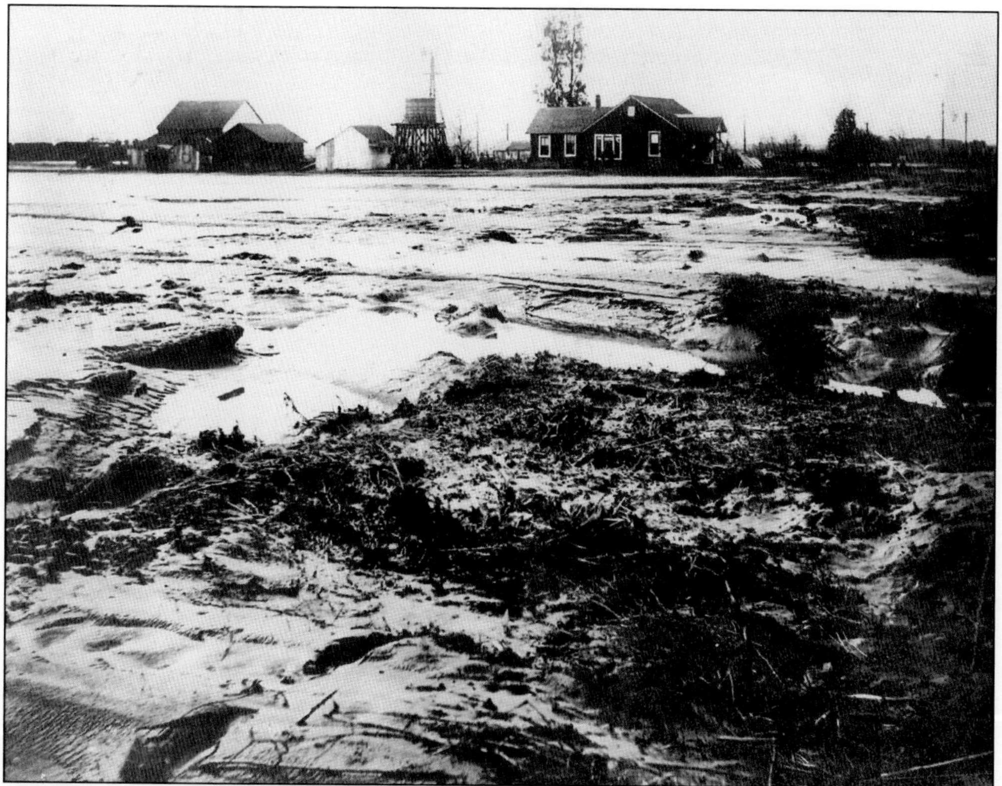

The Bangle Farm was located in present-day Carson, about one mile south of the Dominguez Water Company. During the 1916 flood, the entire area was underwater, and the Bangle family, like many others, had to be rescued by boat. (Courtesy Special Collections and Archives, California State University, Dominguez Hills.)

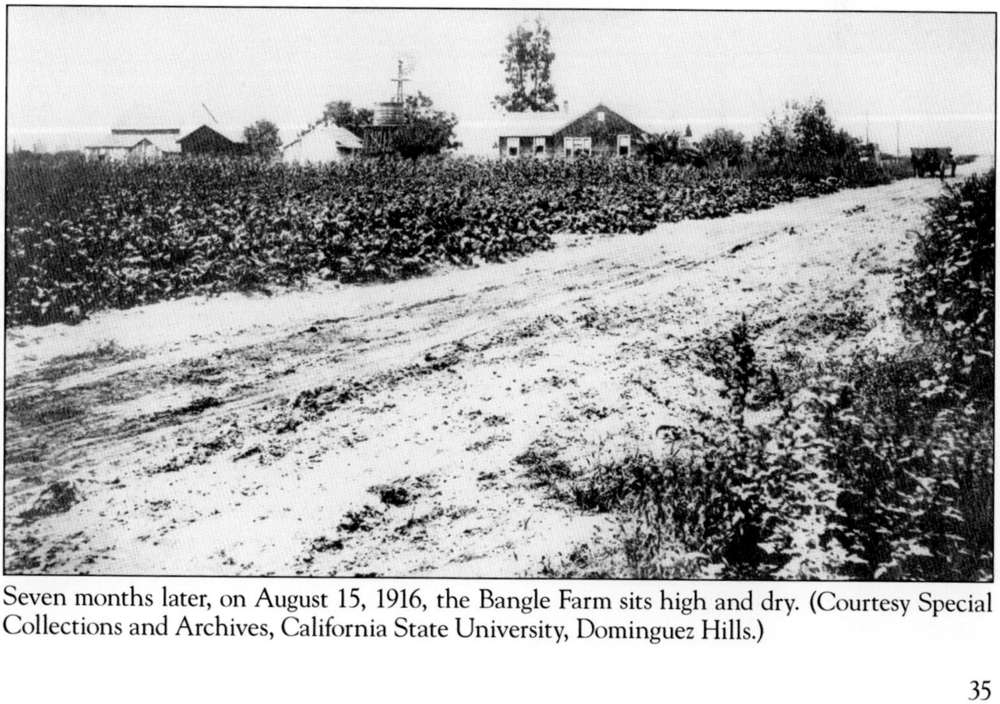

Seven months later, on August 15, 1916, the Bangle Farm sits high and dry. (Courtesy Special Collections and Archives, California State University, Dominguez Hills.)

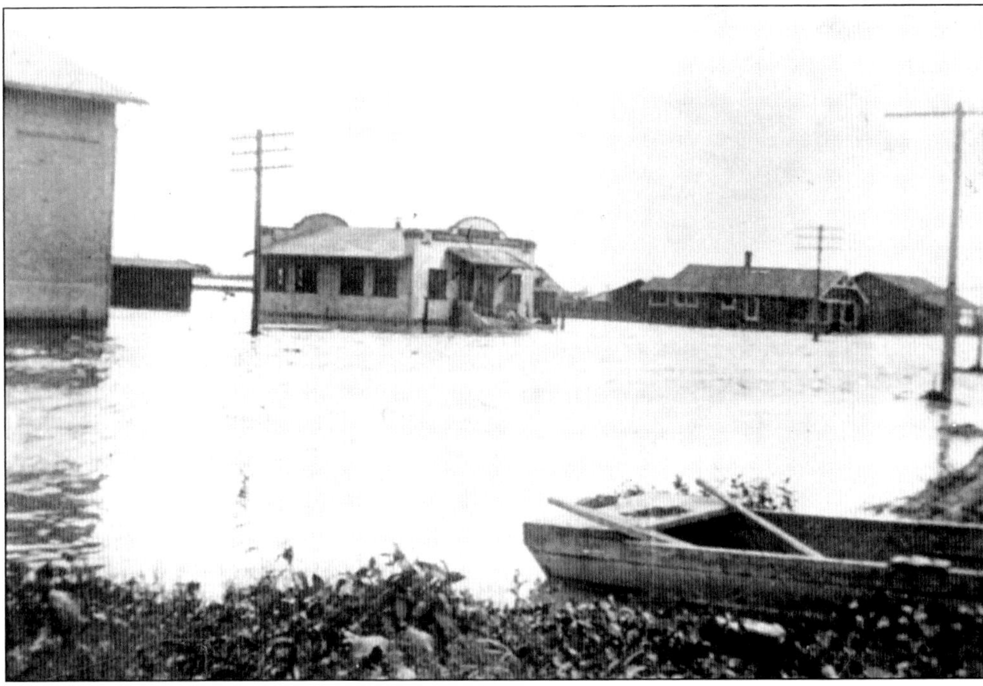

Ironically this 1914 flood inundated the Dominguez Water Company. The office is in the center, while homes can be seen at right and the pump station is at left. (Courtesy Special Collections and Archives, California State University, Dominguez Hills.)

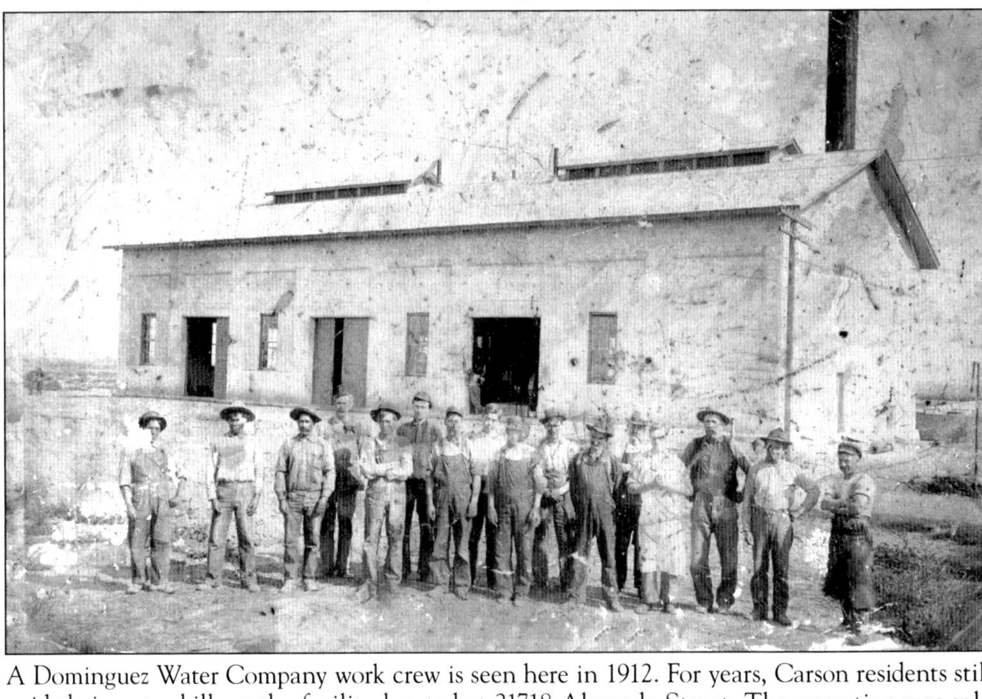

A Dominguez Water Company work crew is seen here in 1912. For years, Carson residents still paid their water bills at the facility located at 21718 Alameda Street. The operation was sold to Cal Water some years later. (Courtesy Special Collections and Archives, California State University, Dominguez Hills.)

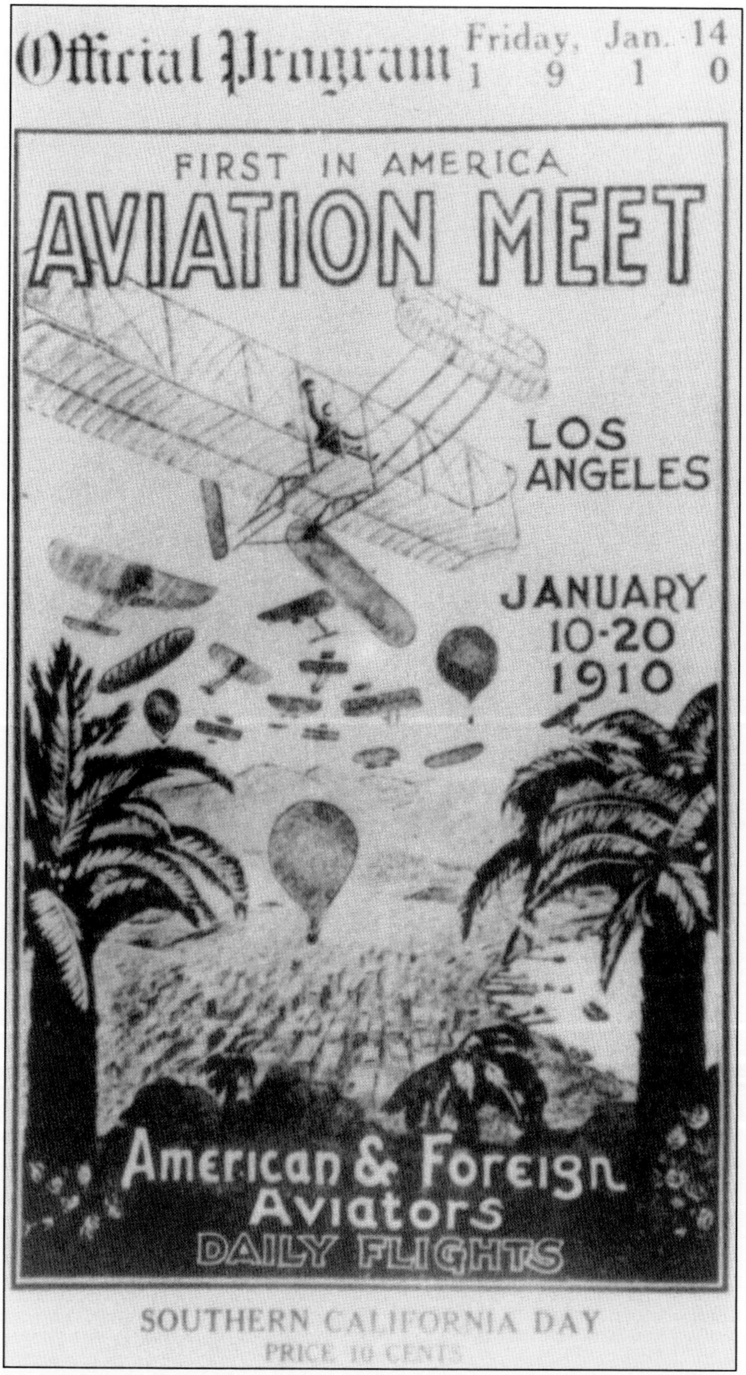

This official program from the Dominguez Air Meet offers up a fantastic scene of a sky fringed by palms and filled with all manner of floating and flying machines. In reality, these were the earliest days of flying and did not quite live up to the fantasy. Of the 43 airplanes entered, only seven actually took flight on the barren hilltop. Other entries included six dirigibles and blimps and nine hot-air balloons. Still the event was a huge success of international prominence. (Courtesy Special Collections and Archives, California State University, Dominguez Hills.)

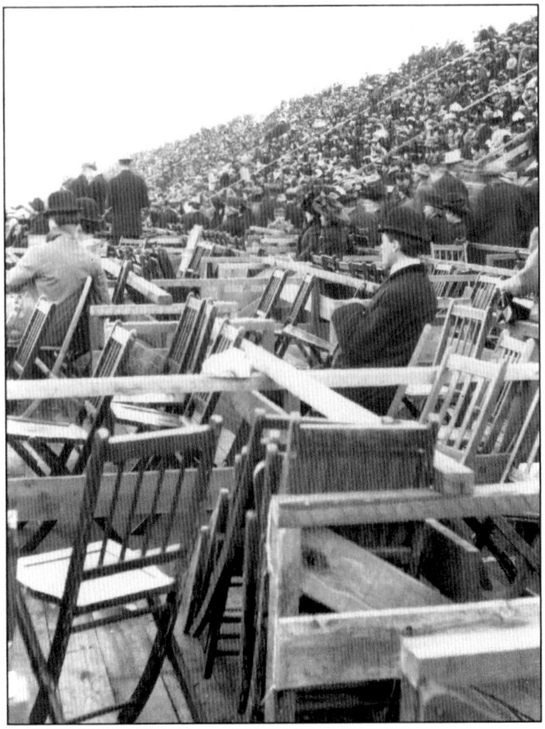

The 1910 Dominguez Air Meet, also known as the United States National Air Meet, employed a grandstand that was constructed on-site and measured 600 feet in length. An estimated 100,000 spectators attended, many by rail from Los Angeles. (Courtesy Special Collections and Archives, California State University, Dominguez Hills.)

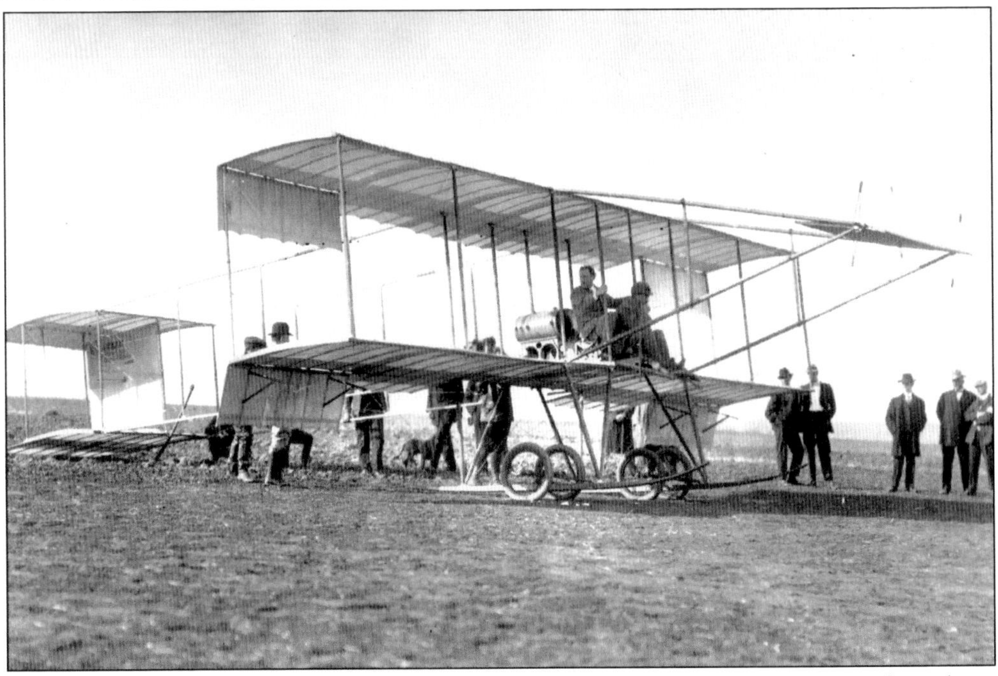

The fourth day of the Dominguez Air Meet featured passenger-carrying aircraft, a then-revolutionary concept in aviation. Here Frenchman Louis Paulham takes on eight passengers, including meet promoter Dick Ferris and his wife, who by virtue of the event became the first woman to fly in a plane. (Courtesy Special Collections and Archives, California State University, Dominguez Hills.)

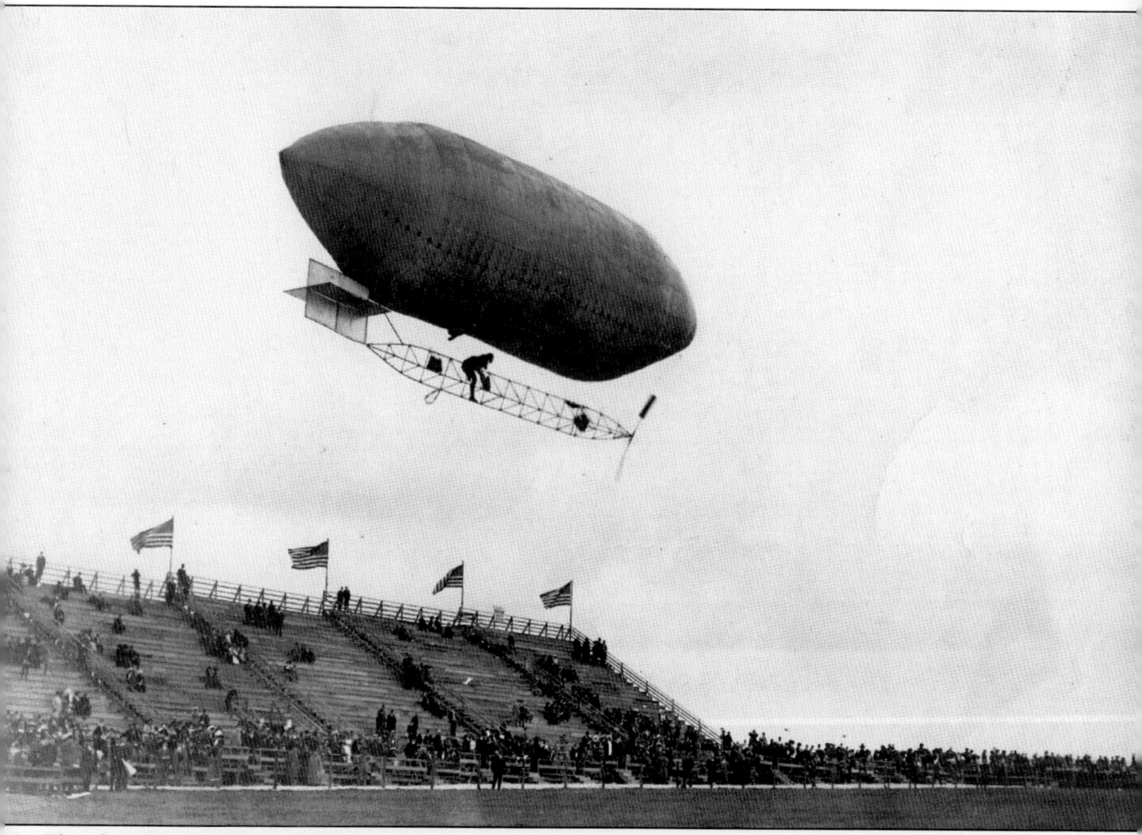

This dirigible was flown in 1910 in Carson by Roy Knabenshue, who died in 1960. Airships owned by Goodyear would later moor in Carson for decades and be used in the 1960s, 1970s, and beyond in the coverage of sporting events. (Courtesy Special Collections and Archives, California State University, Dominguez Hills.)

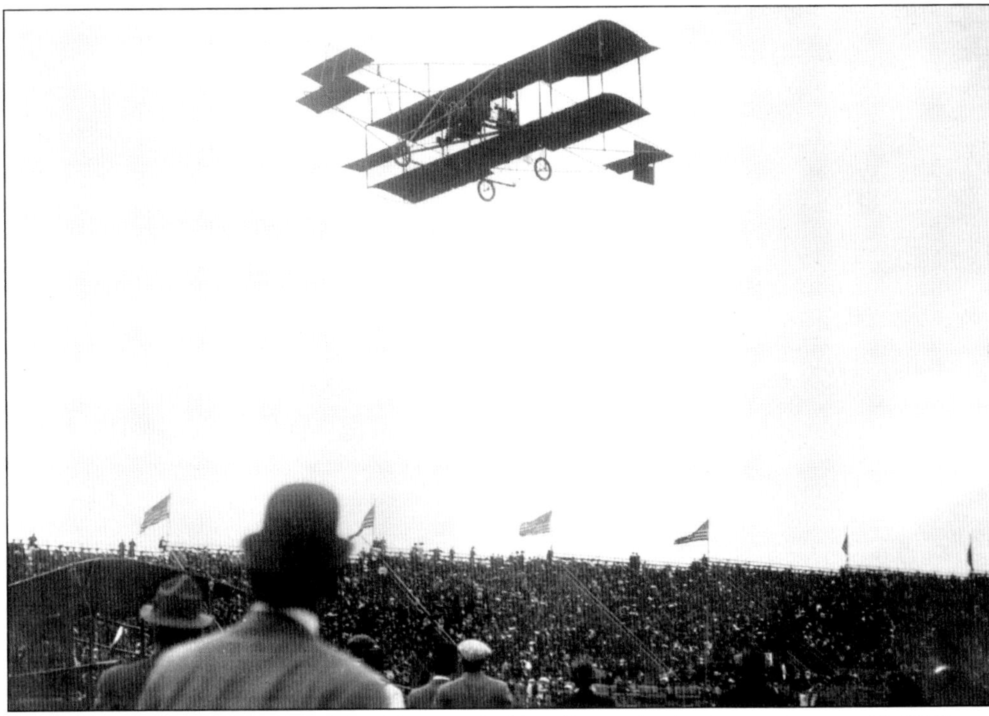

The first United States National Air Meet was held in Carson beginning on January 10, 1910, and ran for 10 days. It was an event of international prominence and a day of many firsts in aviation. The Dominguez family made a portion of Dominguez Hill available as a venue free of charge to the promoters. Pictured here is the Curtiss biplane during the first successful airplane flight in the West. The first plane to fly in California, it flew on the first day of the meet, soaring 50 feet above spectators and making bank turns during its five-eighths of a mile, 28-second flight. (Courtesy Special Collections and Archives, California State University, Dominguez Hills.)

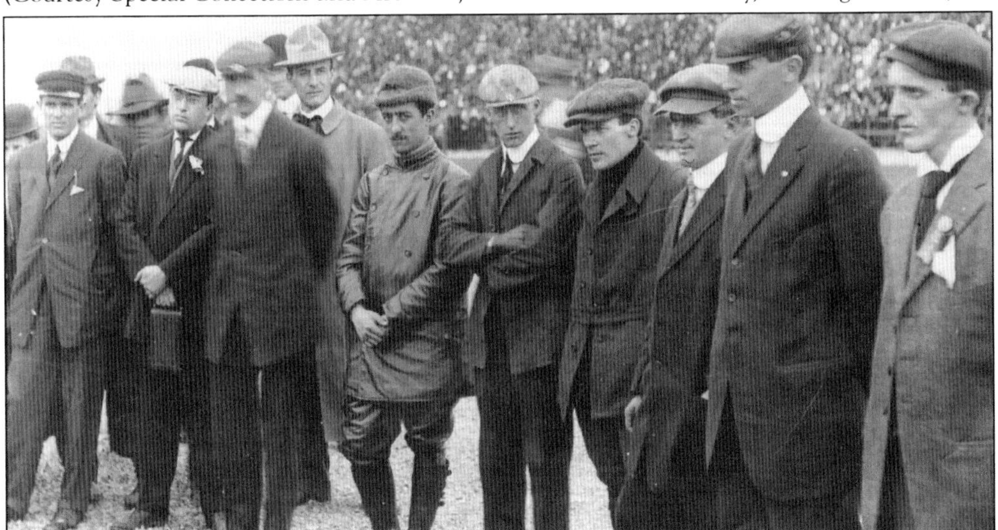

This historic gathering of aviators at the air meet included, from left to right, Colonel Johnson, unidentified, "F. K.," "F. H.," Glenn Curtiss, Louis Paulhan, Charles Willard, D. Matson, Lincoln Beacy, Roy Knabenshue, and Charles Hamilton.

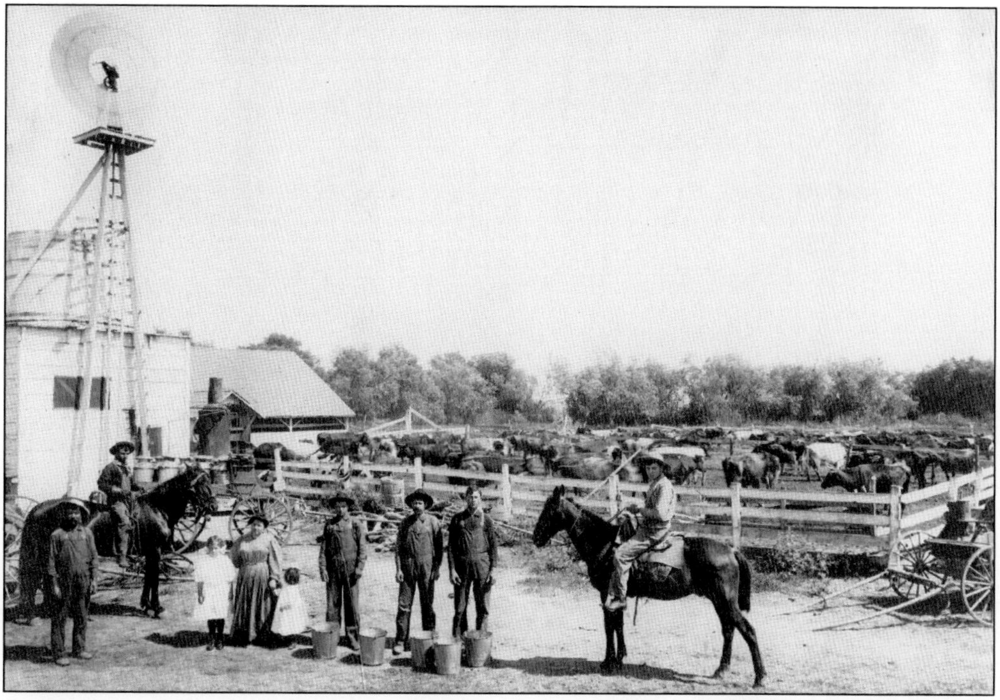

During the same era as the air meet, farming, rather than livestock ranching, had become the mainstay of the rancho. Carson Estate dairy operations form the subject of this 1908 photograph. (Courtesy Special Collections and Archives, California State University, Dominguez Hills.)

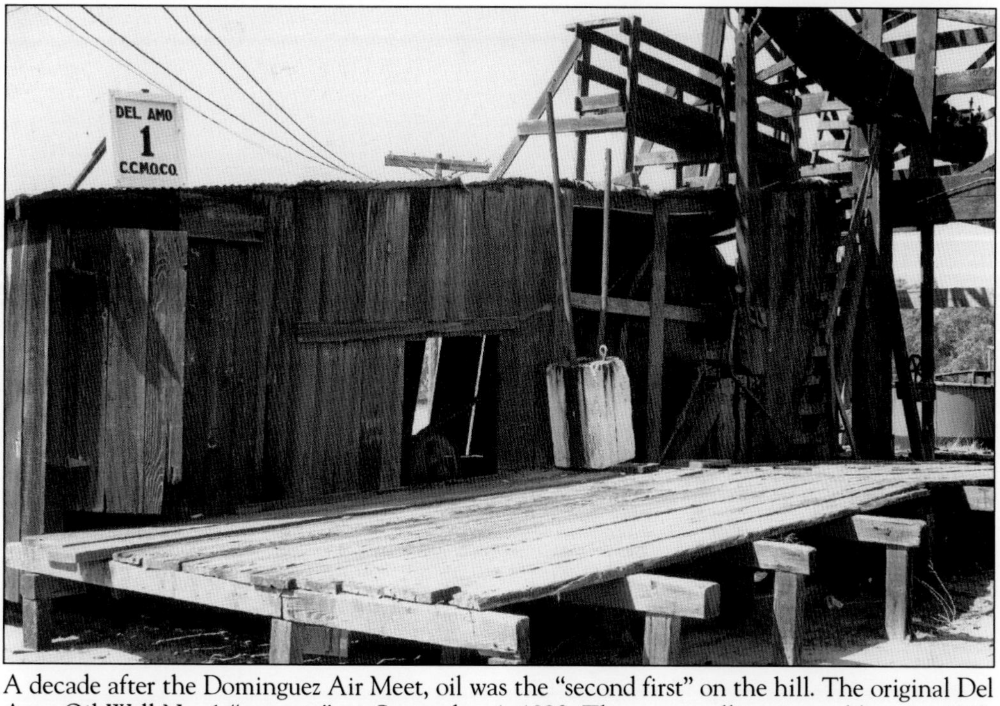

A decade after the Dominguez Air Meet, oil was the "second first" on the hill. The original Del Amo Oil Well No. 1 "came in" on September 1, 1923. The same well is pictured here in 1945. (Courtesy Special Collections and Archives, California State University, Dominguez Hills.)

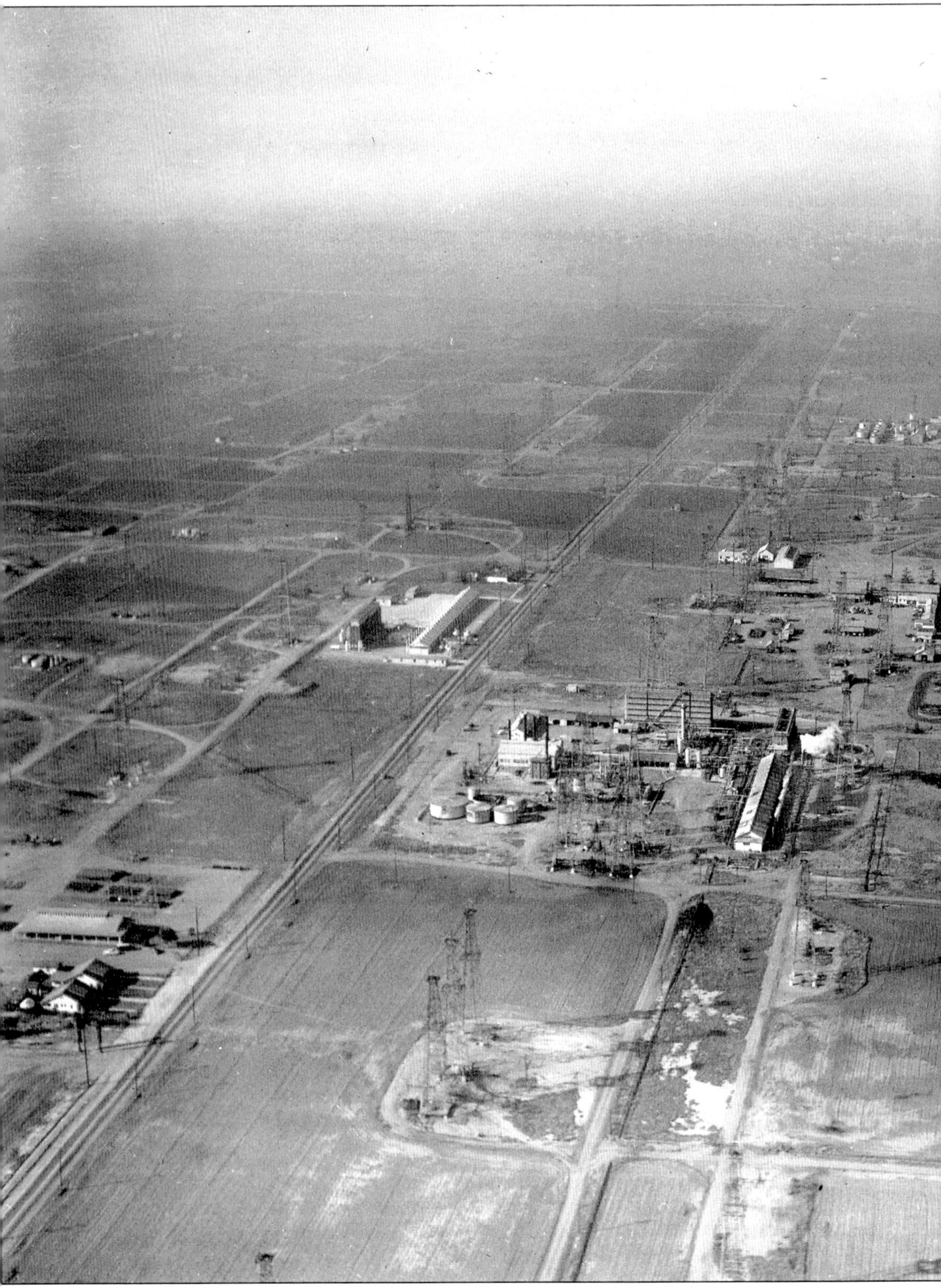

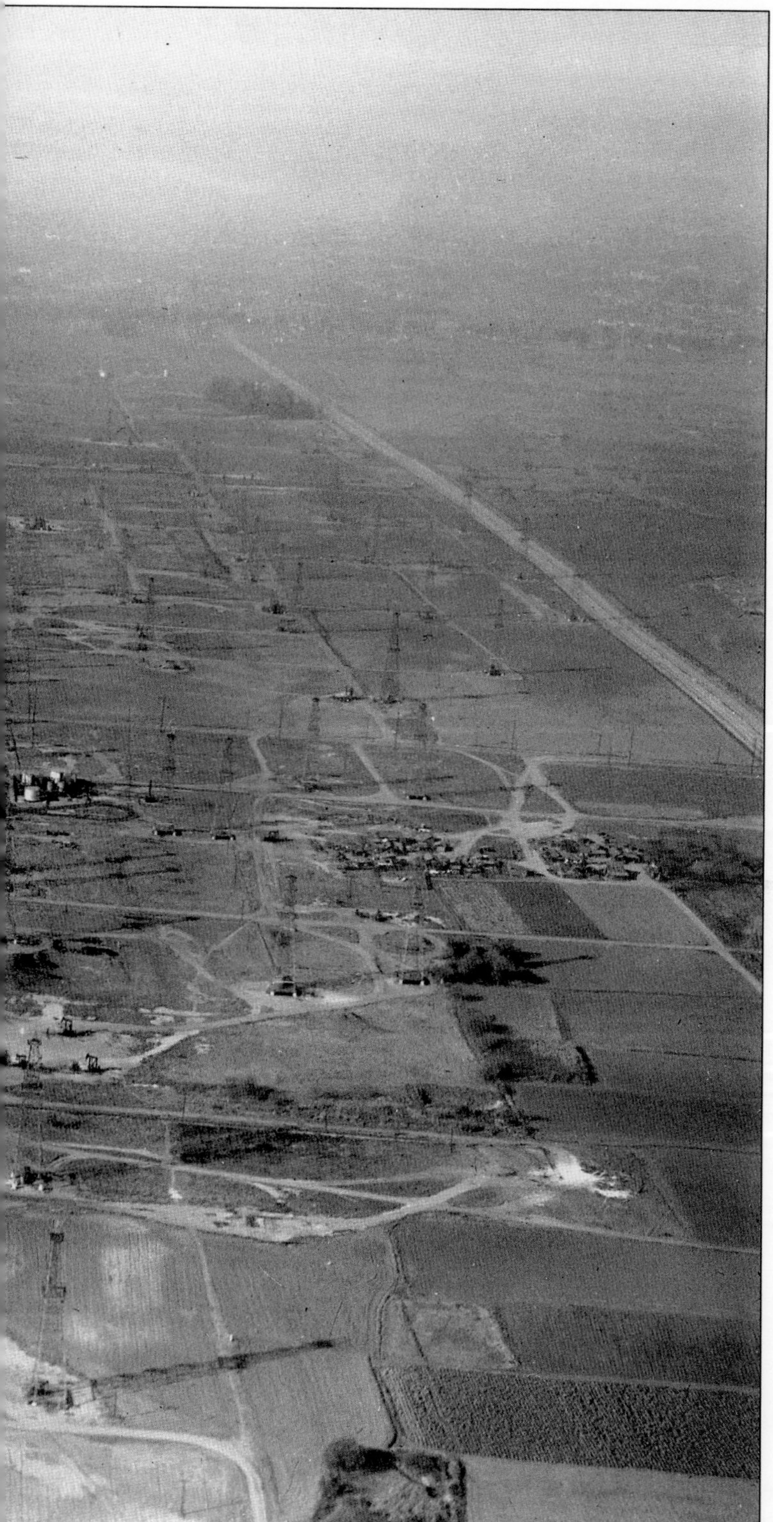

This aerial photograph shows oil development on Dominguez Hill in 1945. The site contained more than 350 wells and spanned 1,200 acres. (Courtesy Special Collections and Archives, California State University, Dominguez Hills.)

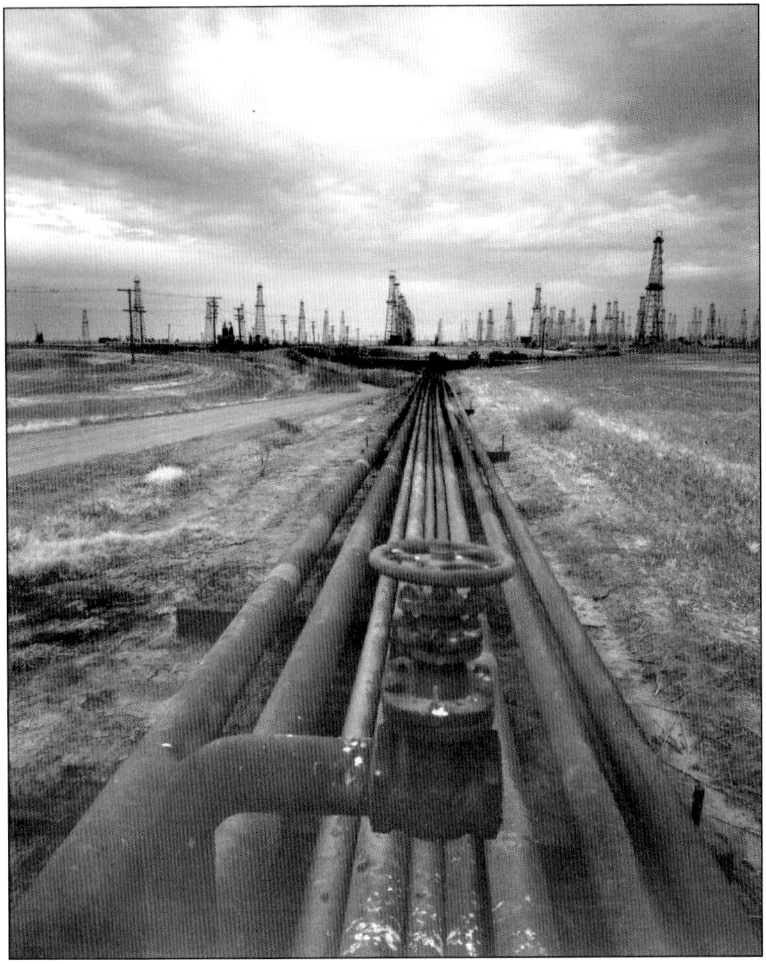

An oil pipeline and derricks stretch into the distance on Dominguez Hill, the high point of the surrounding Dominguez Hills, pictured here in 1945. Oil provided the major source of income for the Dominguez heirs after the ranching era and before the real estate development boom. (Courtesy Special Collections and Archives, California State University, Dominguez Hills.)

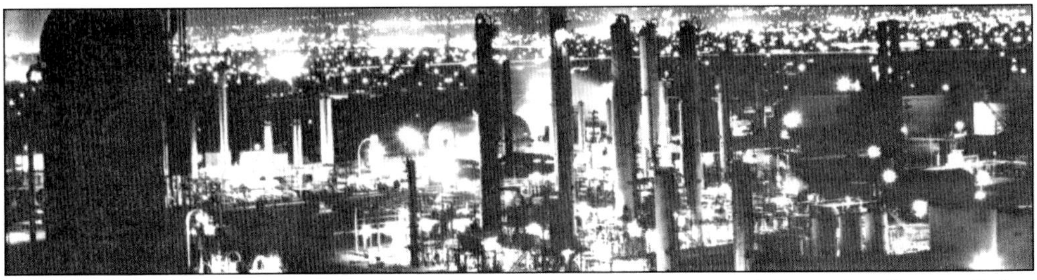

In 1975, a mere 30 years after the above photograph was taken, one of Carson's refineries lights up the night sky, illustrating the city as a major petroleum industry location north of both of the enormous Ports of Los Angeles and Long Beach.

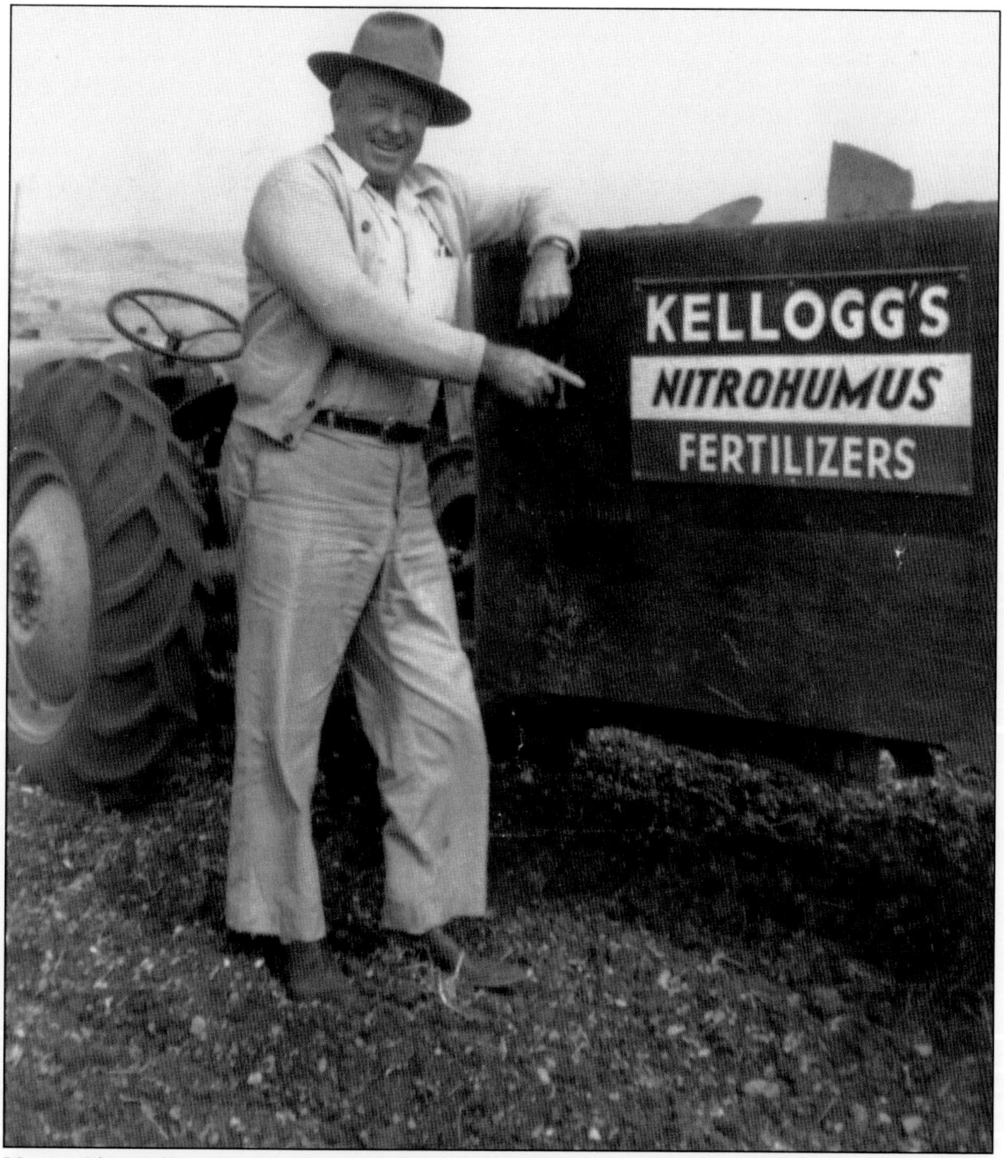

Hiram Clay Kellogg Sr., founder of Kellogg Garden Products, established his business in Carson on a handshake agreement to lease land from the Los Angeles County Sanitation District in 1925. The Kellogg family holds a distinguished place in California history, descending from the Battle Creek, Michigan, "cereal" Kelloggs. One of these Kelloggs, Mark, traveled west as far as Salt Lake City with the doomed Donner party. Hiram Sr.'s father, H. K. Kellogg, was a civil engineer whose works included intensive planning for the City of Corona, Riverside County, and work on dams and aqueducts in Southern California and Hawaii.

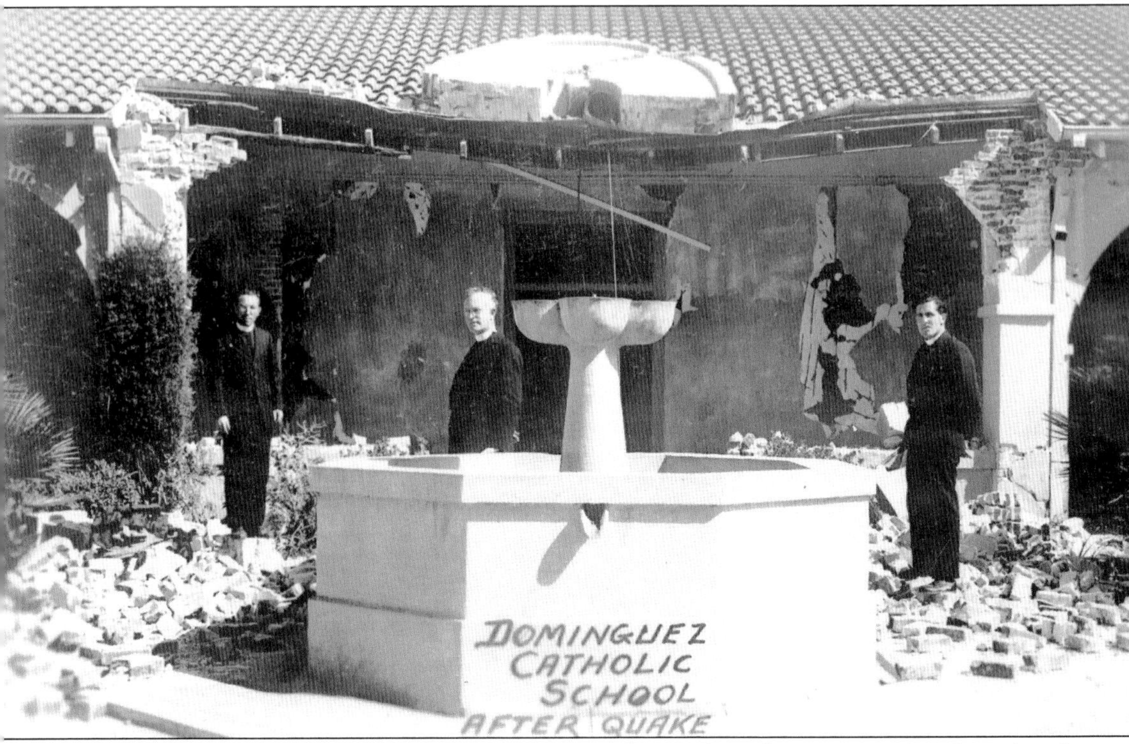

The Rancho San Pedro adobe sustained significant damage from the 1933 Long Beach earthquake, which actually had its epicenter in Compton. It registered 6.3 on the Richter scale and 120 people were killed in the region. (Courtesy Special Collections and Archives, California State University, Dominguez Hills.)

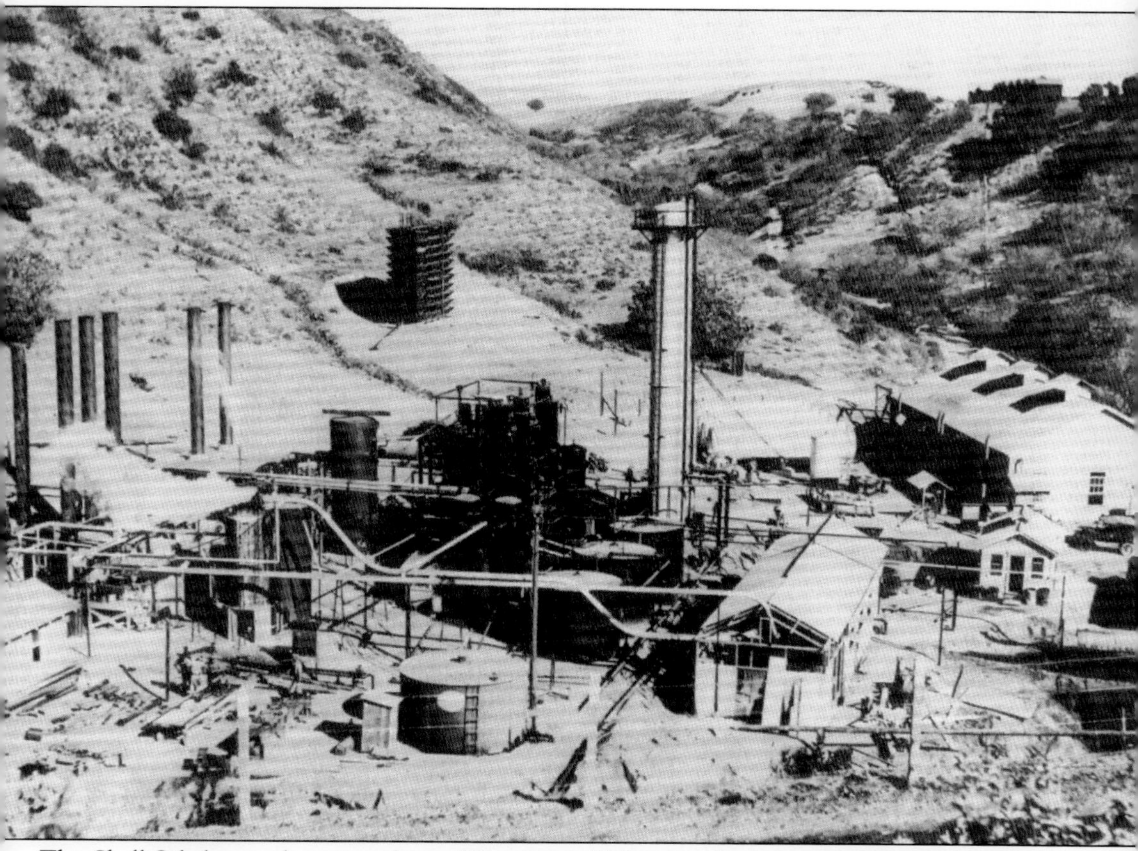

This Shell Oil plant at the eastern base of Dominguez Hill was under construction in 1927. Today its space is filled with industrial development, and a vast mobile home park sits above it.

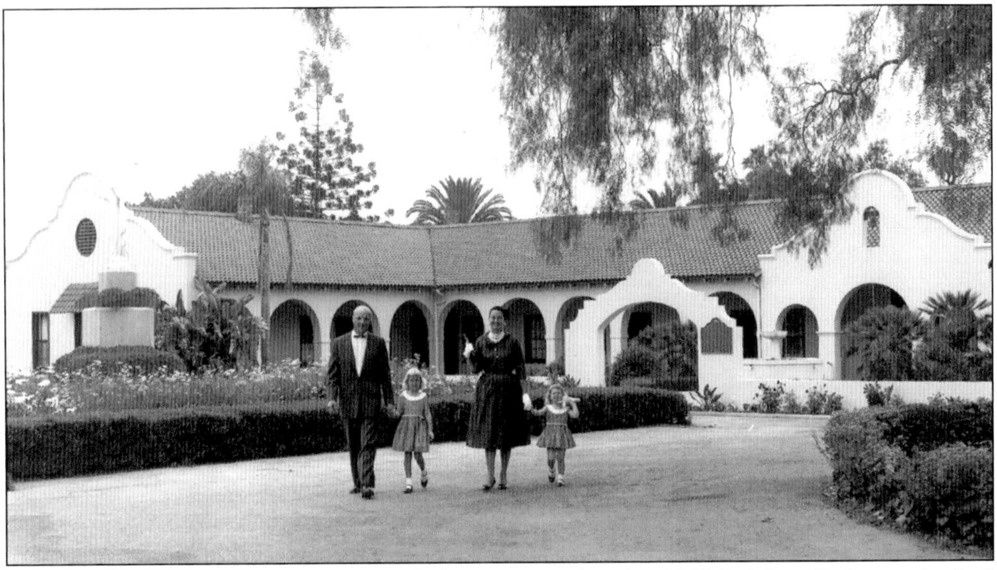

The old flat roof on the Dominguez family home was replaced in 1907 by Maria Dolores, who had moved back to the rancho two years earlier. Her other Mission Revival modifications were the round arches and white stucco gables. (Courtesy Special Collections and Archives, California State University, Dominguez Hills.)

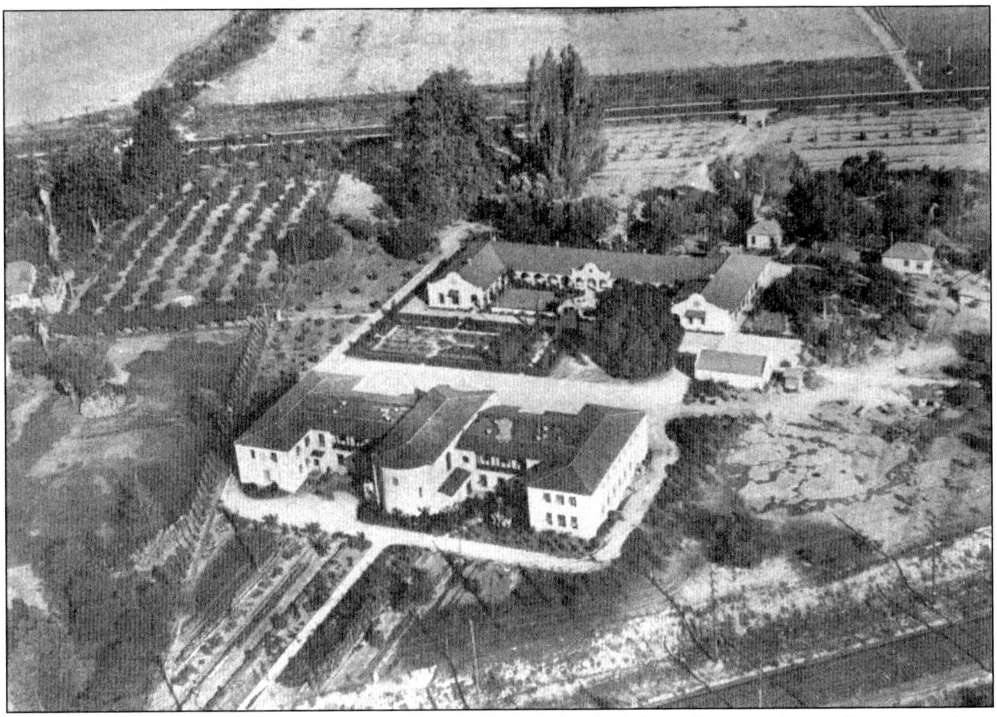

In 1922, the Dominguez family, with no male heirs, deeded the adobe and the 17 surrounding acres to the Claretian Brothers. In 1927, Gregorio Del Amo built the Casa Claret Seminary, which is at lower left in this 1930s photograph. The adobe itself eventually became a museum through a generous donation by the Claretians, who discontinued its use in 1974. (Courtesy Special Collections and Archives, California State University, Dominguez Hills.)

Three

BEFORE AND AFTER INCORPORATION

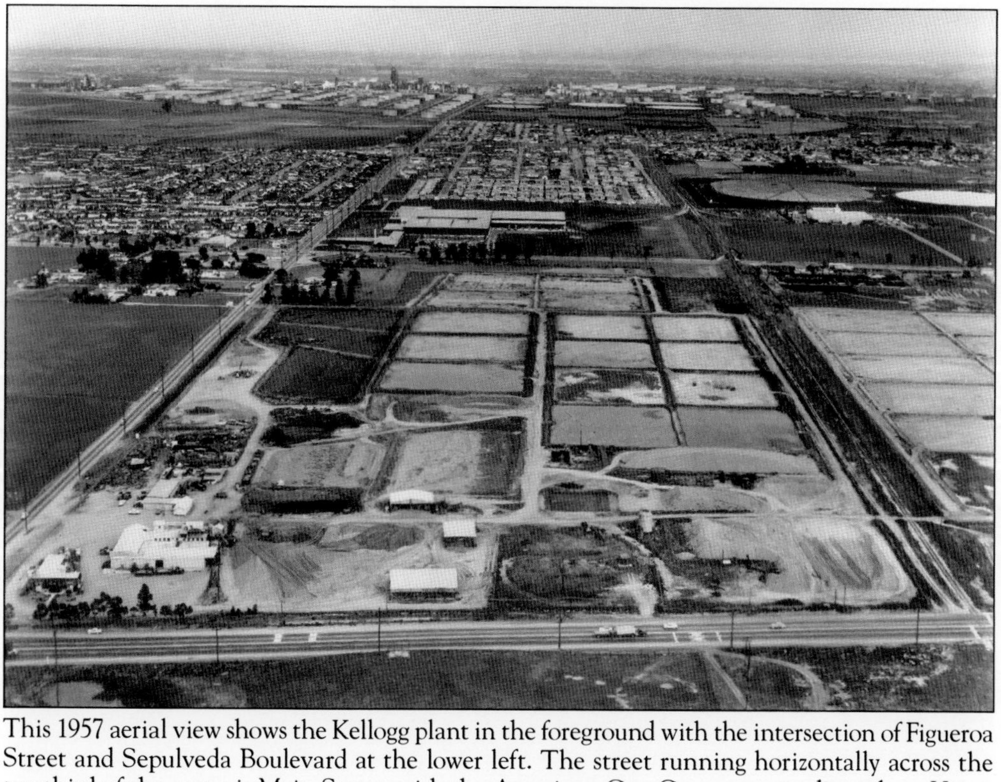

This 1957 aerial view shows the Kellogg plant in the foreground with the intersection of Figueroa Street and Sepulveda Boulevard at the lower left. The street running horizontally across the top third of the scene is Main Street, with the American Can Company standing where Home Depot and Albertson's shopping center are today. Signal Hill and a forest of oil derricks can be seen in the far, shadowy distance. (Courtesy Special Collections and Archives, California State University, Dominguez Hills.)

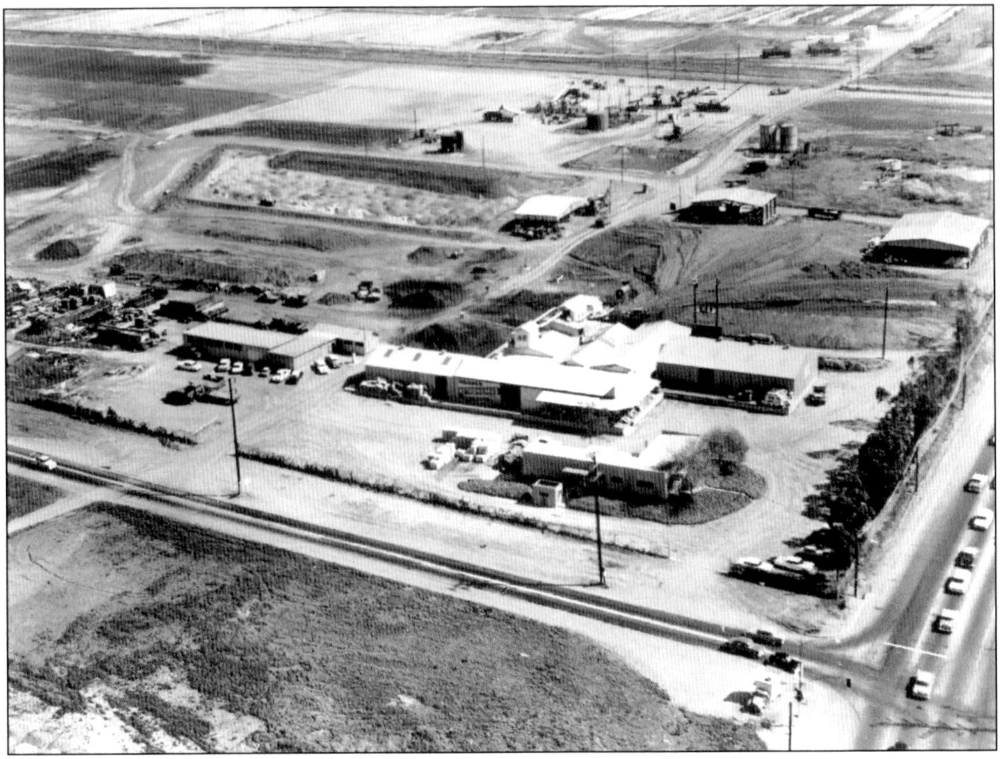

A look from above the intersection of Sepulveda Boulevard and Figueroa Street shows the relative emptiness of the future Carson area in 1957, which is still occupied today by Kellogg Garden Products, although the company no longer produces fertilizers at the Carson site.

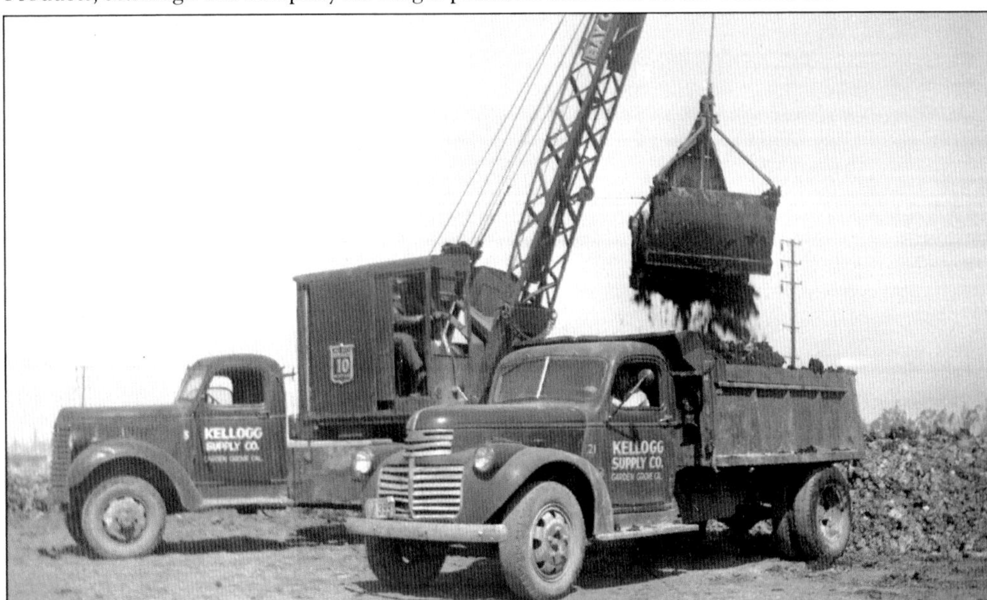

Trucks are loaded with the Kellogg product, which has been used in the landscapes and gardens of many California landmarks such as Disneyland, the Hearst Castle, the Getty Museum, Dodger Stadium, and the Coliseum, as well as the Tropicana in Las Vegas.

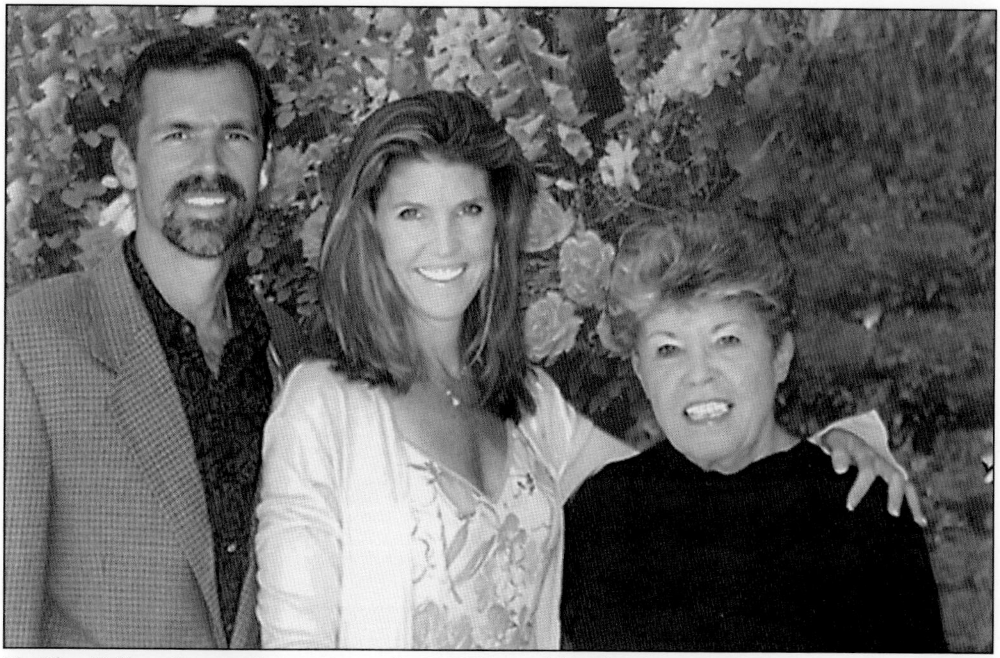

H. Clay Kellogg Jr. ran the company from 1958 until his death in 1987. Before he died, Kellogg surprised his wife, Janice, by insisting that, in the event of his death, she would be in charge. According to Mrs. Kellogg, "It turned out to be the kindest thing he could have done." The Kellogg family still runs the company and is today represented by, from left to right, Hap Kellogg, Kathy Johnson Kellogg, and Janice Kellogg.

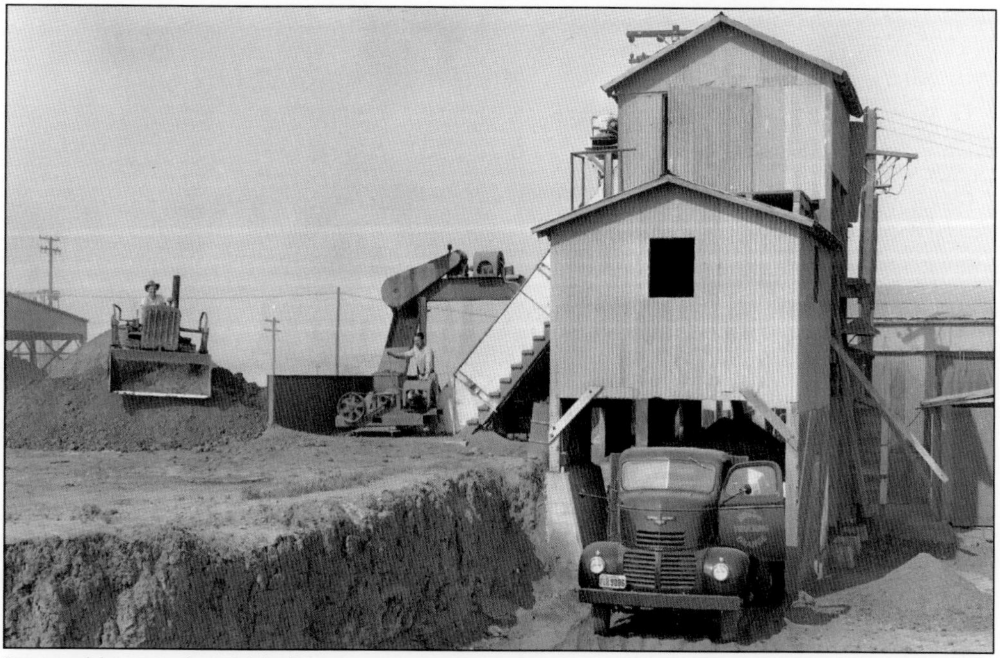

Pictured here is the old bulk screening and grinding operation, where trucks are loaded from above with the finished product. In earlier days, Kellogg used horses and wagons in the beds to transport materials for screening and grinding.

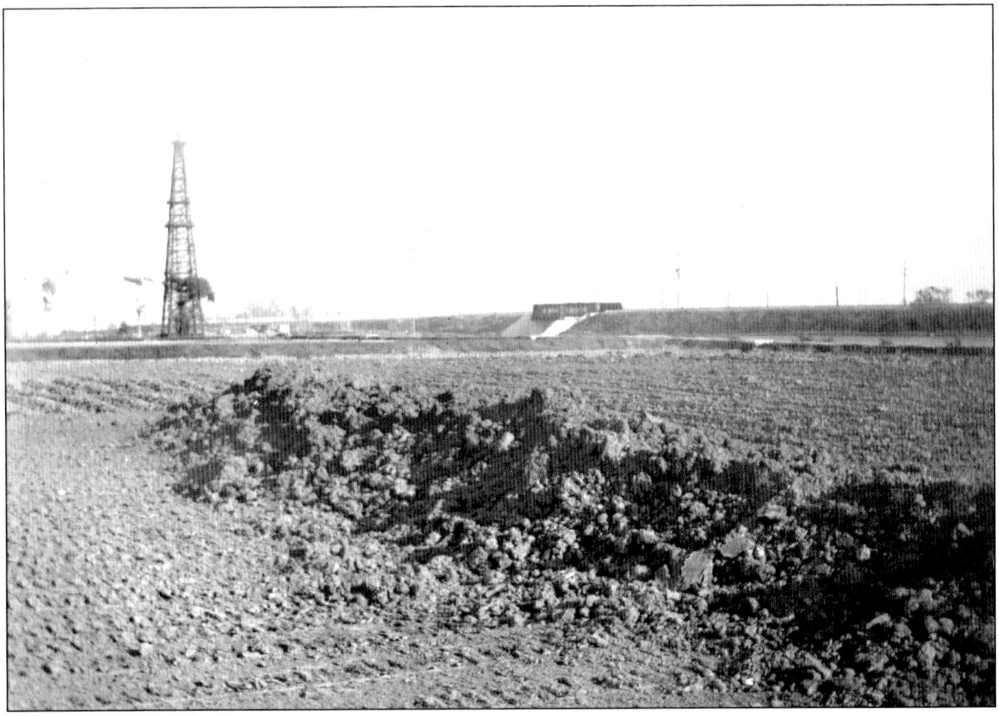

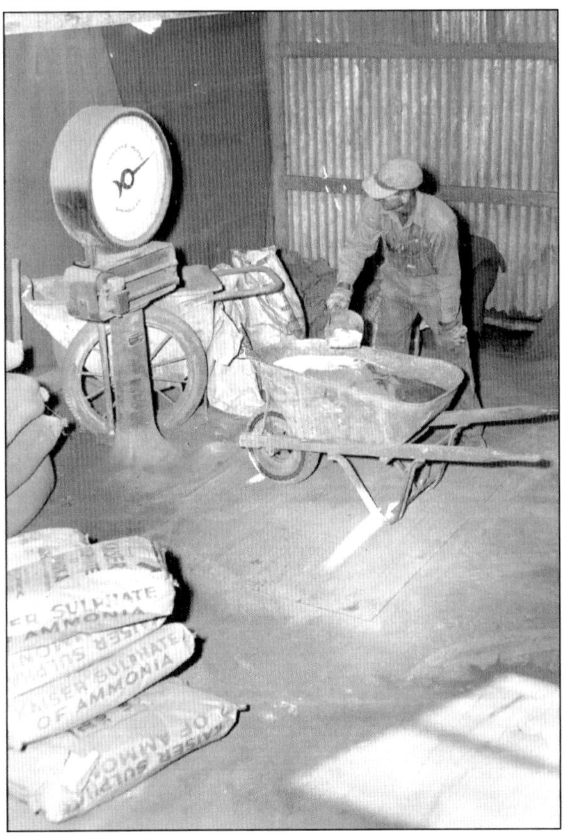

Looking southeast from Figueroa Street and Sepulveda Boulevard lies a sewage drying bed, with the still familiar Main Street railroad bridge in the background.

Fertilizer components were hand-mixed in the 1930s at Kellogg Garden Products on the Los Angeles County lands that became the city of Carson.

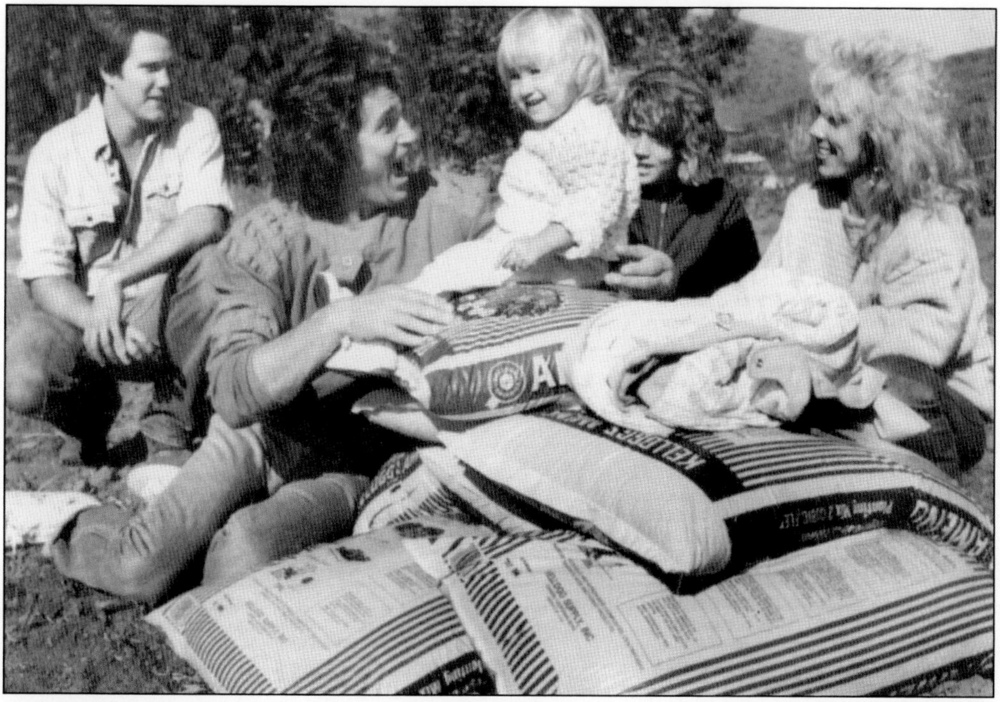

In the 1970s, actor Michael Landon and his family participated in a promotional shoot for Kellogg. Landon, second from left, starred in the television series *Bonanza*, *Little House on the Prairie*, and *Highway to Heaven*.

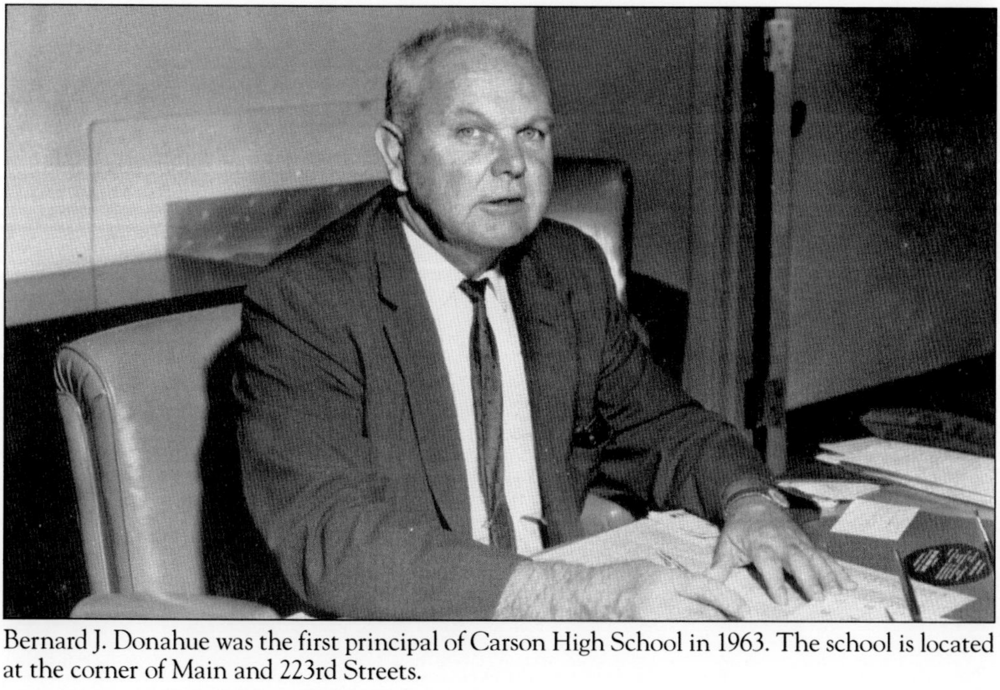

Bernard J. Donahue was the first principal of Carson High School in 1963. The school is located at the corner of Main and 223rd Streets.

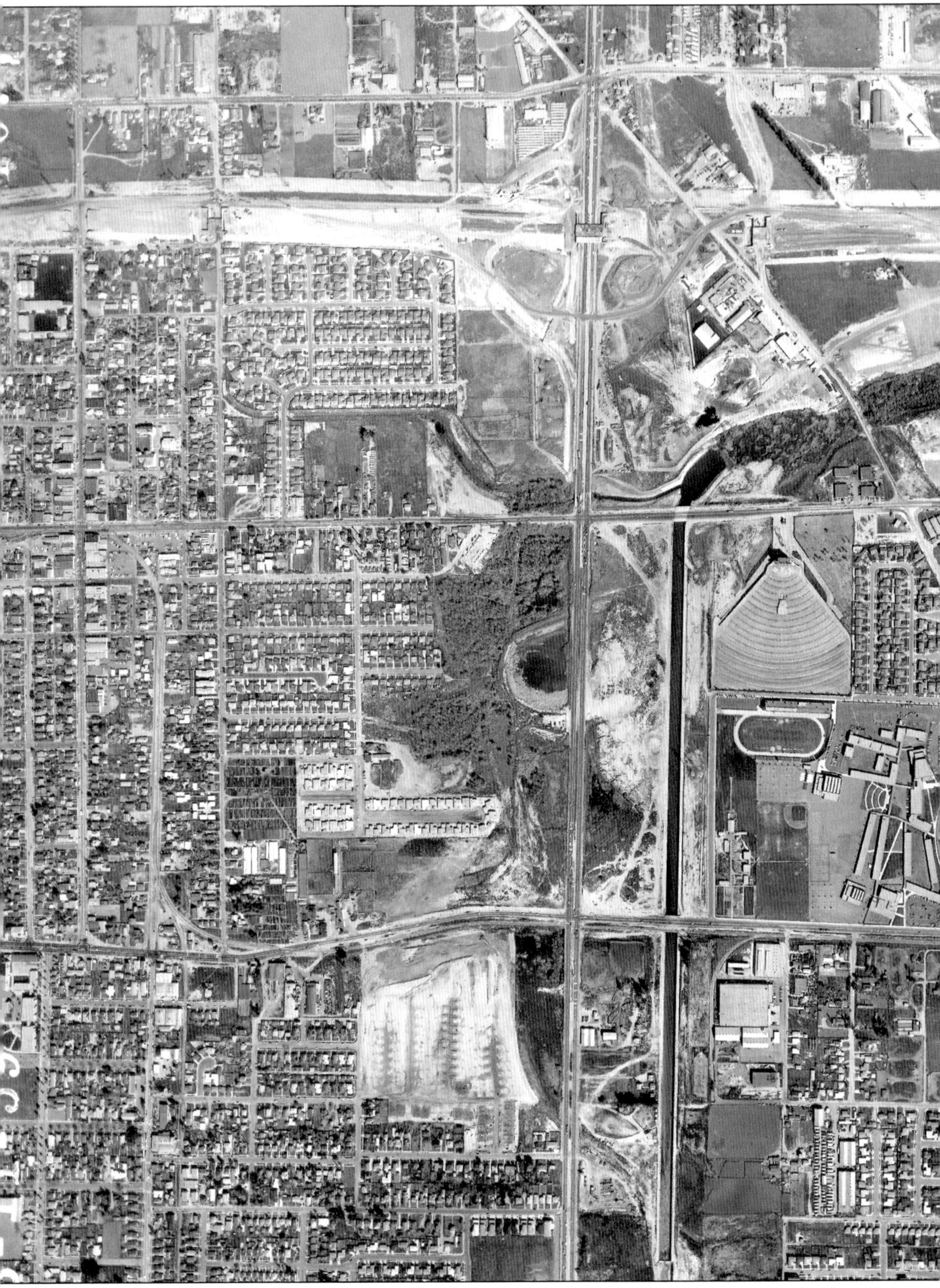

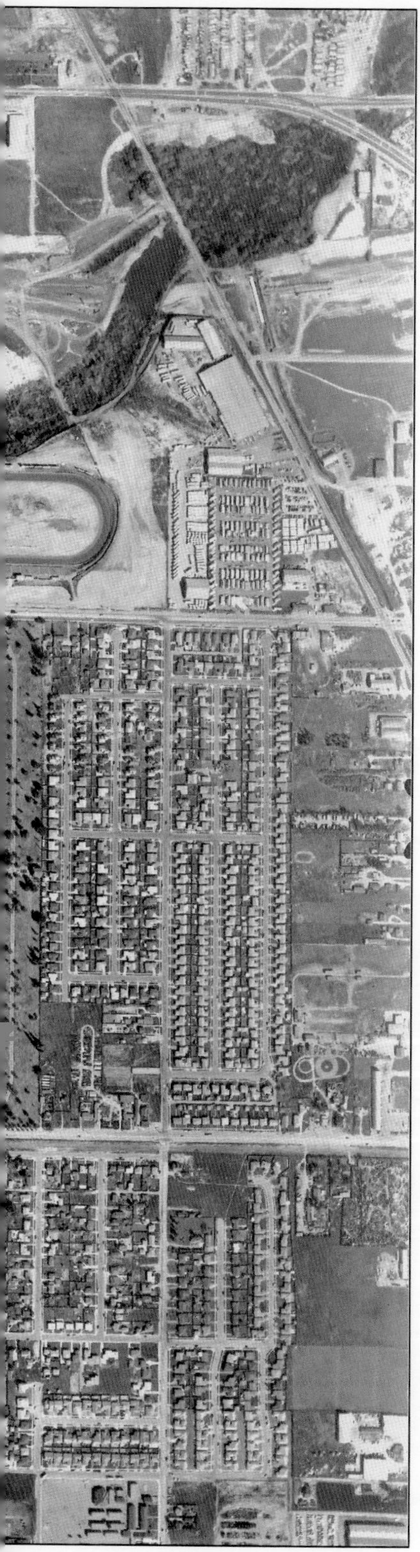

This 1959 aerial image depicts the southernmost portion of the Harbor Freeway still under construction, traversing the area from left to right along the top quarter. The first part of the freeway opened in 1952, and it was finally completed in 1970. Today the Harbor Freeway is a vital transportation link between the Ports of Long Beach and Los Angeles and other connecting freeways, as well as the city's downtown. (Courtesy Special Collections and Archives, California State University, Dominguez Hills.)

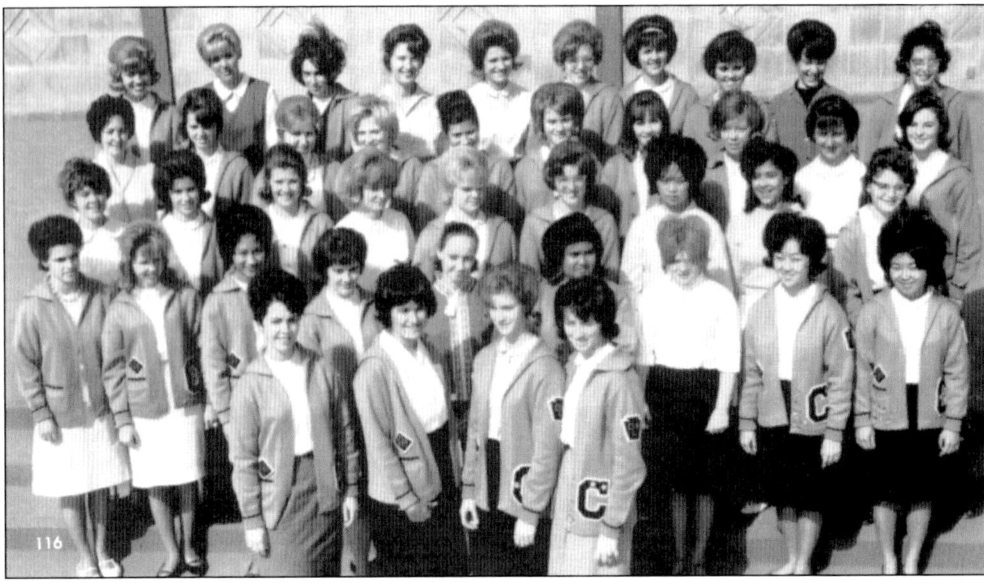

The 1963 Carson High School Letter Girls pose for their group photograph during the year that the school opened. (Courtesy Carson High School.)

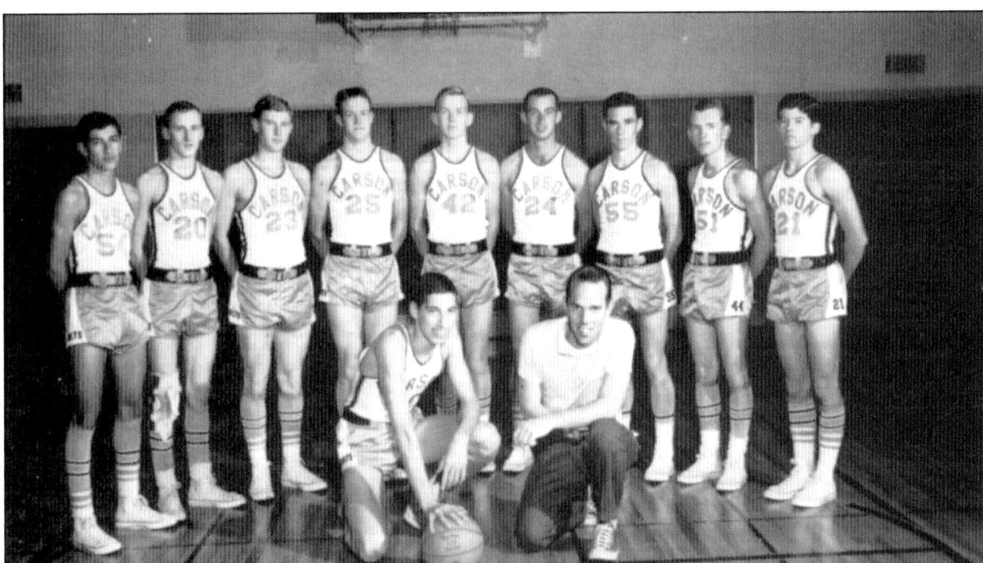

Carson Varsity Basketball in 1963 included, from left to right, (first row) Pat Holmes, coach Ezell; (second row) Harvey Holmes, Mike McFarline, Lee Miller, Gary Roller, Buddy Brown, Nick VanLue, Steve Mead, Robert Crisp, and Ken Fenton.

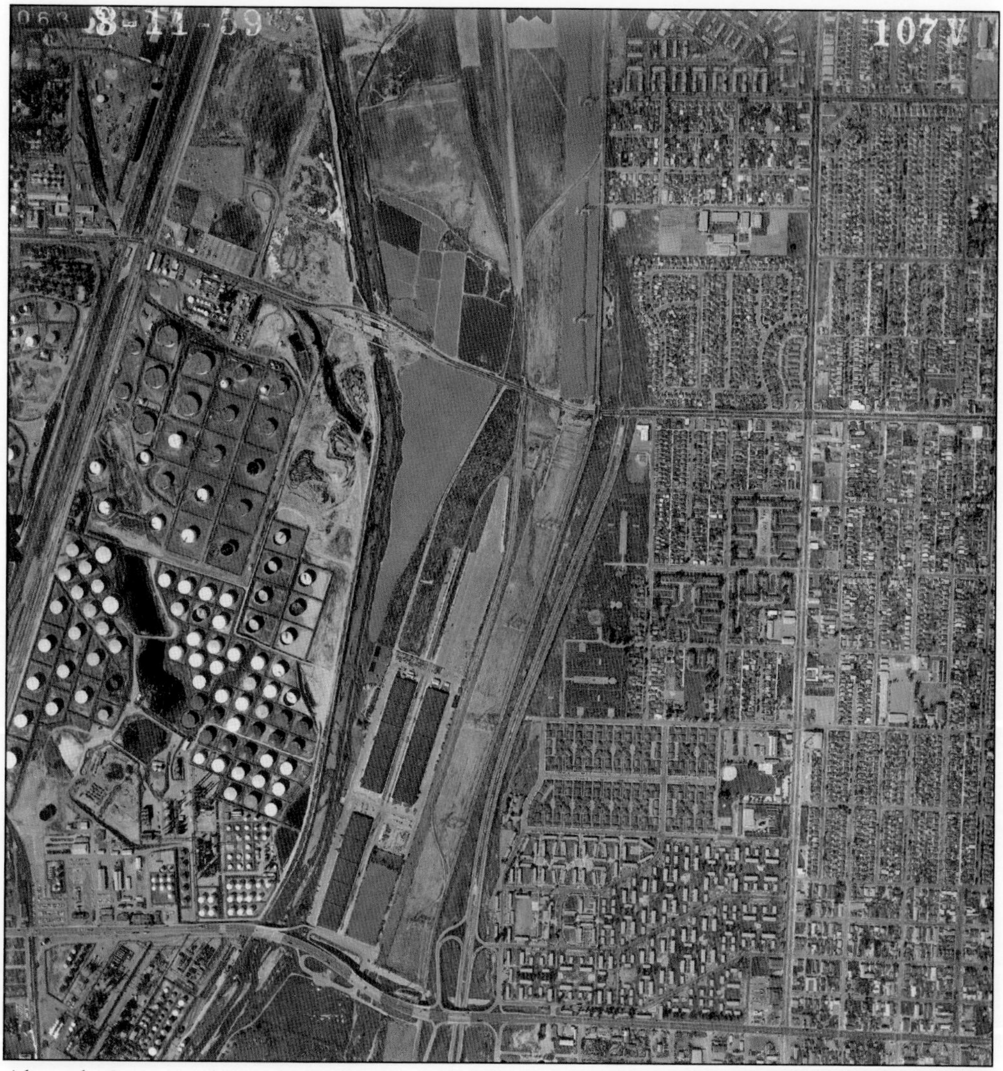

Alameda Street and Sepulveda Boulevard can be seen in the upper left quadrant of this 1959 aerial photograph, with the Cal Cartage trucking yard running down the center of the image and the Pacific Coast Highway running horizontally across the bottom. (Courtesy Special Collections and Archives, California State University, Dominguez Hills.)

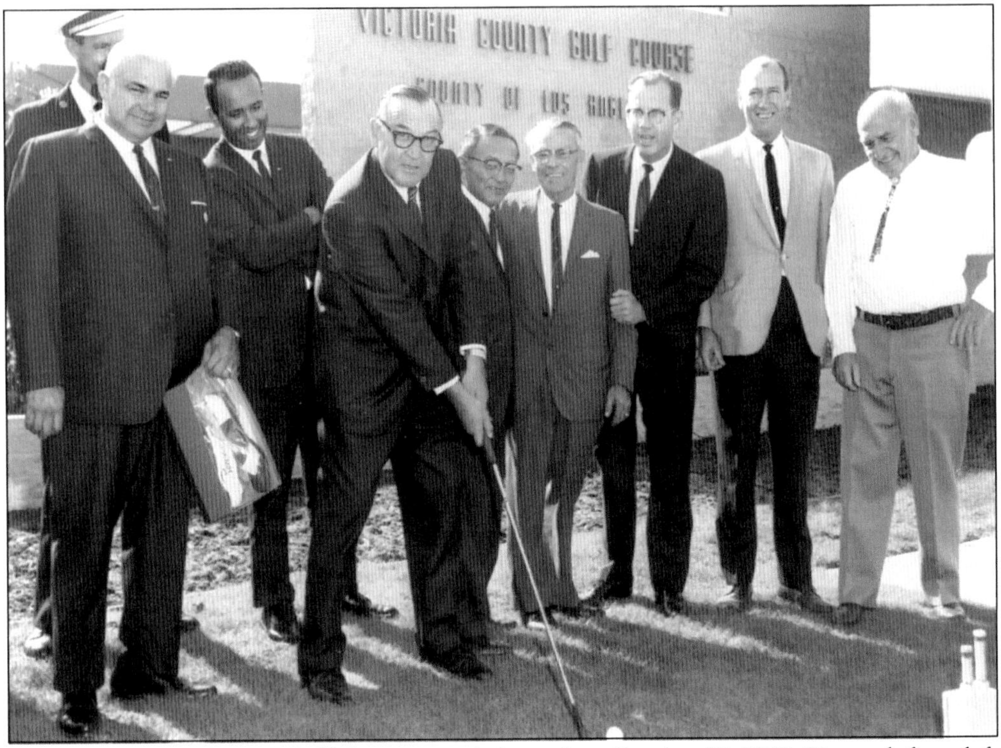

The new Victoria County Golf Course was dedicated on October 10, 1966. Pictured, from left to right, are fire battalion chief Paul Schneider (also the first chamber of commerce president), John Calas, Gil Smith, California governor Edmund G. Brown, Sak Yamamoto, an unidentified Los Angeles County parks and recreation representative, Kenneth Hahn, "Mr." Harvey (sports shop owner), and Art Fritzen.

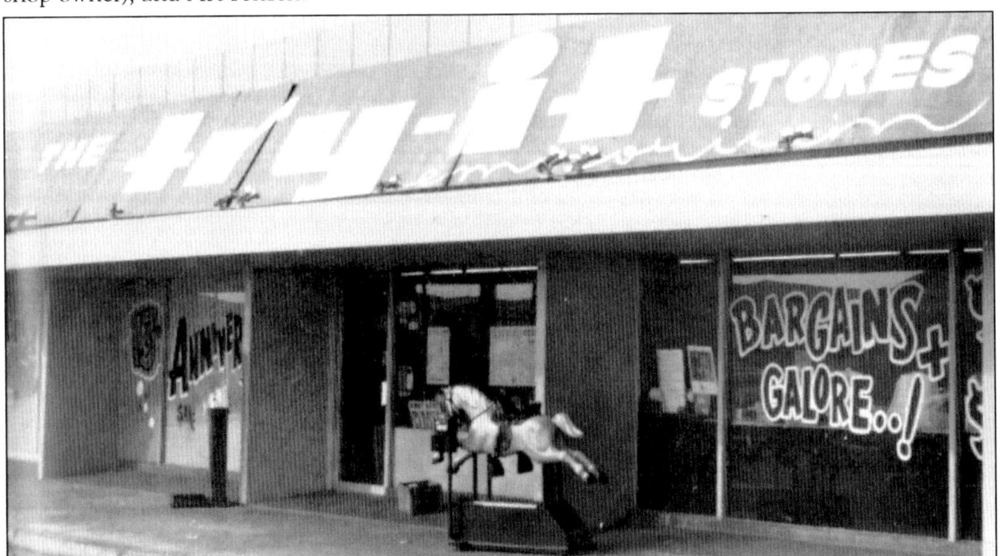

The Try-It Stores Emporium in 1965 was located at 23027–33 South Avalon Boulevard. Once a thriving retail center, it was later abandoned and became the scene of gang activity, vandalism, and arson fires in the late 1990s and early 2000s. A new gated community has since taken its place.

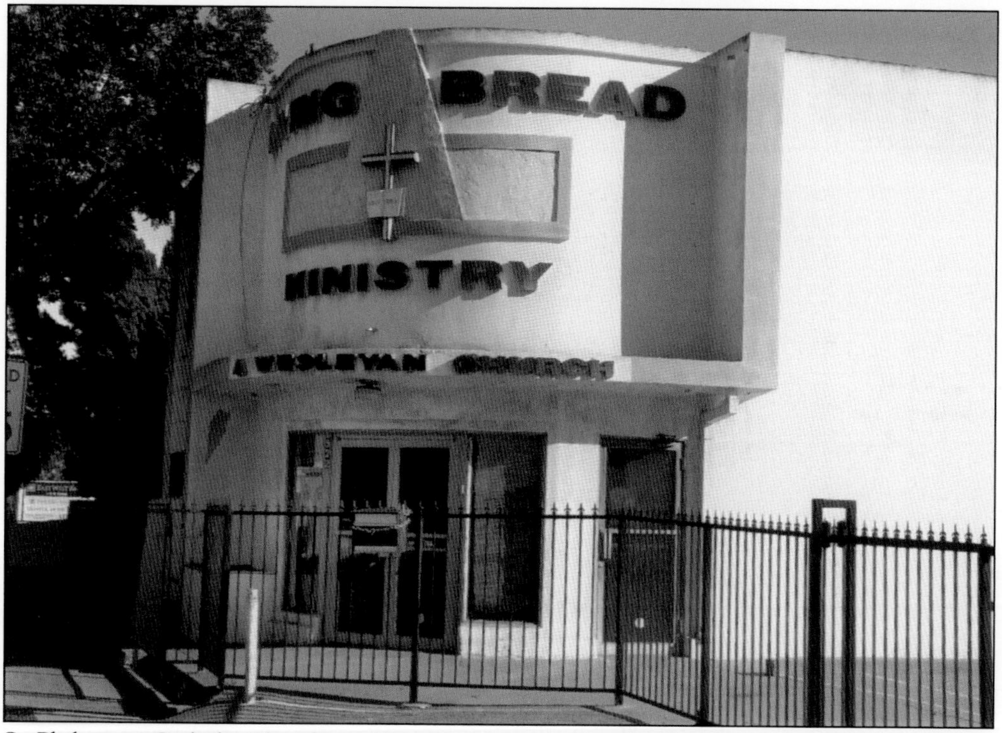

St. Philomena Catholic Church's earliest masses were held at the Plasterers' Union Hall on Carson Street before the church was built. The old art deco-style building now houses its own church, the Living Bread Ministry, and retains its classic, although crumbling, facade.

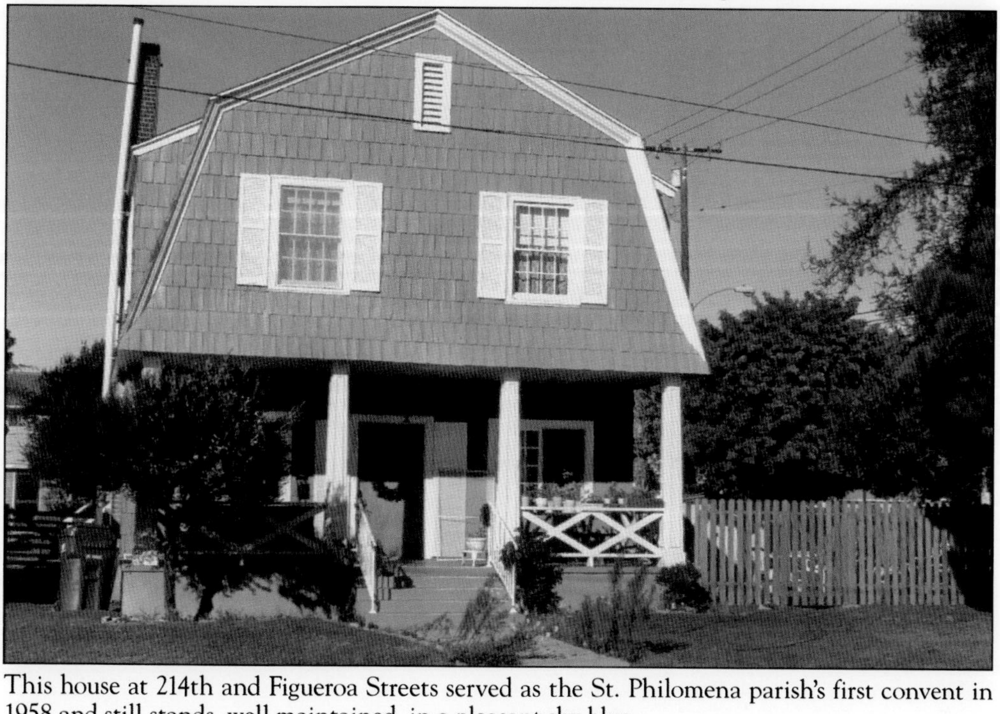

This house at 214th and Figueroa Streets served as the St. Philomena parish's first convent in 1958 and still stands, well maintained, in a pleasant sky blue.

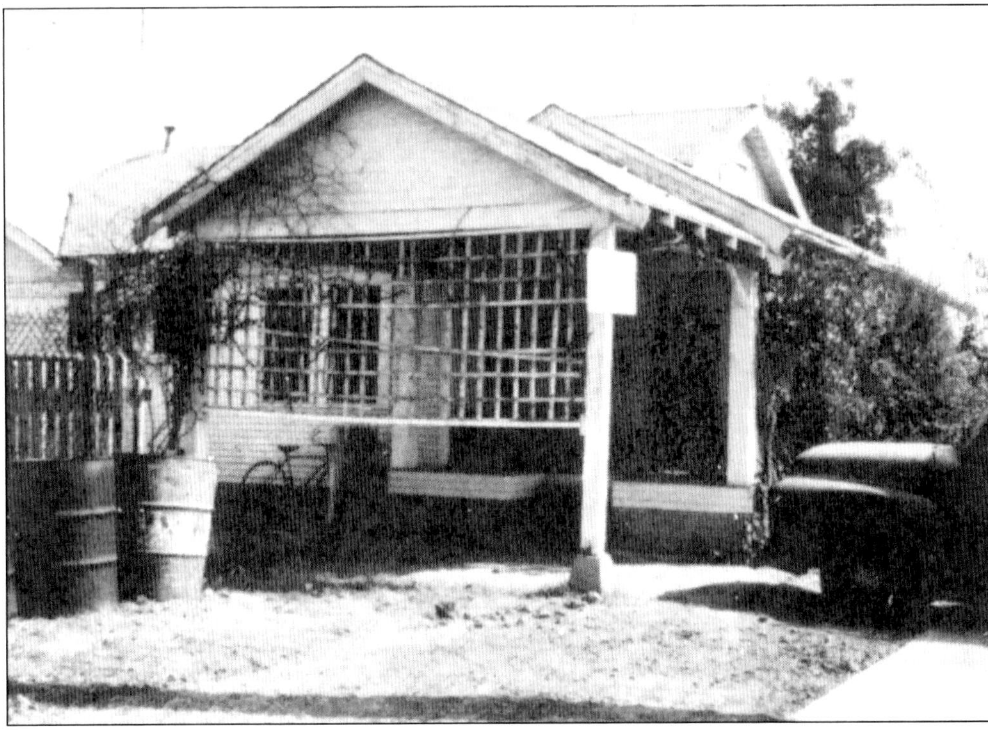

Pictured here is Carson's first city hall, a converted residence located at 625 East Carson Street. Its second location was a modular unit at the edge of a large vacant lot on Avalon Boulevard and 228th Street. The third site was at 21919 South Avalon Boulevard.

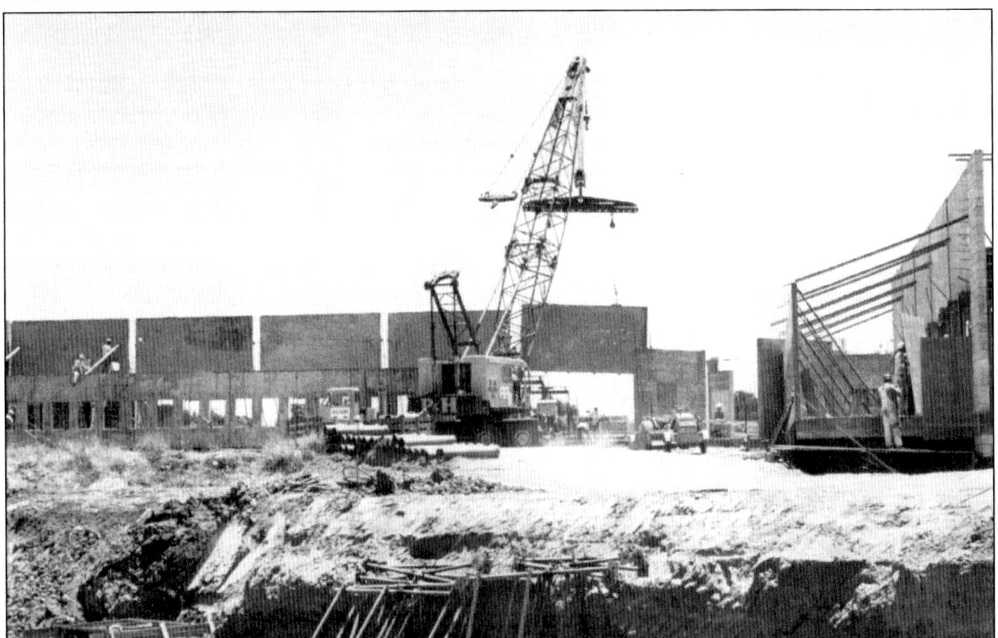

Today's Carson City Hall is under construction here in 1975. The new facility contained over 60,000 square feet and was dedicated on February 21, 1976.

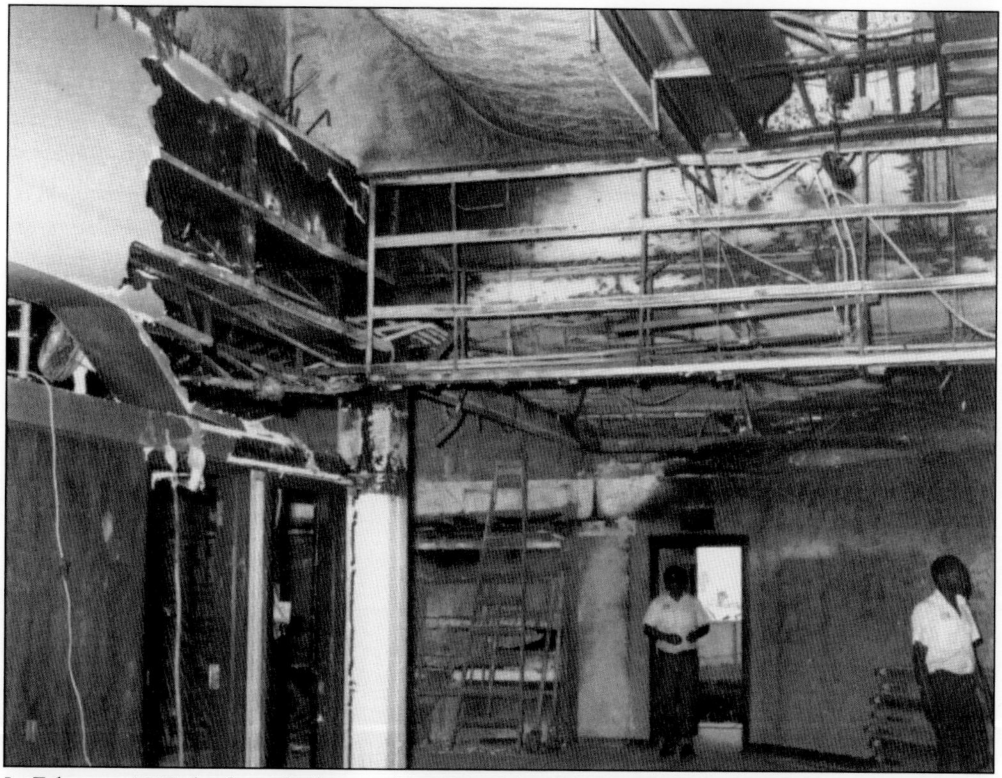

In February 1987, fire heavily damaged a wing of the new facility. Losses included many archived historic documents and photographs. The City of Carson Archival Committee has recently been formed to restore and renew the city's collection of memorabilia.

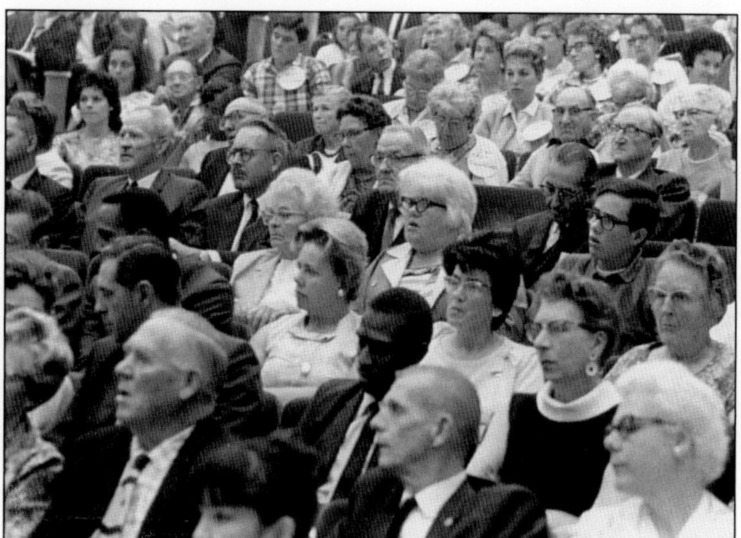

Citizens gather before the Los Angeles County Board of Supervisors for a hearing on Carson's impending incorporation. Pictured in the audience are Al Sims, Bill Salyers, Mary Santiago, Glenn Henderson, Bill Snudden, Irv Hulse, Peg Hulse, and R. Green. The city was finally established in 1968.

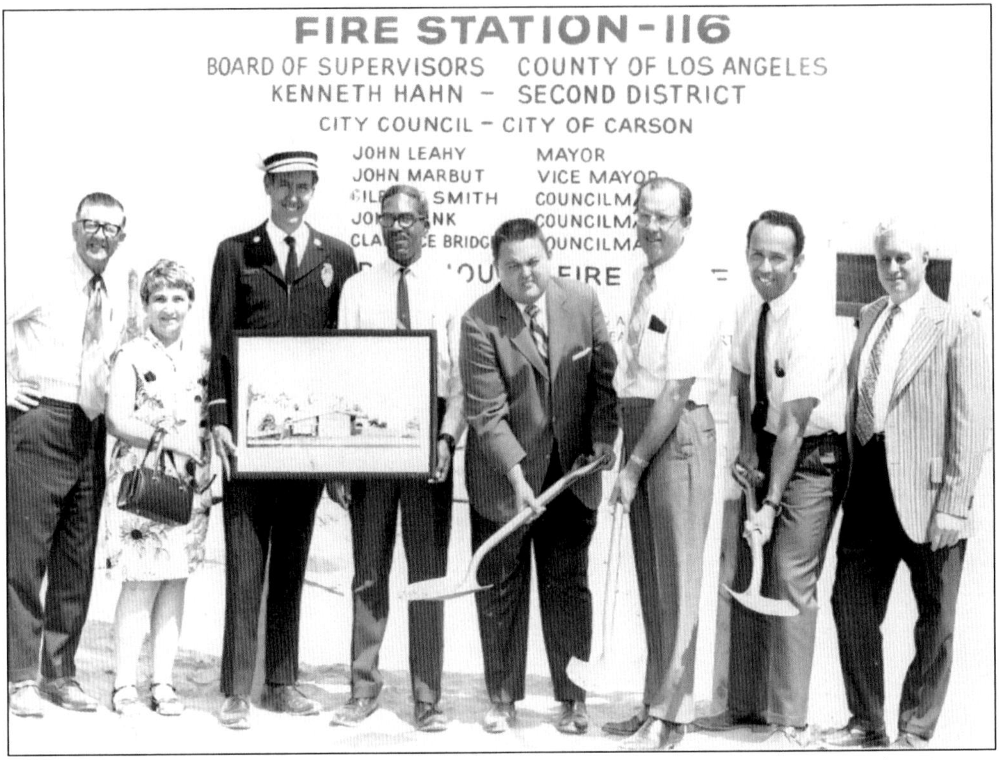

Ground was broken for Fire Station No. 116 at Victoria Avenue and Avalon Boulevard in August 1971. Pictured, from left to right, are John Marbut, Thelma Strelitz, battalion chief Paul Schneider, Clarence Bridgers, John Leahy, county supervisor Kenneth Hahn, Gil Smith, and Dan Jhanke.

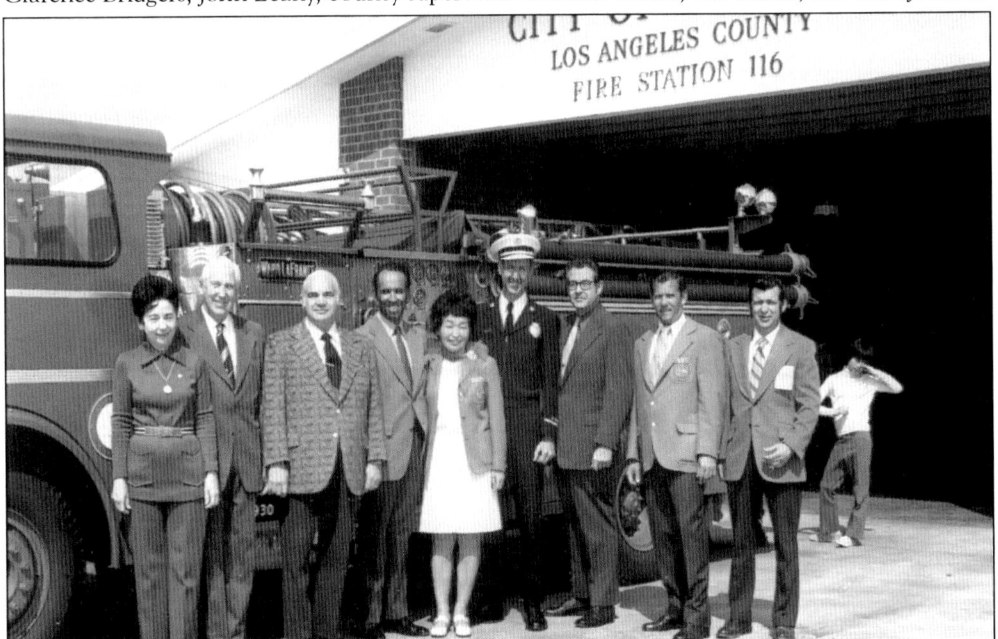

The completed fire station at Victoria and Avalon is being dedicated here in 1972.

Santa has been a familiar sight on the streets of Carson at Christmastime. In earlier days, he was driven around on a fire truck. In this 1962 photograph, former mayor John Leahy plays Santa. For many years, prominent citizen and local dairyman Ben Cluff put on the red suit.

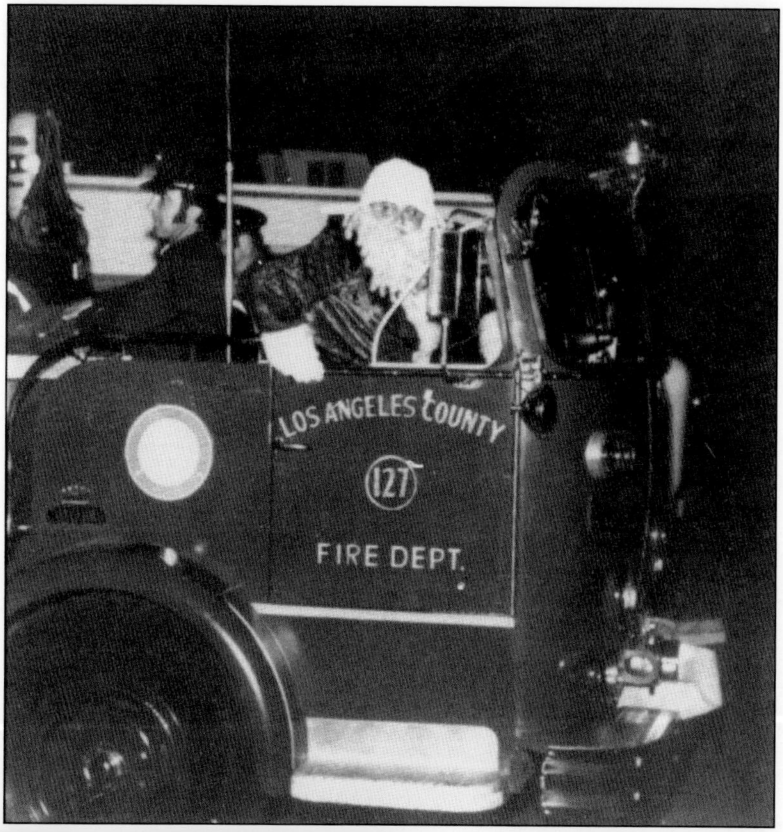

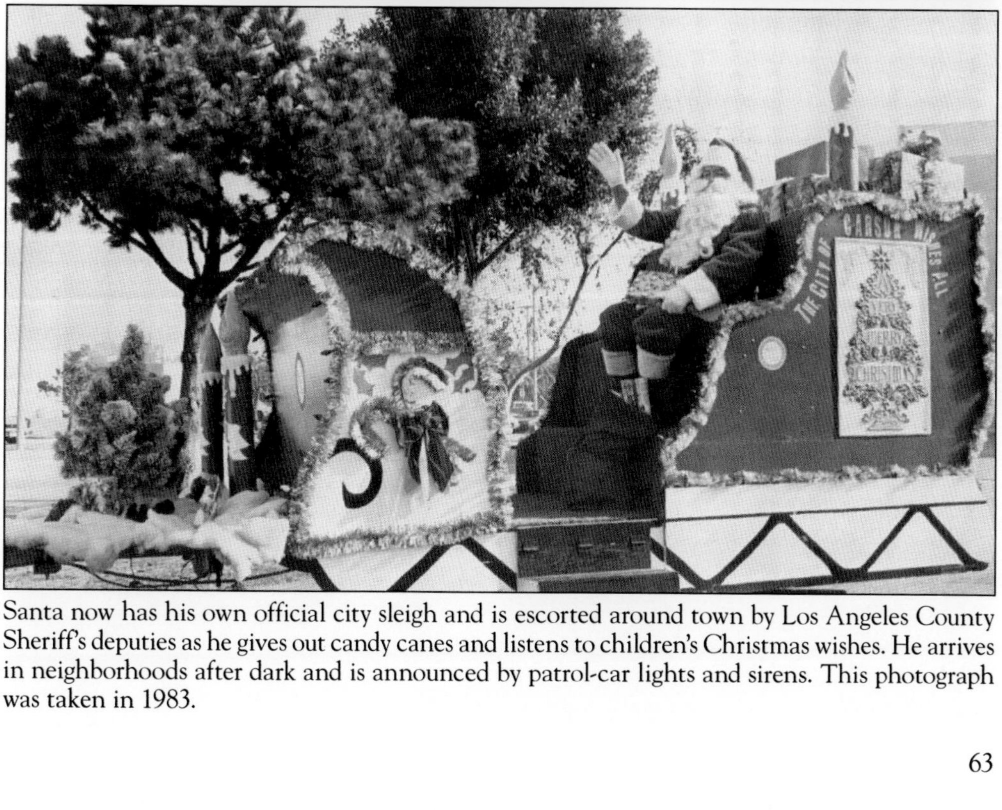

Santa now has his own official city sleigh and is escorted around town by Los Angeles County Sheriff's deputies as he gives out candy canes and listens to children's Christmas wishes. He arrives in neighborhoods after dark and is announced by patrol-car lights and sirens. This photograph was taken in 1983.

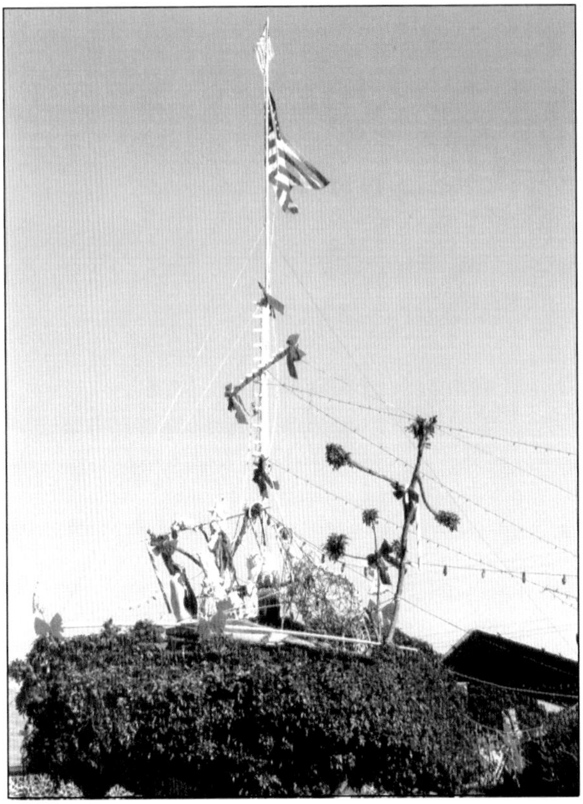

A familiar sight to Carson residents year-round is this Christmas display in a tree at a home in the Scott Park neighborhood. This ship bobs proudly in the breeze and seems to be a tongue-in-cheek tribute to Carson's diversity. It features, among other symbols not pictured, Santa, the Virgin Mary, penguins, an American eagle, turtledoves, crosses, Christmas bells, and a tall "mast" that flies the Stars and Stripes.

Carson Day at Santa Anita Racetrack on February 12, 1975, had community representatives greeting "Shoe" himself, Willie Shoemaker, at the sixth race. Shoemaker, generally considered the greatest jockey of all time, won four Kentucky Derbies, five Belmont Stakes, and three Preakness Stakes.

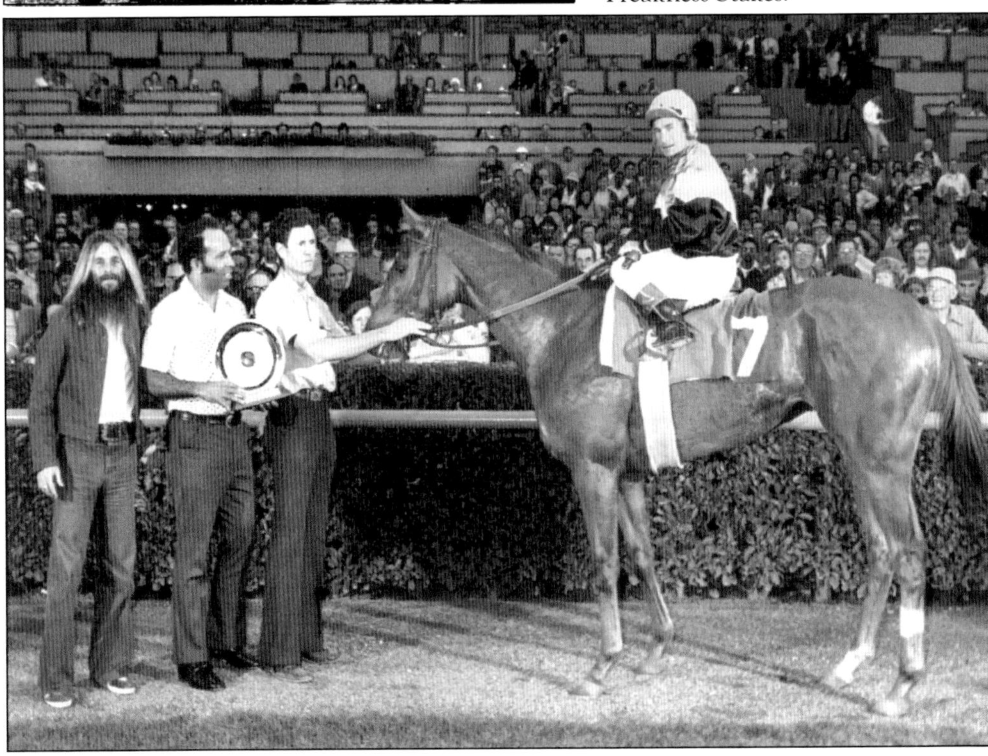

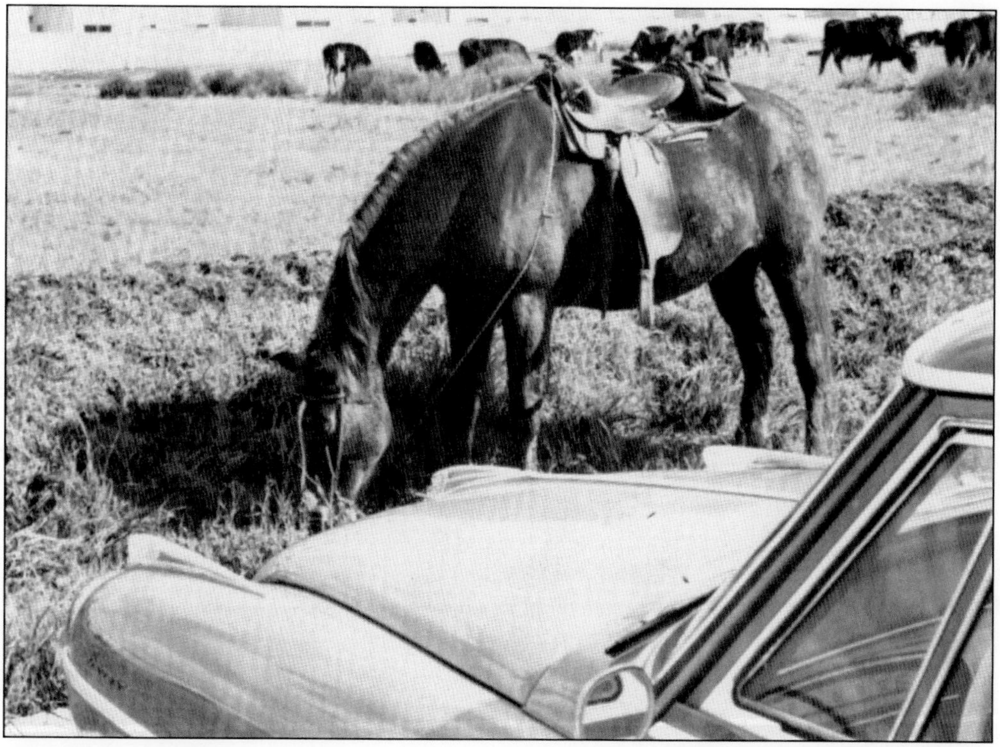

Academia meets agriculture at California State University, Dominguez Hills, in 1969, as seen by the livestock boundary between the parking lot and residences. Former mayor and councilman Gil Smith recalls renting horses for 50¢ an hour in the neighborhood.

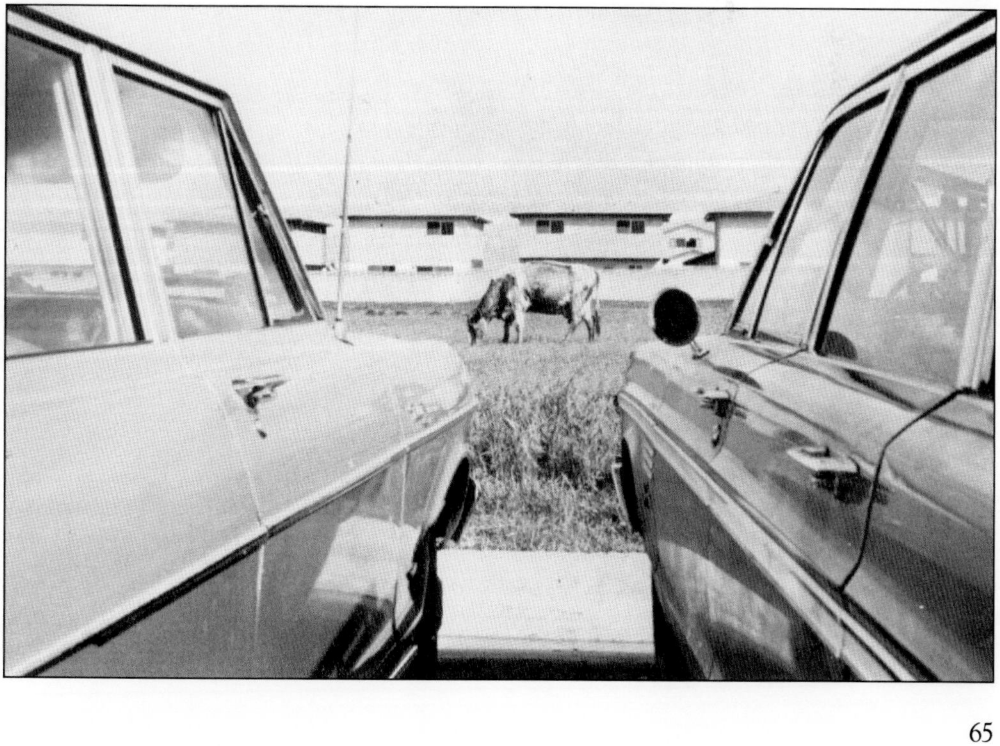

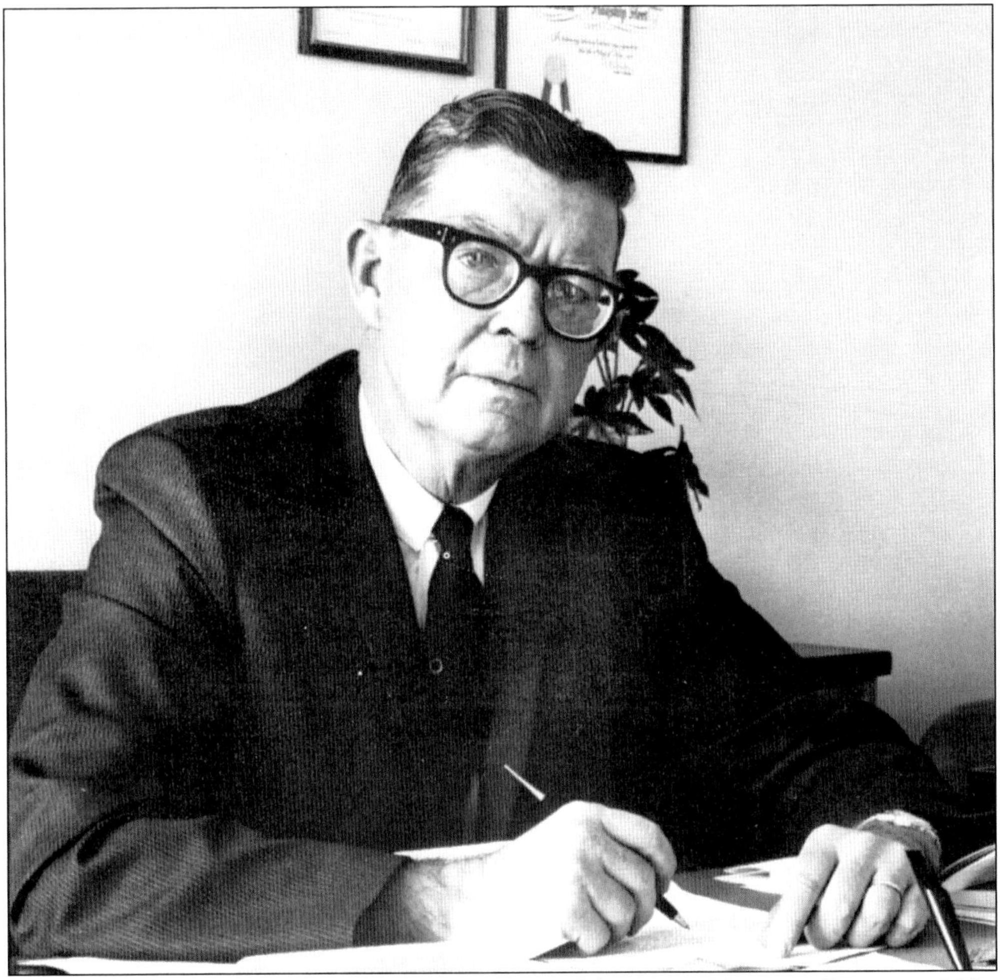

In the 1960s, Leo F. Cain served as the first president of California State University, Dominguez Hills. (Courtesy Special Collections and Archives, California State University, Dominguez Hills.)

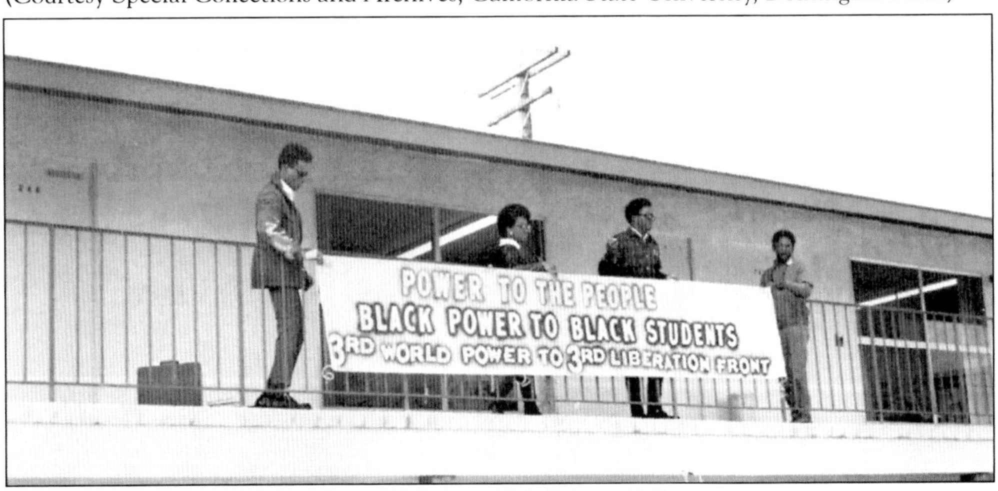

The CSUDH Black Student Union celebrates Club Day in 1969.

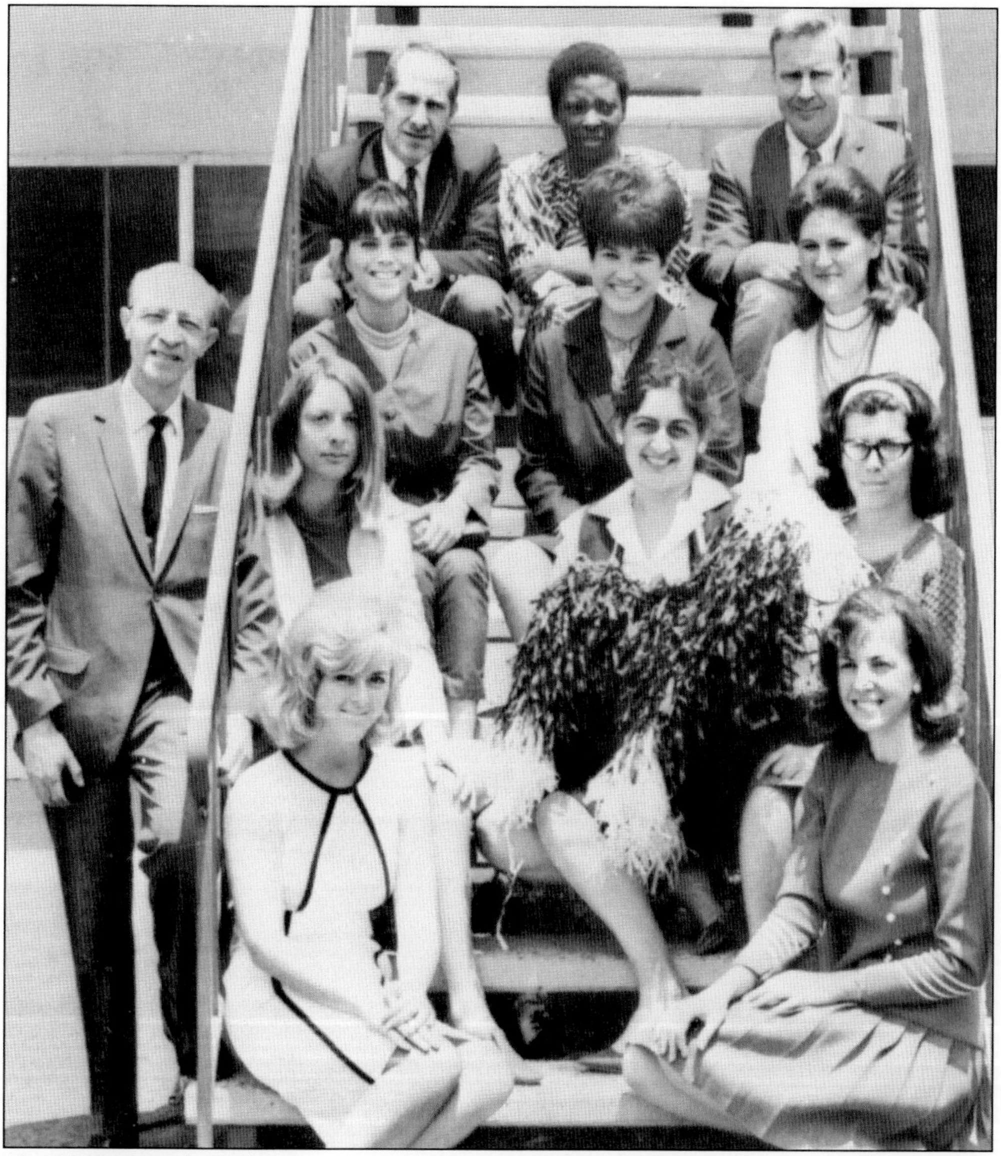

The 1968 Spanish Club was under the direction of Dr. Adolfo Monsanto and Alba Moeser at CSUDH.

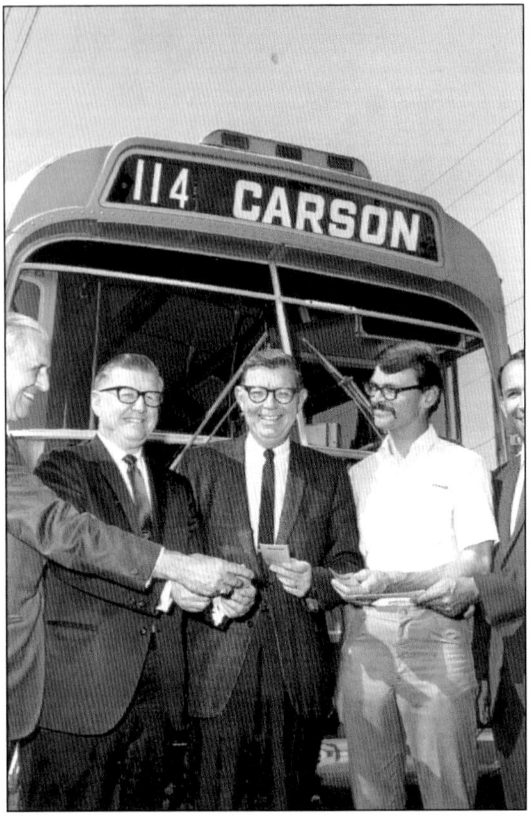

University president Leo Cain (center) councilman Gil Smith (far right), and representatives of the RTD are commemorating the Southern California Rapid Transit District (RTD) extension to CSUDH on November 8, 1968.

The new Carson City Hall was officially dedicated during the country's bicentennial year on February 21, 1976. Preparing to cut the celebratory cake are, from left to right, Clarence Bridgers, Gil Smith, John Marbut, and Sak Yamamoto.

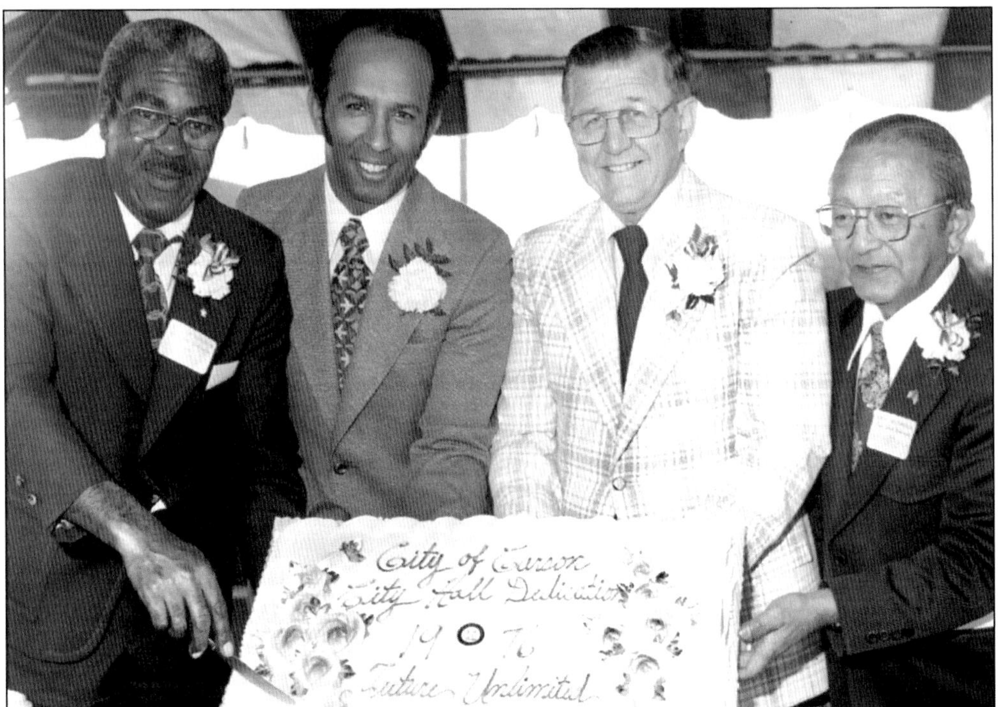

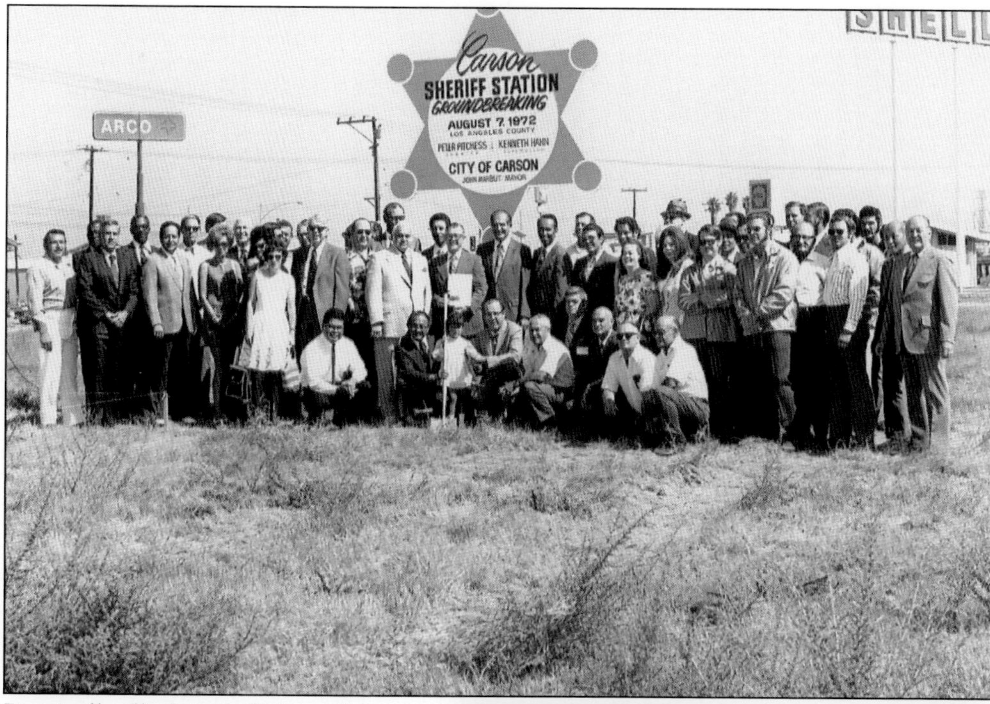

Practically all of city hall showed up for the groundbreaking of the new Los Angeles County Sherriff Station.

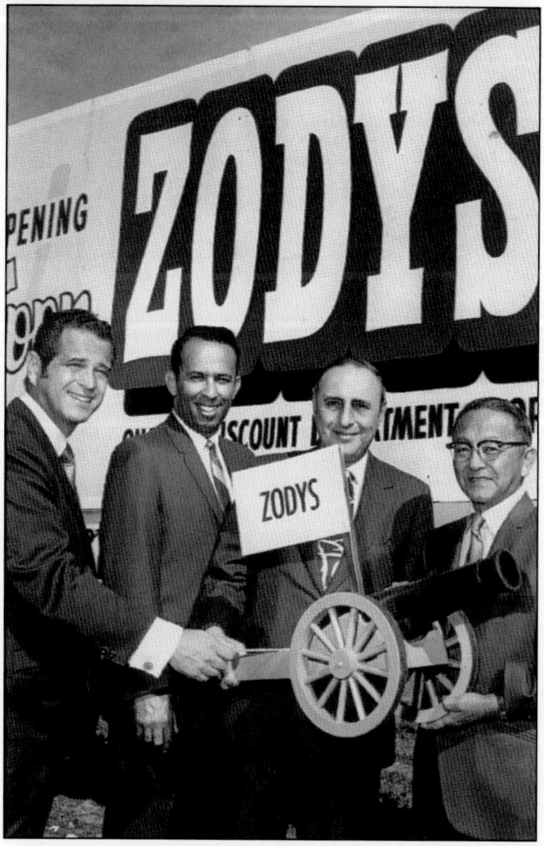

Zody's Discount Department Store was once located at the corner of Vermont Avenue and Sepulveda Boulevard. Former mayors Gil Smith, second from left, and Sak Yamamoto, right, were at the grand opening in the late 1960s.

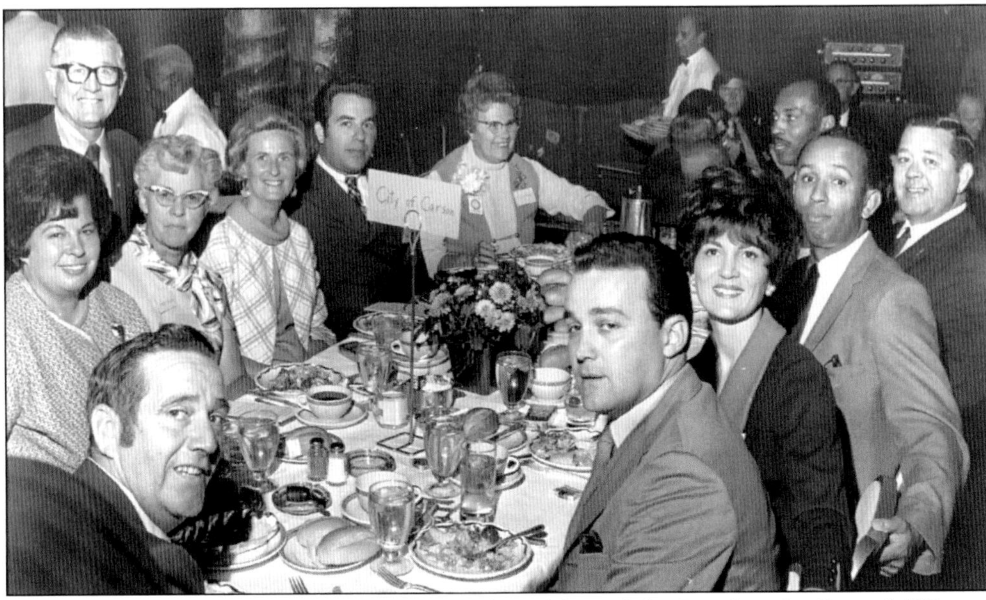

It was a stylish group of city representatives who celebrated the Los Angeles Beautiful/Carson Beautiful Award in 1969. Combating the blight inherited with the area before city hood has long been a community concern, with both residents and businesses rewarded for their efforts. From the left end of the table are Andy McCormack, John Junk, Mary Custer, Gil Smith, and Bob Scanlon. At the far right end of the table is Fred Ex, with Gertrude Schwartz to the left. On top left is John Marbut. The woman at left end is Jane Wyman, and next to her is Virginia Smith.

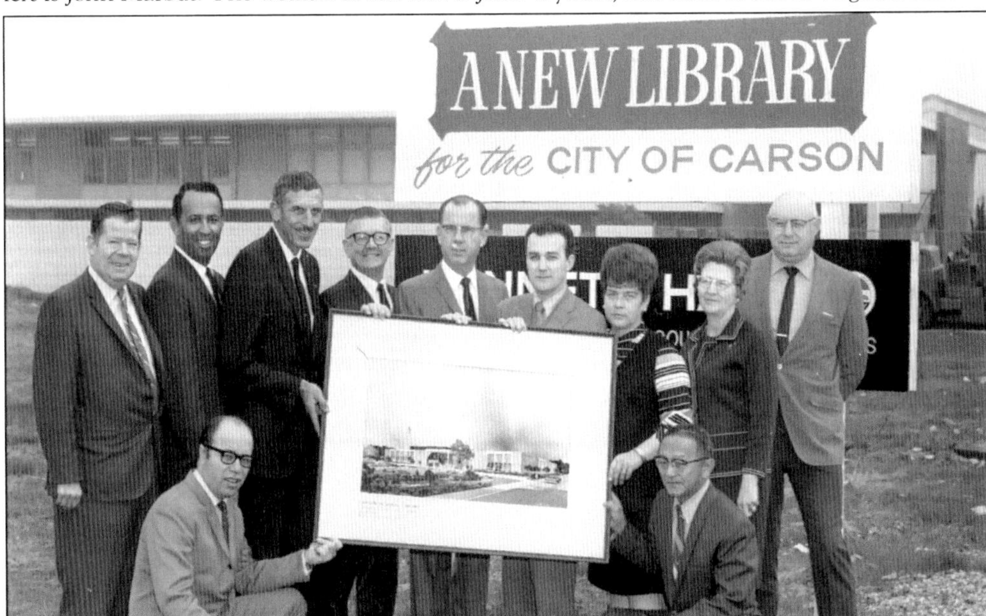

Groundbreaking for the new Carson Regional Library at Carson and Main Streets was celebrated in February 1970. Pictured, from left to right, are (first row) Rick Clark, and Sak Yamamoto; (second row) the deputy to Burton Chase, Gil Smith, Bill Jonelli of Southern California Gas, John Marbut, Kenneth Hahn, John Junk, Jean Fox, Dorothy Carter (first city treasurer), and Fred Bien (first city administrator).

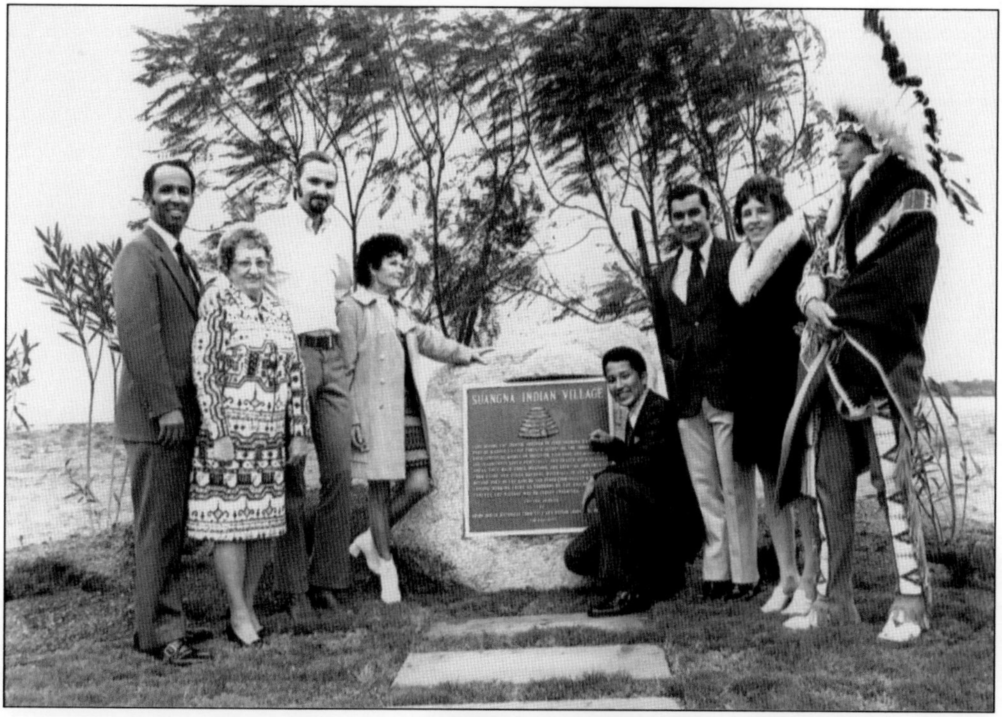

A Suangna Indian village once stood in the area known today as the Watson Industrial Center. Descendants of these Native Americans occupied the Los Angeles Harbor basin for 6,000 years before the arrival of the Spaniards. On October 20, 1972, the Carson Indian History Advisory Committee was successful in recognizing the site with Los Angeles Historical Marker No. 13. The group includes City of Carson and Native American representatives, as well as Iron Eyes Cody, the famous Native American actor, at far right.

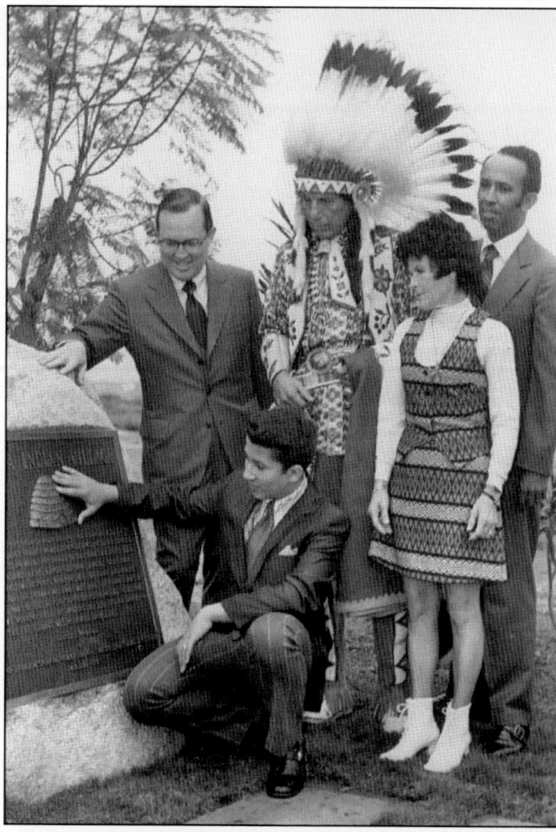

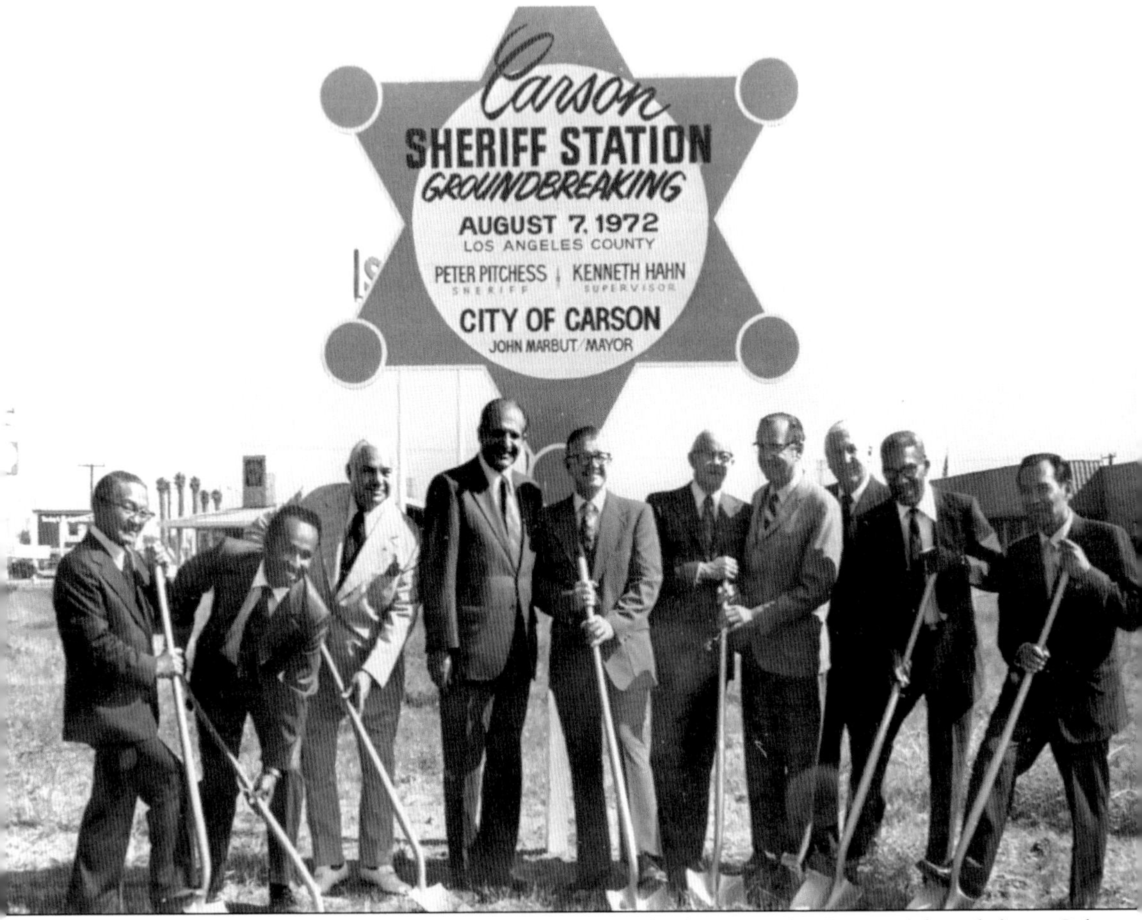

Groundbreaking for the Carson sheriff's station took place in 1972. Pictured from left are Sak Yamamoto, Gil Smith, John Calas, county sheriff Peter Pitchess, architect Paul Williams, Los Angeles County supervisor Kenneth Hahn, unknown, Clarence Bridgers, and a member of the Philippine Consulate. Mr. Williams was the first African American architect in Los Angeles and the designer of many notable buildings in the area. Oddly enough, the site and new station were both mentioned and shown in the cult-classic film, *Gone in 60 Seconds* (the 1974 original). Mayor Yamamoto even has a cameo as himself, and several council members are seen during the big car chase.

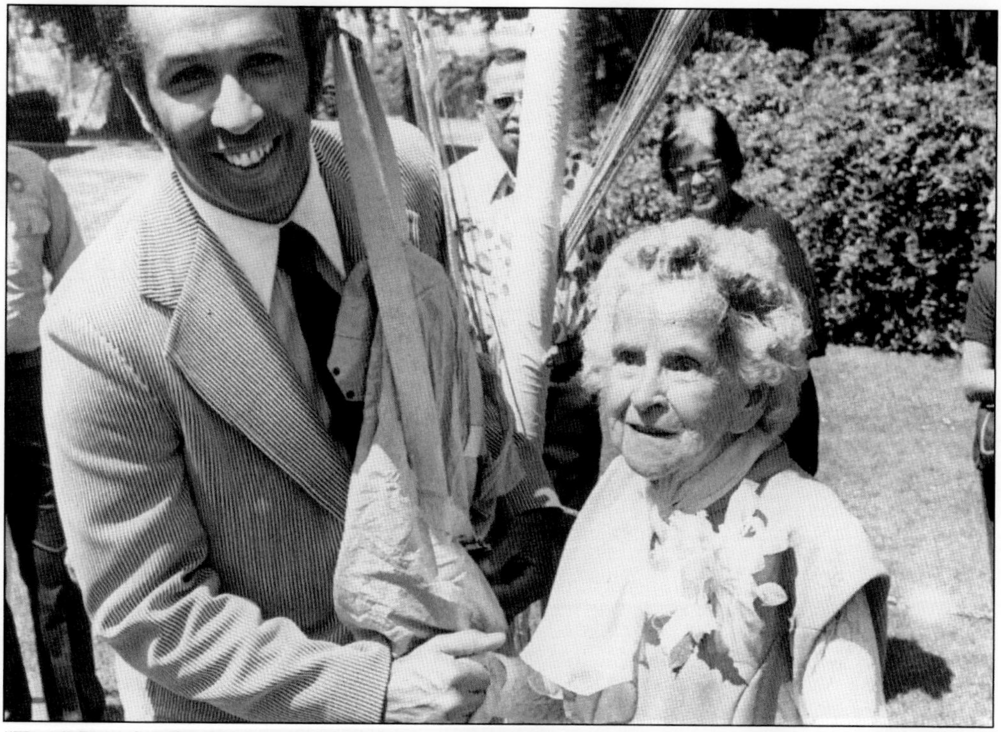

"Tiny" Broadwick, the woman parachutist, is seen here with former mayor and councilman Gil Smith at the historic site recognition ceremony at the Dominguez Ranch adobe on July 10, 1977. Tiny parachuted from balloons during the 1910 Dominguez Air Meet and, in 1912, she became the first woman to jump from an airplane. According to Smith, "Everyone wanted their pictures taken with Tiny."

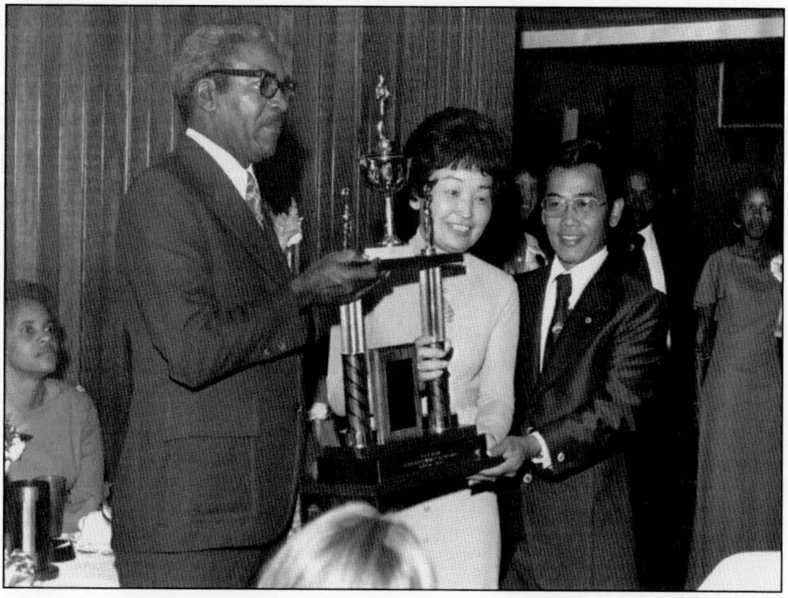

City clerk Helen Kawagoe receives the very first Carson Distinguished Community Citizen's Award at the celebratory banquet in 1974. (Courtesy of Iva Voldase.)

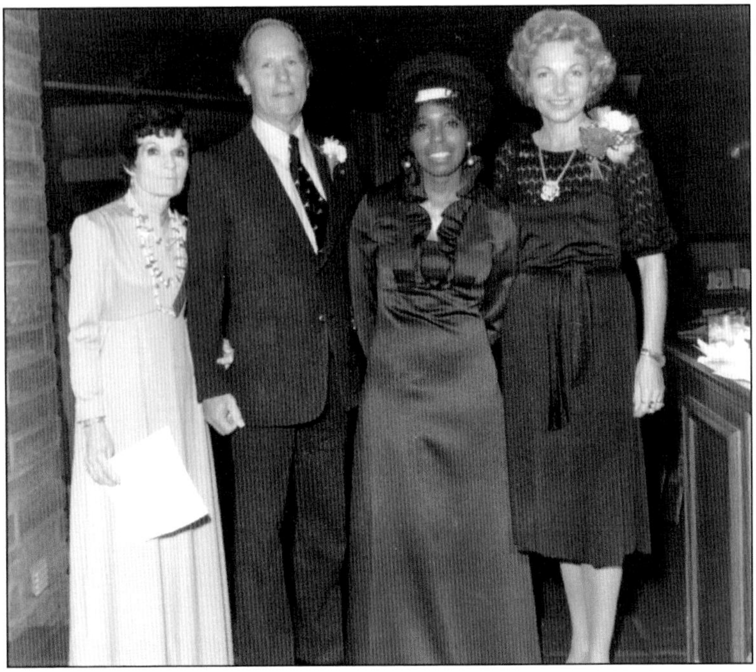

Pictured, from left to right, are Weecie Ford (Native American representative), Congressman Glenn Anderson, Iva Voldase (president of the Carson Black Heritage Association), and Lee Anderson. They are in attendance to celebrate Carson's bicentennial edition of the Distinguished Community Citizen's Award on October 25, 1976. (Courtesy of Iva Voldase)

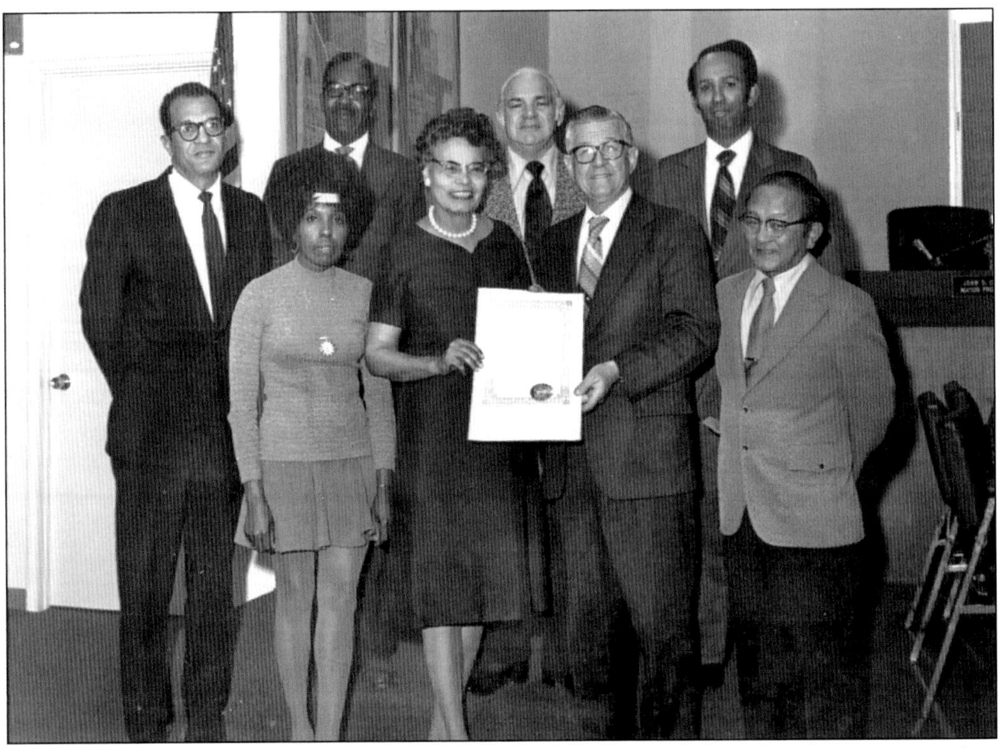

The proclamation for Black History Month in 1973 is presented by the Carson City Council to vice president of the Carson Black Heritage Association Iva Voldase (at left) and president and founder of the association Lillian Duffy (center).

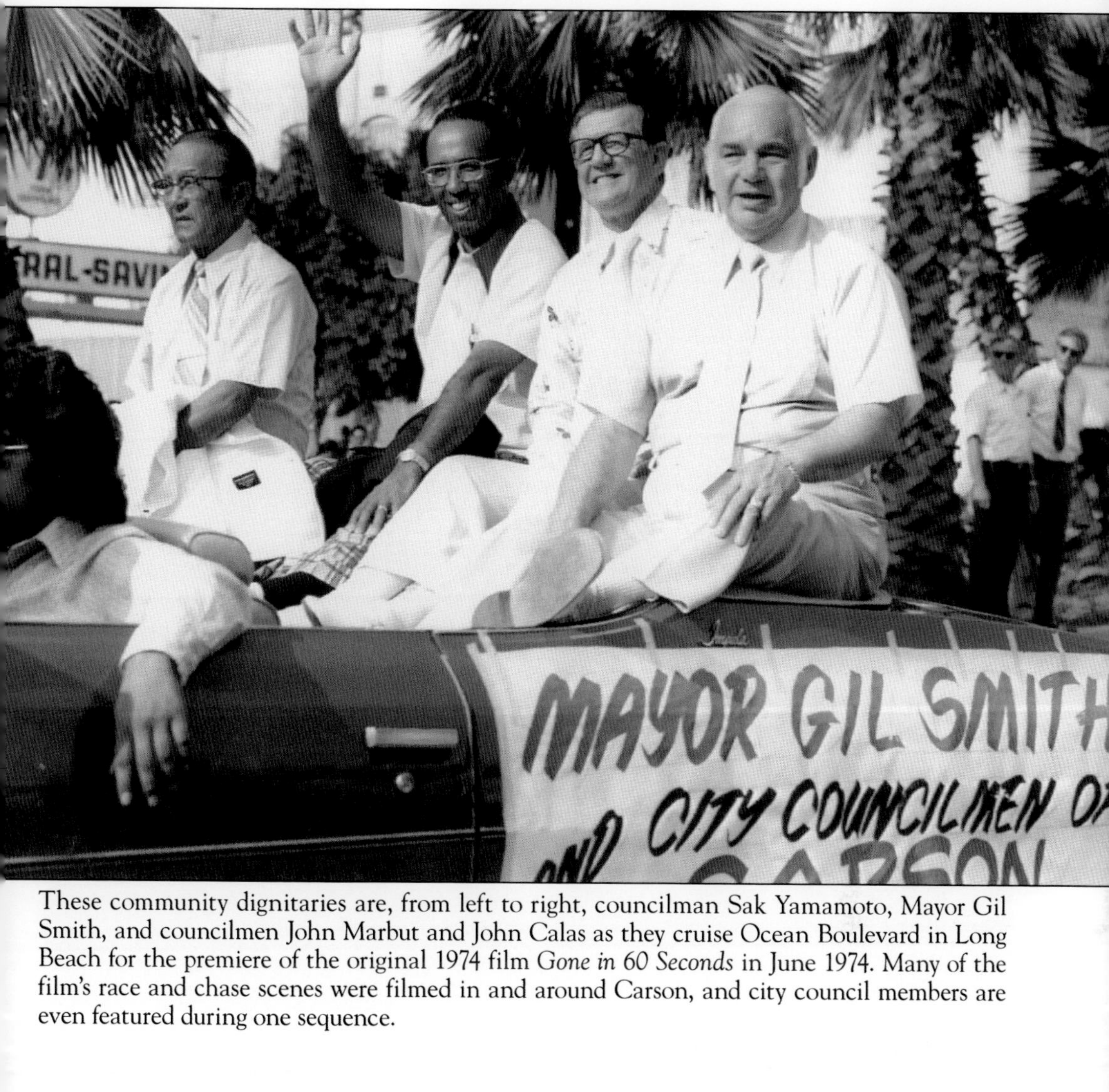

These community dignitaries are, from left to right, councilman Sak Yamamoto, Mayor Gil Smith, and councilmen John Marbut and John Calas as they cruise Ocean Boulevard in Long Beach for the premiere of the original 1974 film *Gone in 60 Seconds* in June 1974. Many of the film's race and chase scenes were filmed in and around Carson, and city council members are even featured during one sequence.

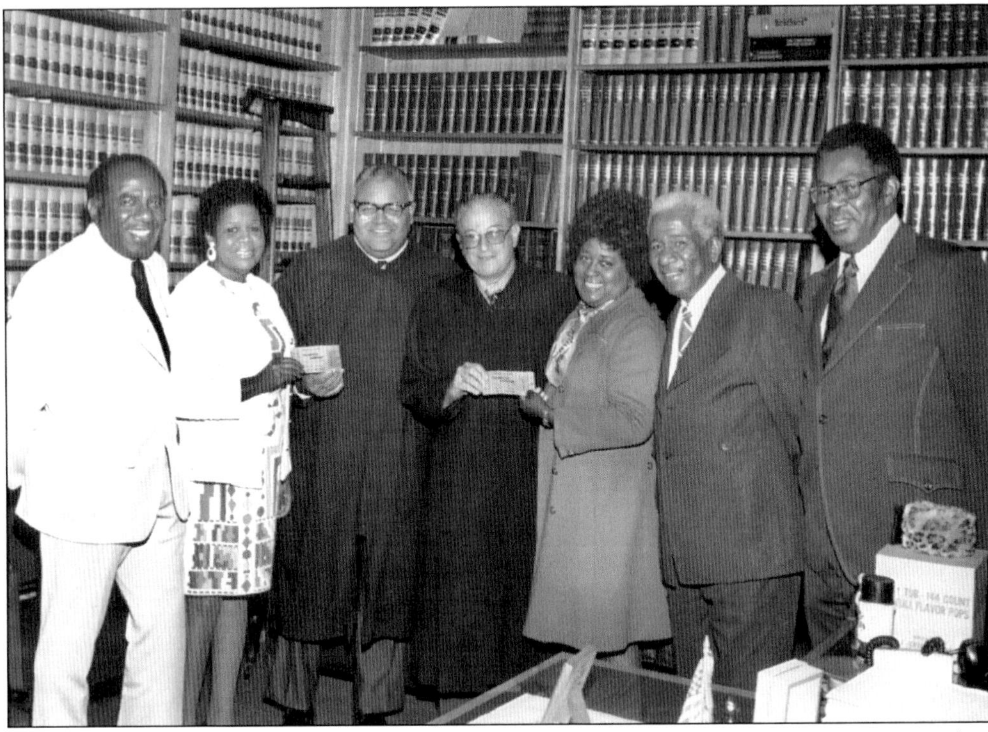

Judges and attorneys at the Compton courthouse accept Black History Month banquet tickets in 1974. (Courtesy of Iva Voldase.)

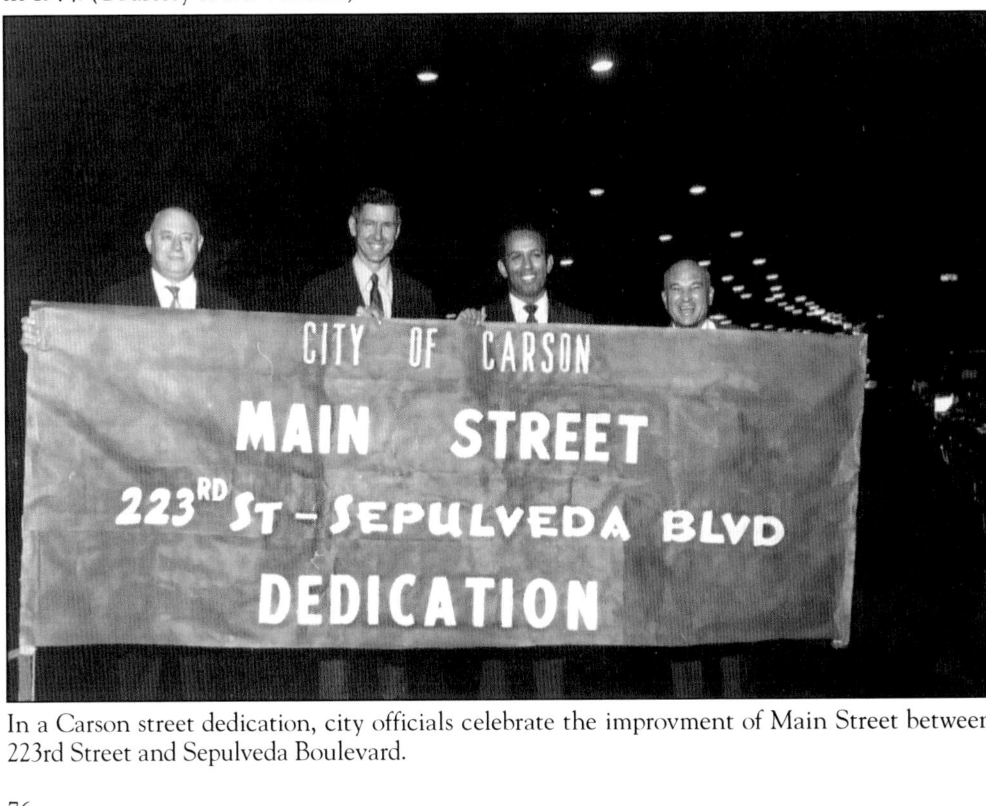

In a Carson street dedication, city officials celebrate the improvment of Main Street between 223rd Street and Sepulveda Boulevard.

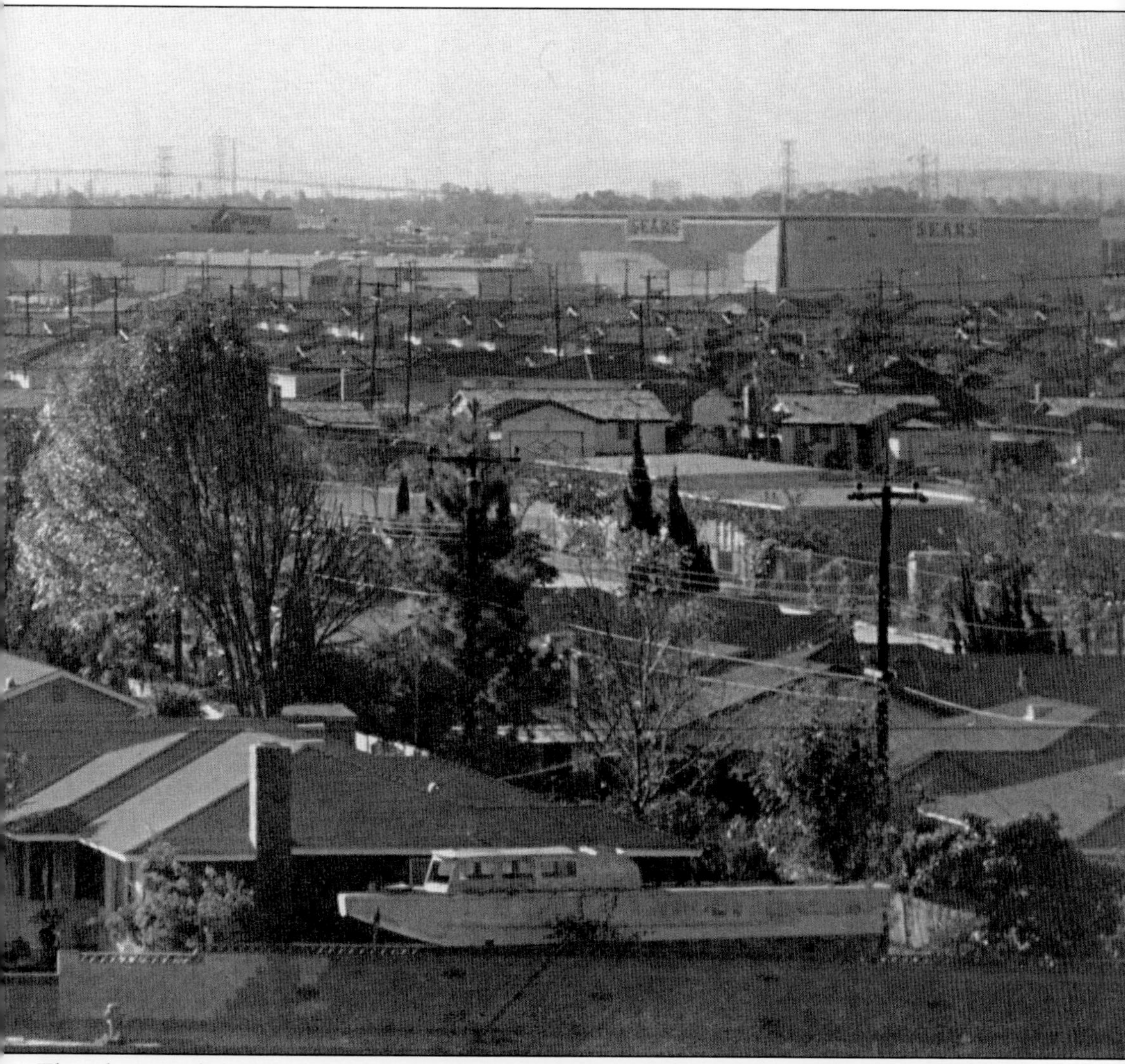

This photograph looks south over the Carson Mall toward San Pedro in 1972. Now known as the South Bay Pavilion, the Carson Mall is undergoing an almost total renovation, adding in the 21st century a new Target store and 24-Hour Fitness gym, with additional stores and restaurants to follow.

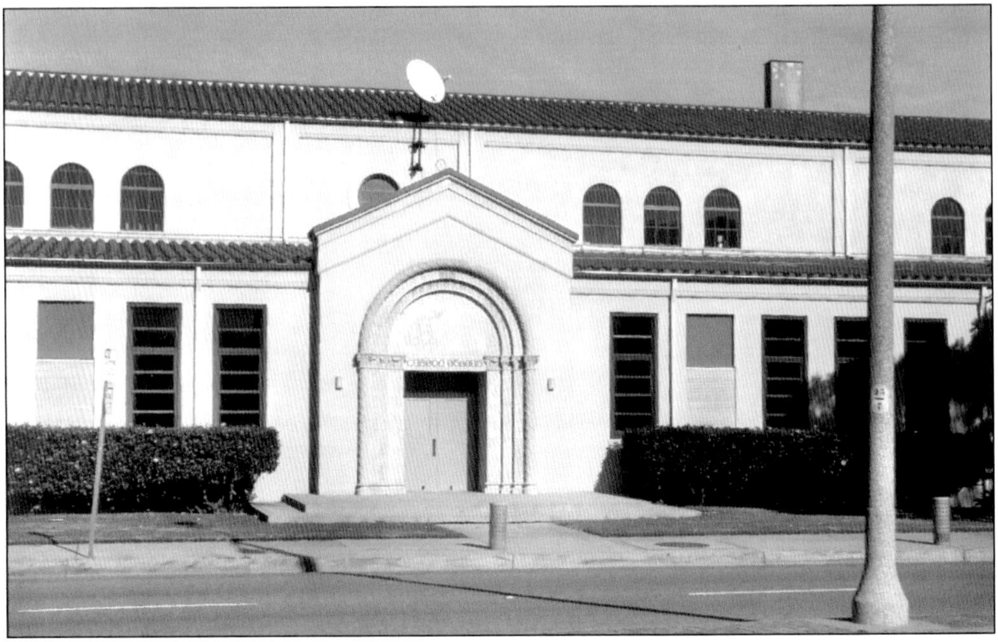

Originally called Boulevard Acres School, Carson Elementary first opened in 1920. Previously area students attended the old Lincoln District School No. 5, which was located at the corner of Sepulveda Boulevard and Main Street. It later became the American Can Company and is presently the site of a new Home Depot and Albertson's shopping center.

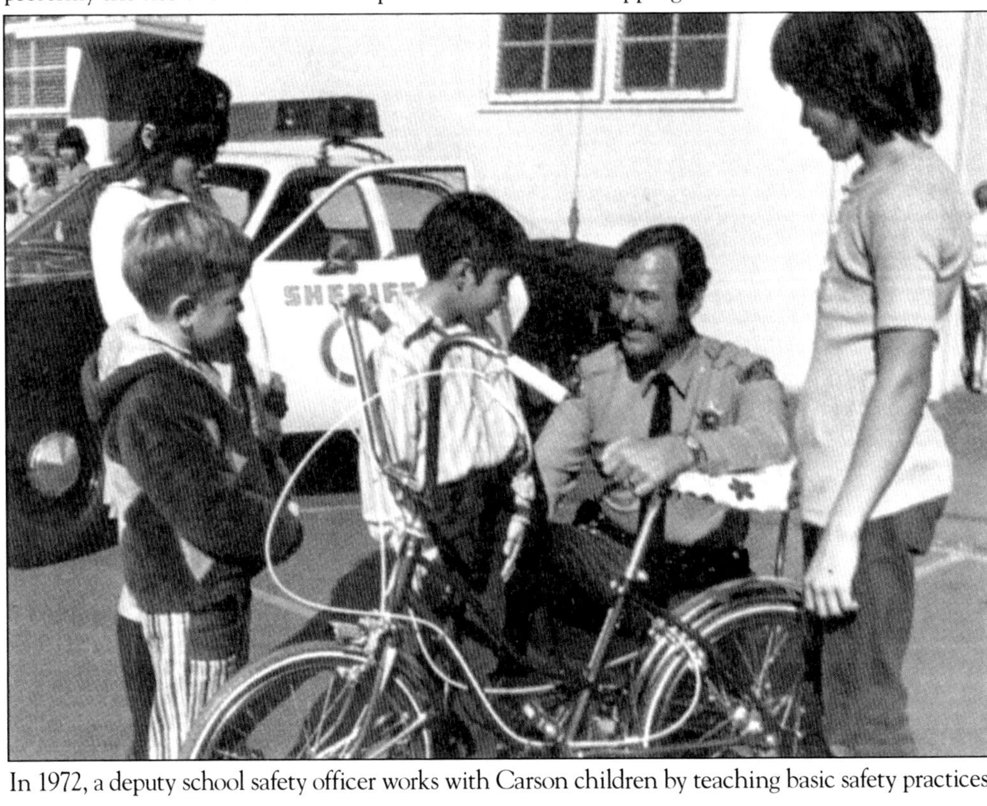

In 1972, a deputy school safety officer works with Carson children by teaching basic safety practices.

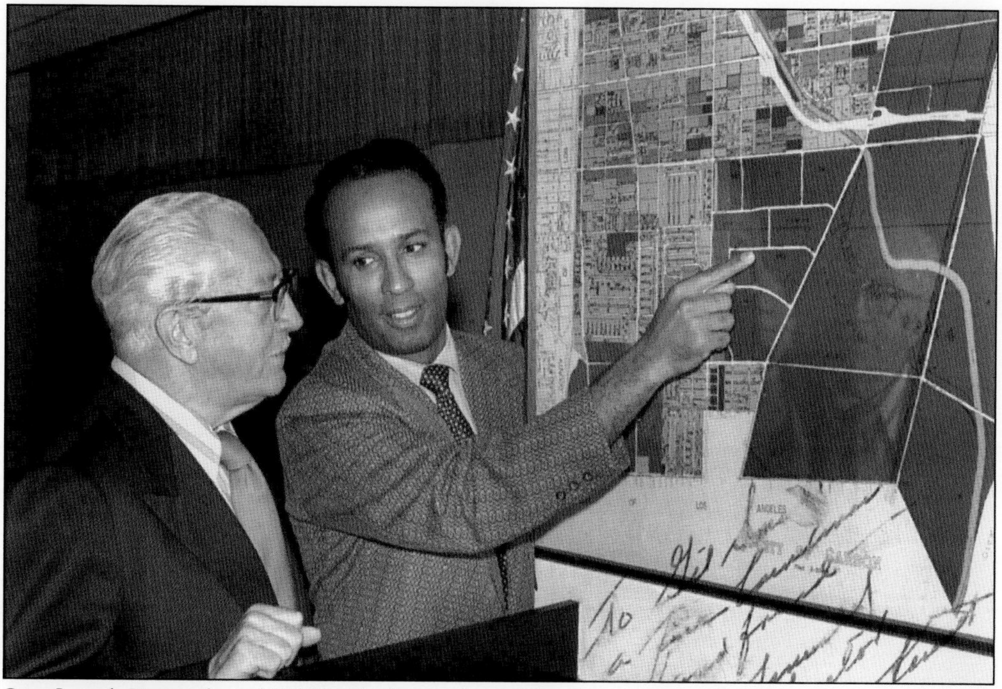

Sen. Joseph Kennick and Gil Smith discuss future developments in the city at Carson City Hall in October 1972.

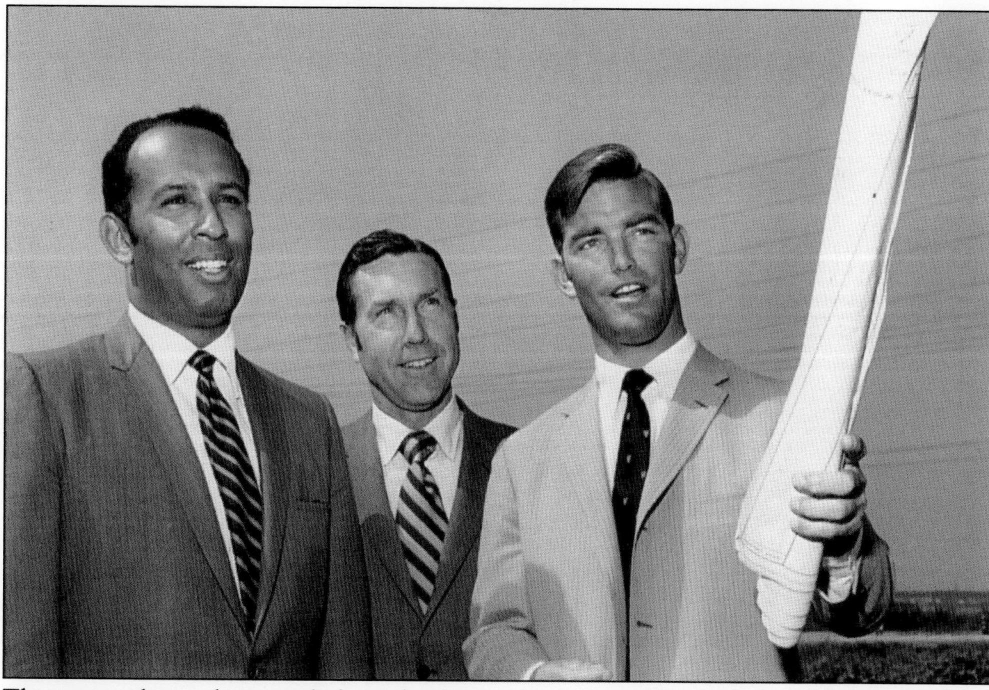

This press release photograph from the Carson Mall groundbreaking in 1971 features, from left to right, Mayor Gil Smith, Bob Hatch from Coldwell Banker, and Roger Severson from Dunn Properties.

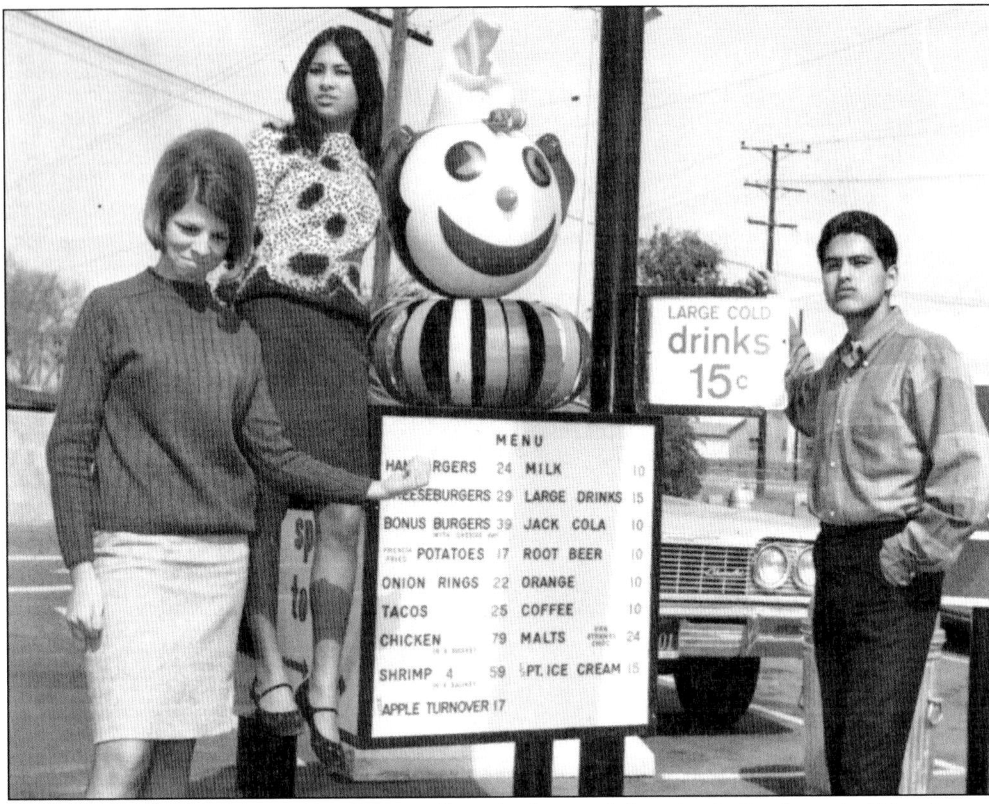

Jack in the Box, seen here in 1967, is still at Avalon and Sepulveda Boulevards. The days of talking to the clown's head to order 10¢ sodas are gone, but Jack in the Box remains one of the few businesses along the stretch of Avalon Boulevard between Sepulveda Boulevard and 228th Street to stay in continuous operation since before the city's incorporation.

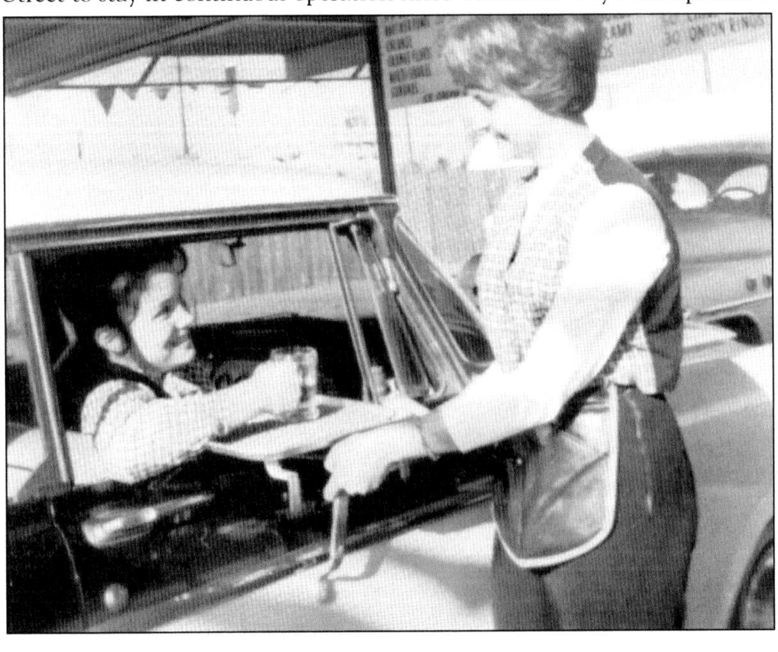

The A&W at 131 West Carson Street was a popular hangout for generations of Carson teenagers.

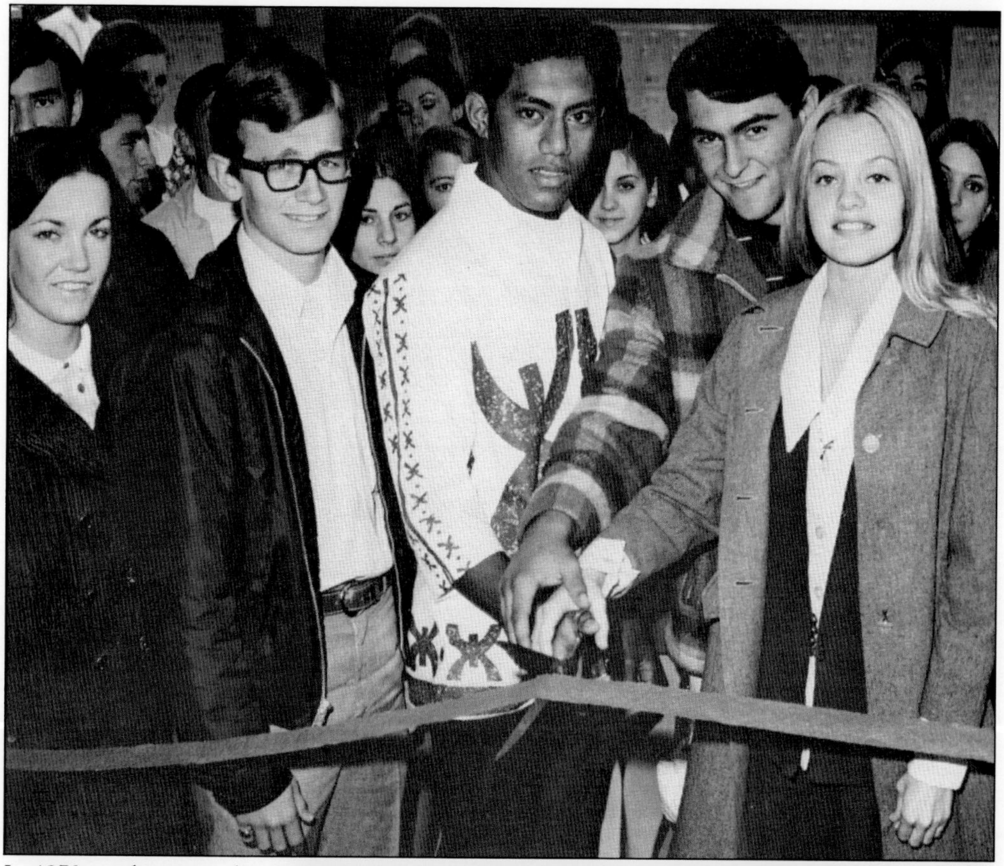

In 1970, students cut the ribbon to open the new Building K, then used for math and the arts, at Carson High School.

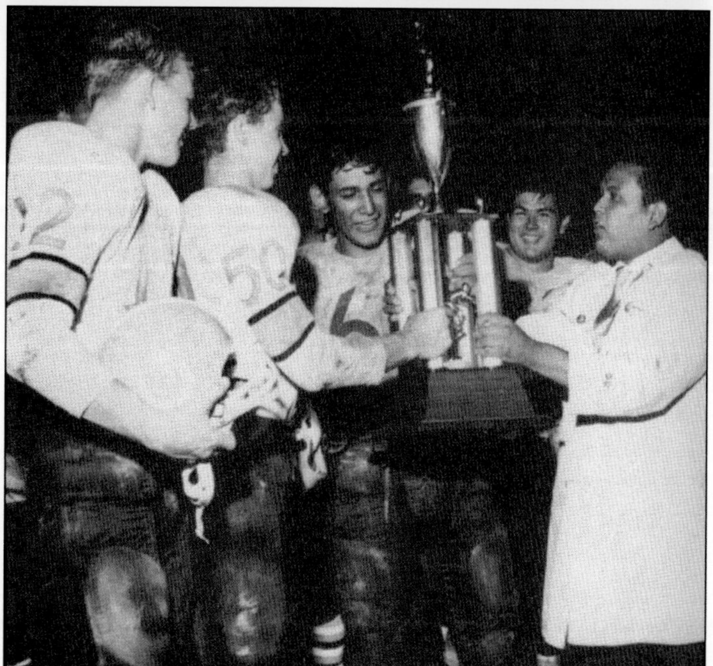

Mr. Coloma presents the 1967 Carson Colts with the perpetual trophy after they defeated the Banning Pilots, 40-21, before a crowd of 12,000 fans at El Camino College Stadium.

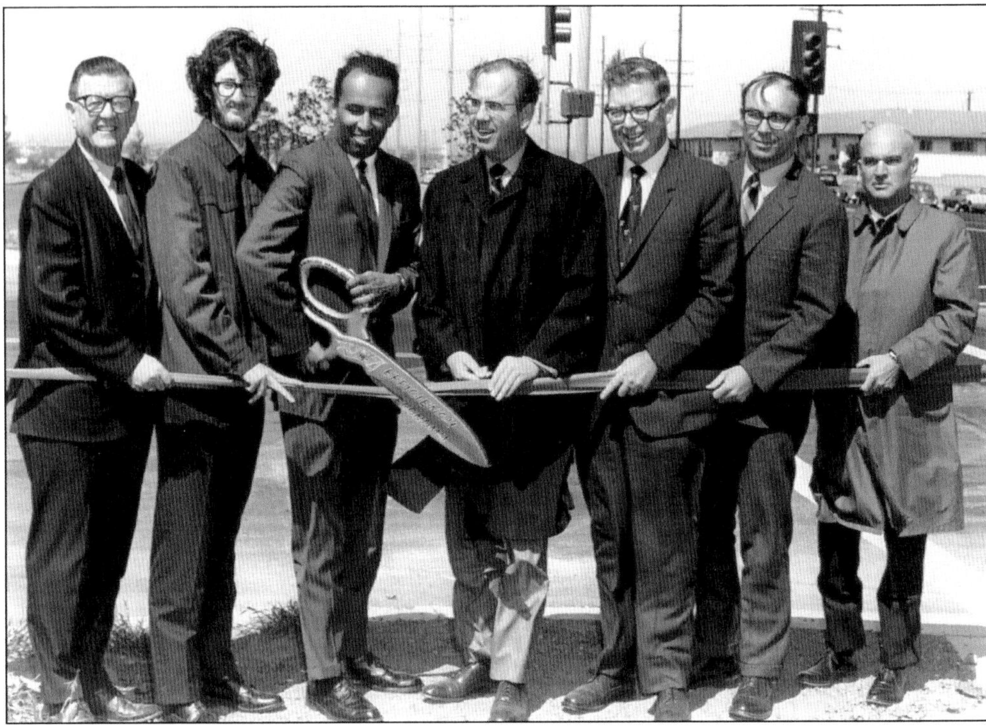

City of Carson officials always strove to be a cut above—a big cut above—other communities. In such a growing city, big doings called for big scissors, and Carson gave theirs a workout in the late 1960s and early 1970s. City officials (above) celebrate street improvements at Victoria Street and Tamcliff Avenue. In November 1969, improvements at Carson Street and Avalon Boulevard are similarly marked (below).

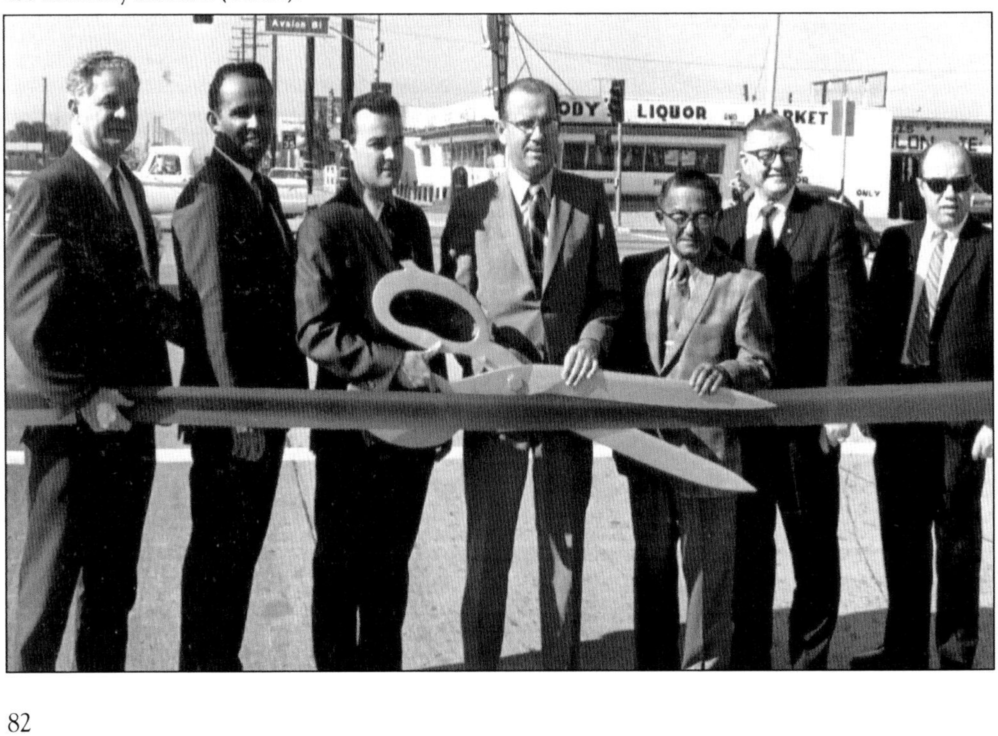

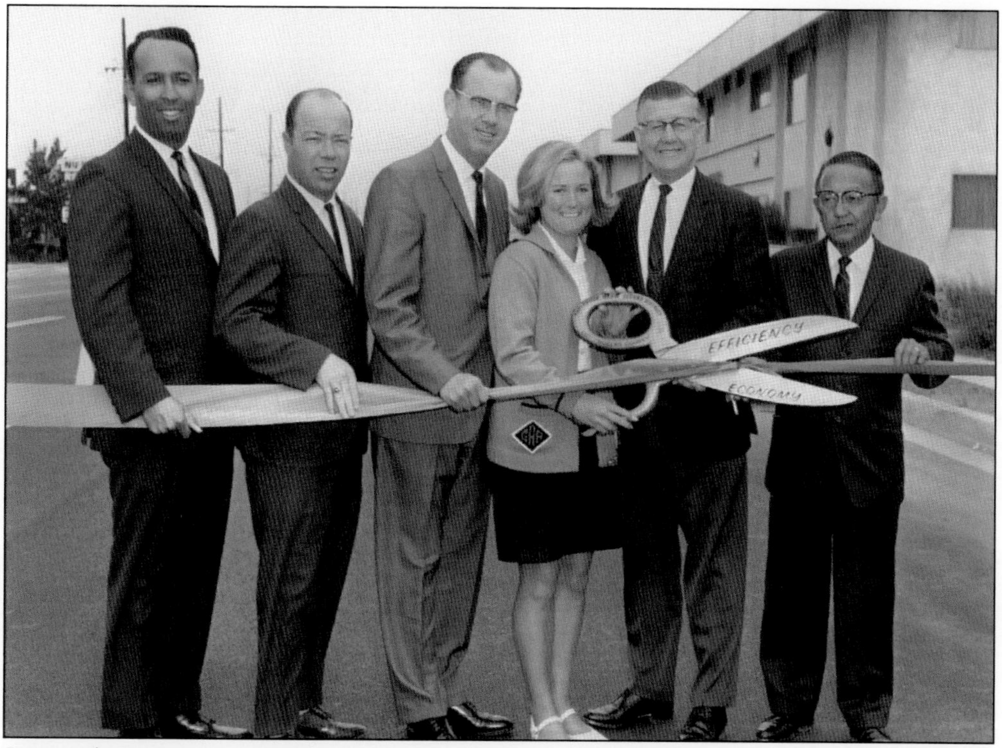

Suits and scissors were again the convention (above) for the improvements at Gardena Boulevard and Figueroa Street in 1968. The big ones are again wielded to dedicate the 223rd Street freeway overpass in 1974 (below). The officials sometimes changed, but note that those big shears weren't always the same ones either.

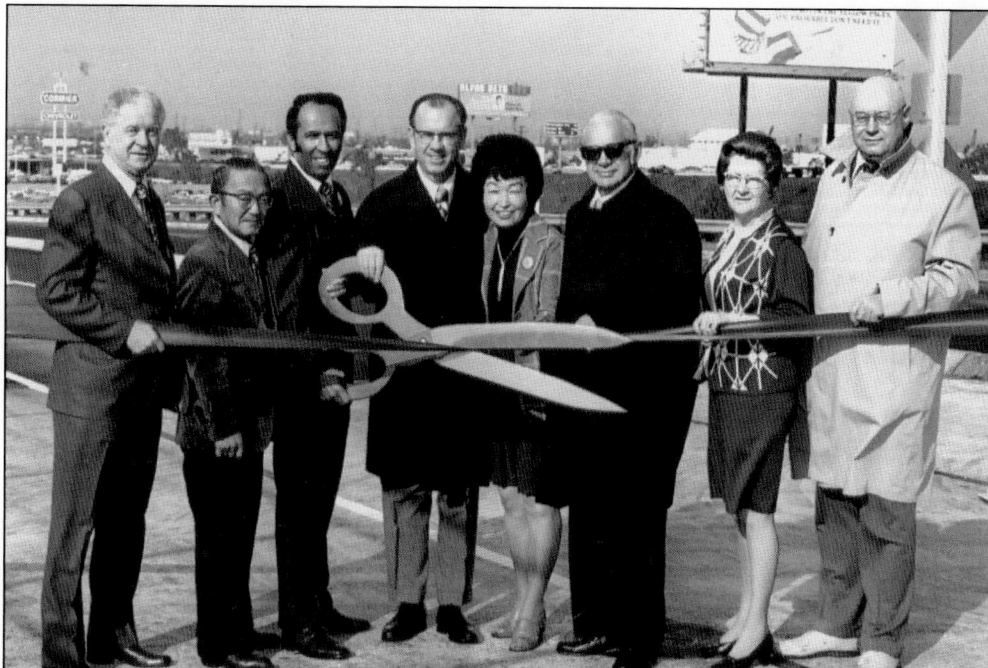

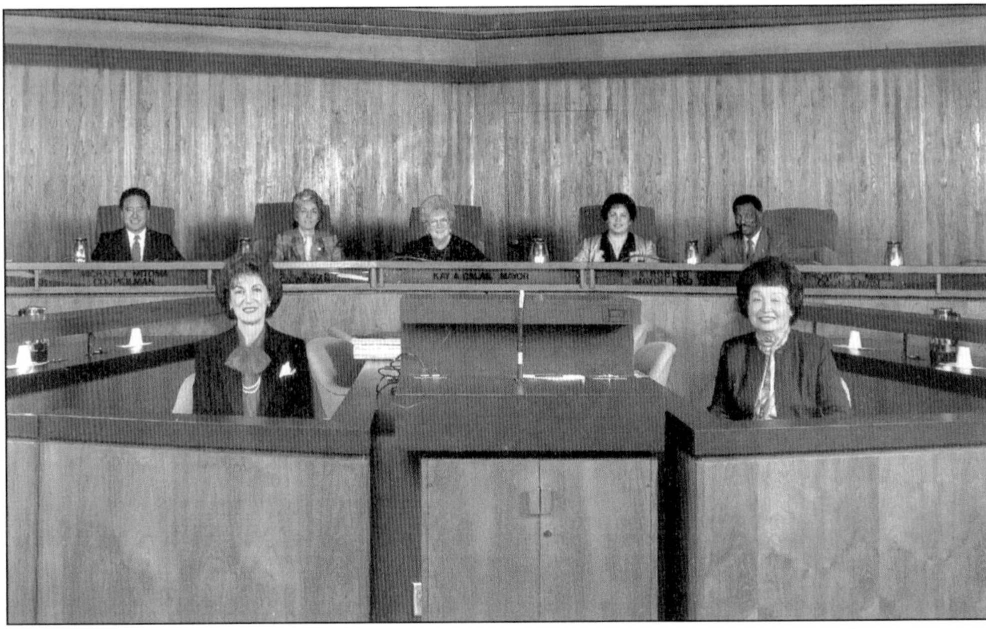

The 1988 Carson City Council is depicted in chambers at the time of the city's 20th anniversary. Included here, from left to right, are (first row) city treasurer Mary Louise Custer and city clerk Helen Kawagoe; (second row) councilman Michael Mitoma, councilwoman Sylvia Muise, Mayor Kay Calas, mayor pro tem Vera Robles DeWitt, and councilman Thomas Mills

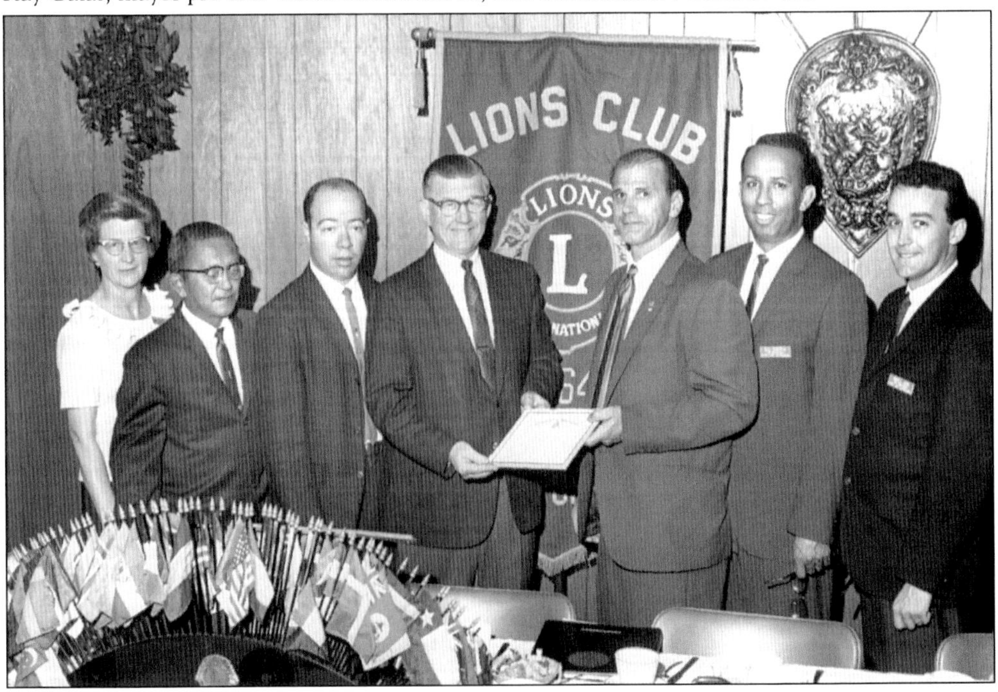

In 1968, the Carson City Council was inducted into the Lions Club. Pictured, from left to right, are Dorothy Carter, first city treasurer; councilman Sak Yamamoto; Rick Clark; John Marbut, first mayor; unidentified president of the local Lions Club; councilman Gil Smith; and mayor pro tem John Junk.

Four

MODERN TIMES

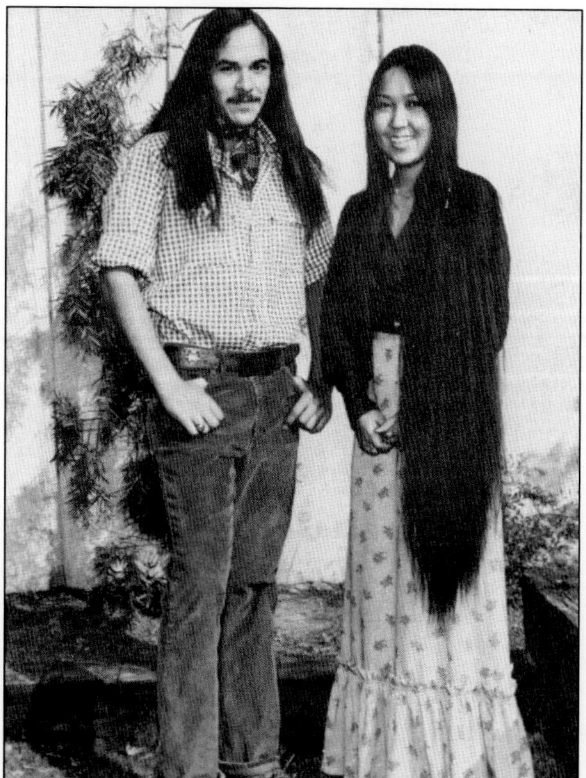

Times were changing in the 1970s. Abe Hernandez and Linda Hernandez were honored for "longest hair" at Carson High School in 1975.

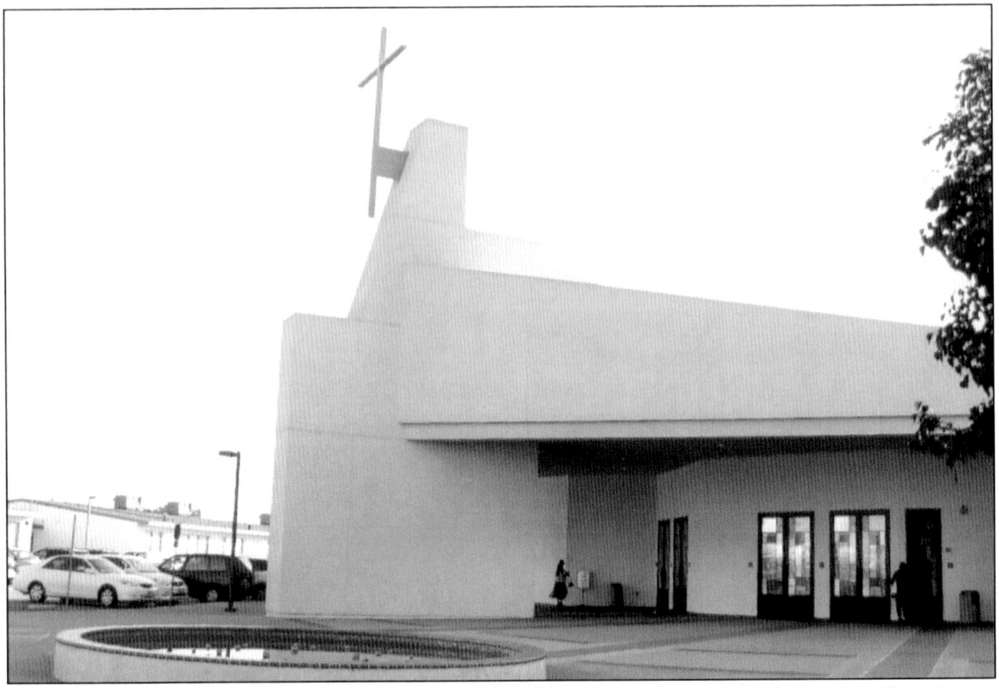

St. Philomena's Catholic Church received a sparkling new sanctuary that opened for Mass in 2002.

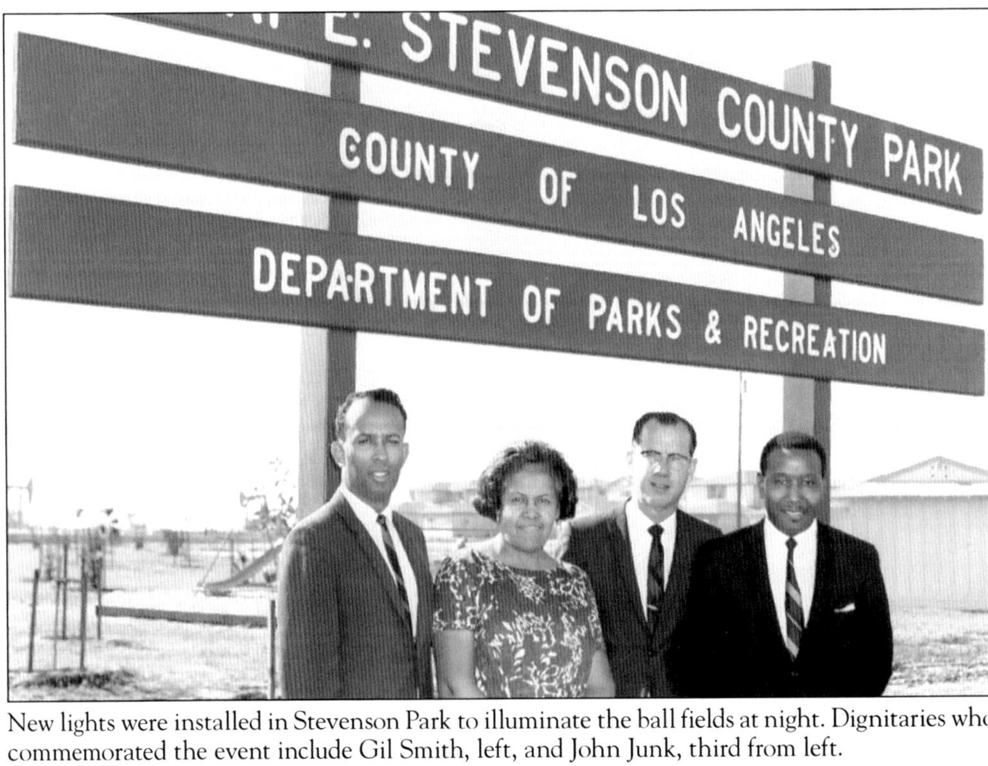

New lights were installed in Stevenson Park to illuminate the ball fields at night. Dignitaries who commemorated the event include Gil Smith, left, and John Junk, third from left.

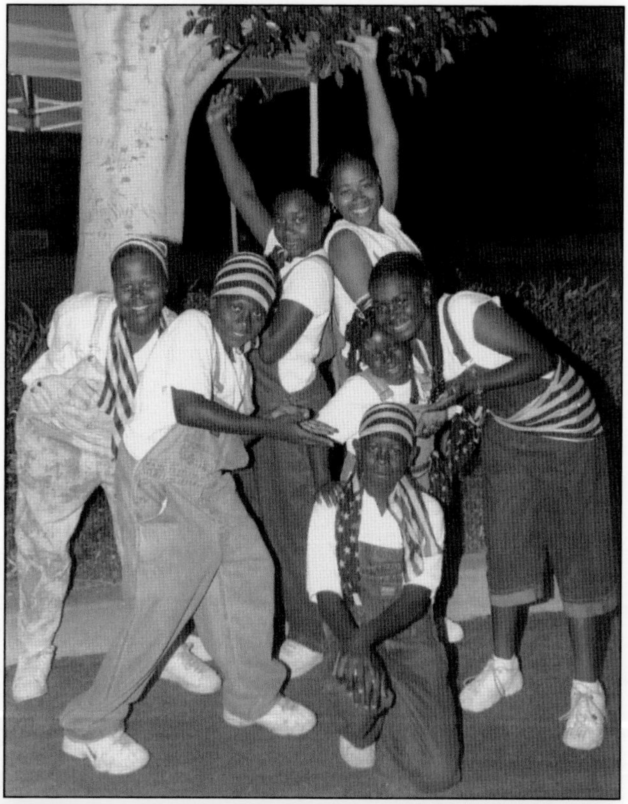

The Apollo West Carson Players, under the direction of Marvin Clayton, always has room for local youngsters to showcase their talents. The group was established in 1974 in order to help its participants build self-esteem, practice group cooperation, and increase poise and self-confidence through cultural and theater arts.

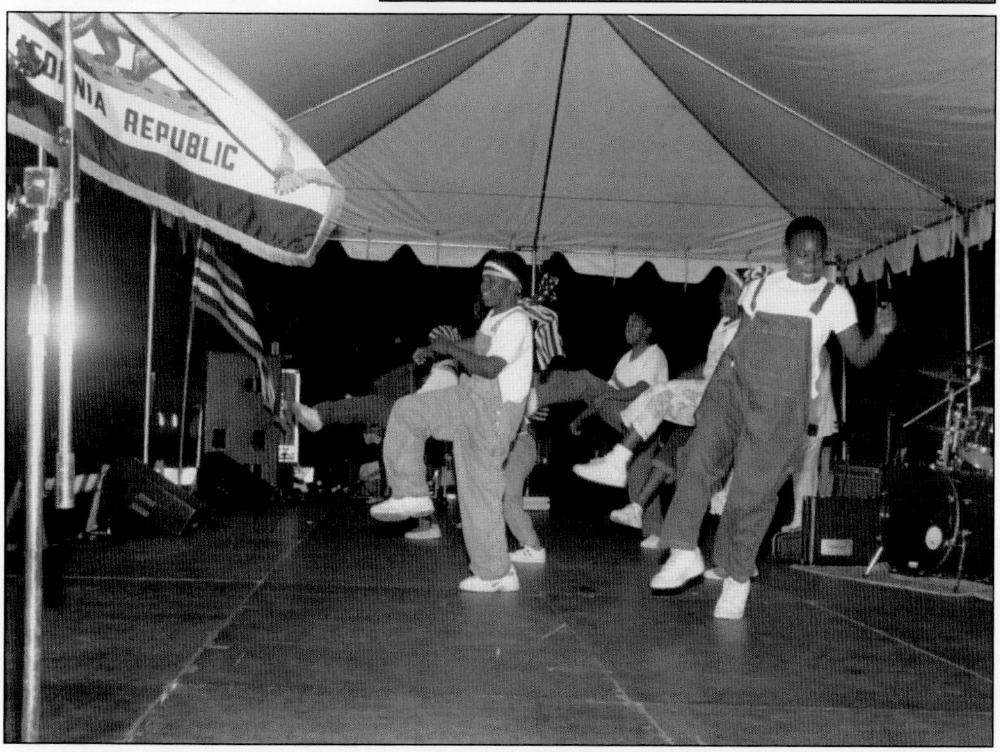

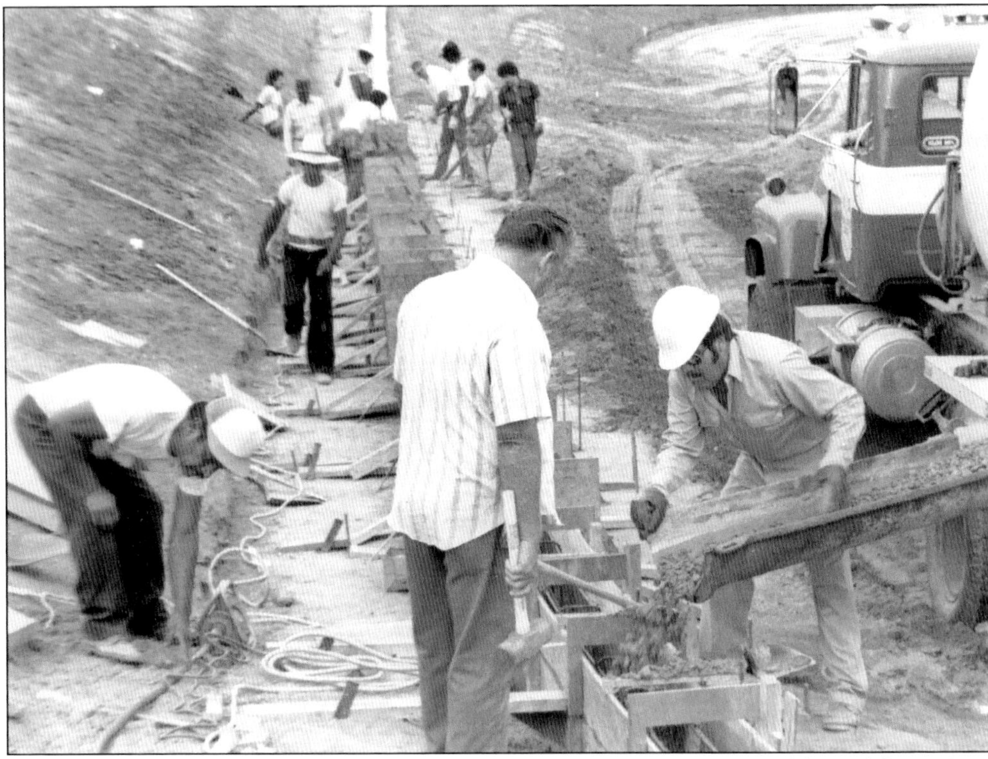

The 1984 7-11 Olympic Velodrome was constructed on the southeast portion of the California State University, Dominguez Hills, campus. Intended as a "permanent landmark of the track cycling events of the 1984 Los Angeles Olympics and as a vital presence in the cycling world," the facility fell into disrepair over the years and was demolished to make way for the Home Depot Center.

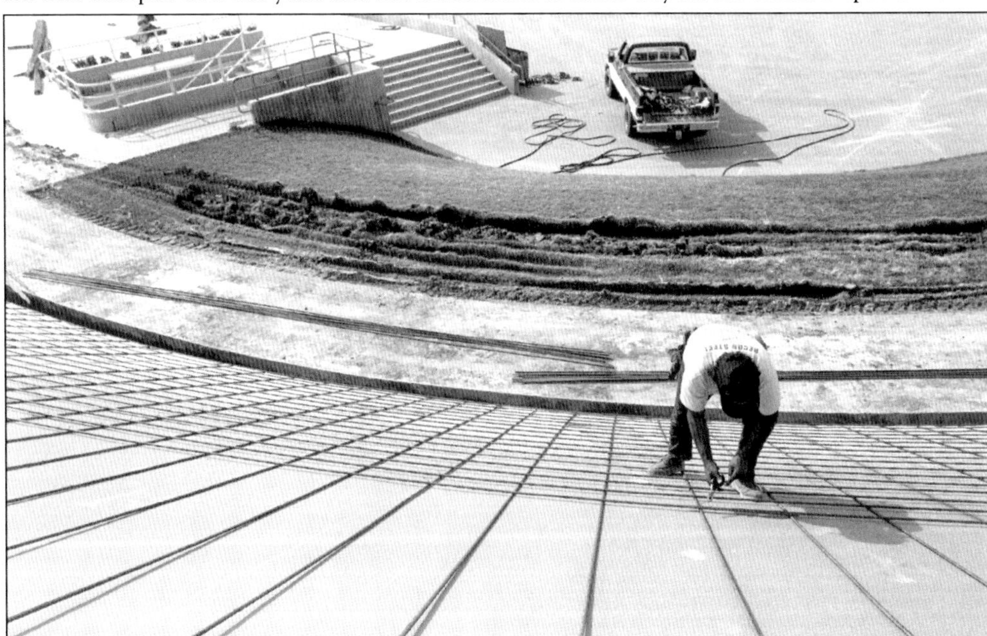

The Olympic Torch passed through Carson on Friday, July 27, 1984, the day before opening ceremonies at the Los Angeles Memorial Coliseum. Thousands of spectators gathered in front of Carson City Hall and at the Velodrome.

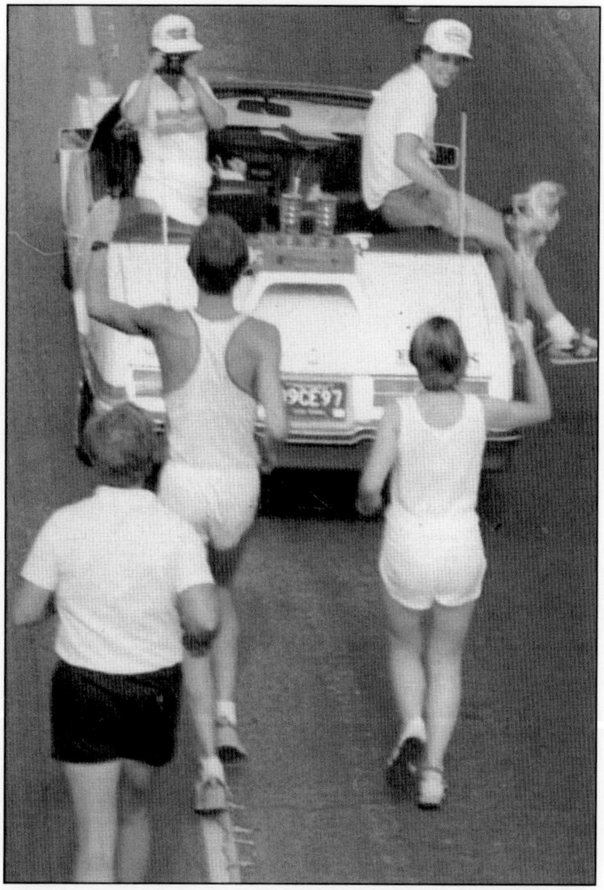

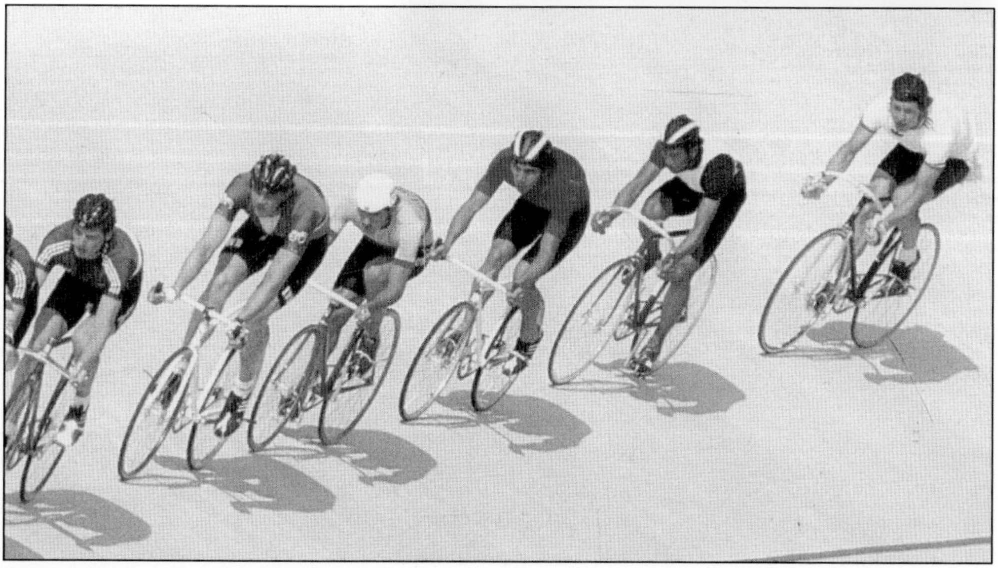

Pictured here is a track cycling event at the Velodrome during the Games of the XXIII Olympiad. Although only the track races were held in Carson, a stretch of the 91 Freeway in the city was closed down on a Saturday morning for road-race training.

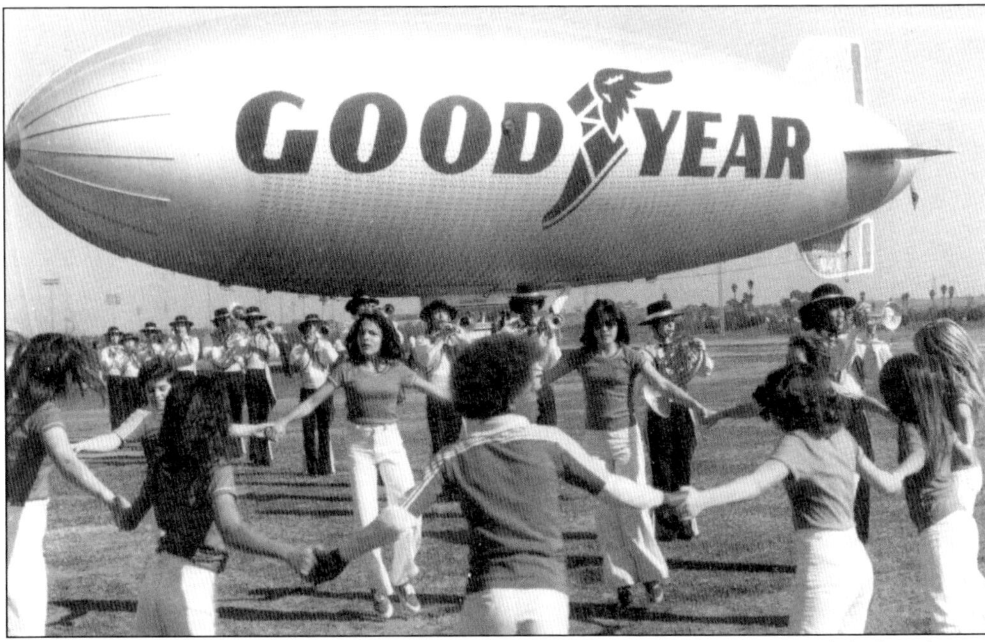

The Goodyear Airship *Columbia* made Carson its home in January 1968, a month before the city was incorporated. Altogether Carson has hosted three of the dirigibles: *Columbia*, 1967–1992; *Eagle*, 1992–2002; and *Spirit of America*, christened on September 5, 2002. City performers, including the Young Life Singers, the Junior Life Singers, and the Los Caballeros Band, celebrate the Goodyear Blimp in the 1980s.

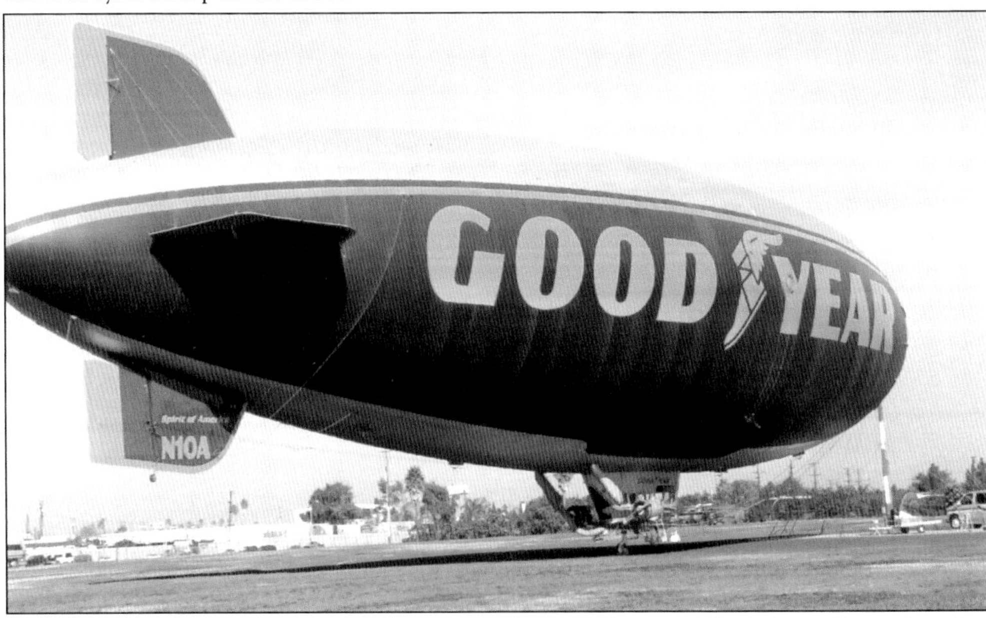

Today the unofficial "bird" of Carson is the airship *Spirit of America*. The behemoth is a cherished floating citizen, visible daily over the South Bay making turns back to its Carson moorings over the Redondo Beach or Hermosa Beach Piers. A landing mishap occurred on December 4, 2003, when the blimp nosed down into a manure pile and crashed. One injury resulted, and the *Spirit* was repaired and returned to Carson 10 months later.

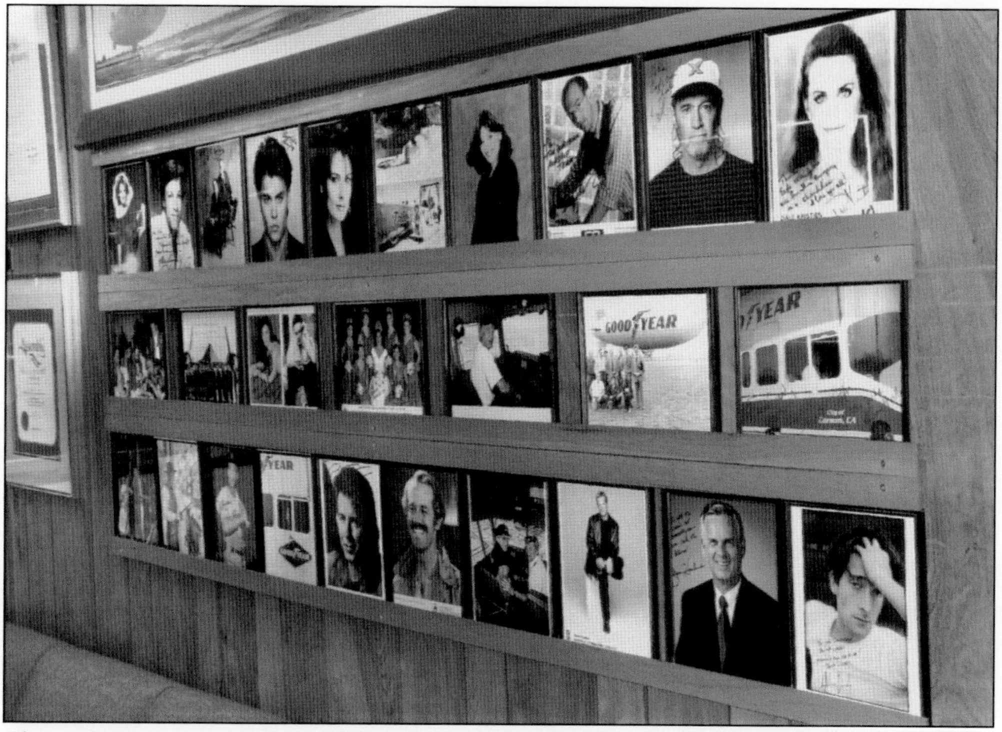

The airship operations office walls are decorated with photographs of famous blimp passengers. Seen most easily from this angle are former Los Angeles mayor James Hahn and actors Mike Farrell, Marilu Henner, Johnny Depp, George Carlin, and Anthony Edwards. At press time, the newly organized Lighter-than-Air Historical Society of Carson had been formed based on an idea by Carole Keen, who dreamed of a Carson "friends of the blimp" organization to unite the airship operations and the community.

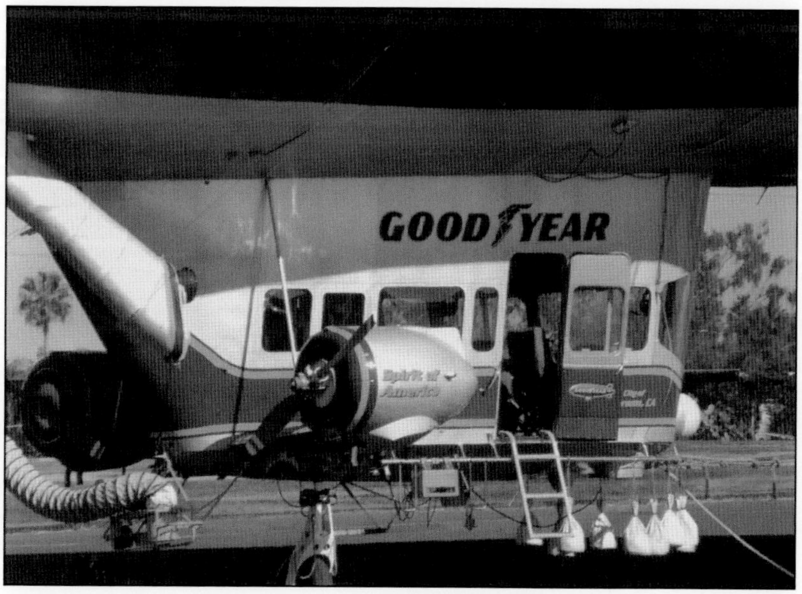

The passenger compartment, or gondola, suspended underneath the blimp is surprisingly smaller than the large passenger vans parked next to it at the time this photograph was taken.

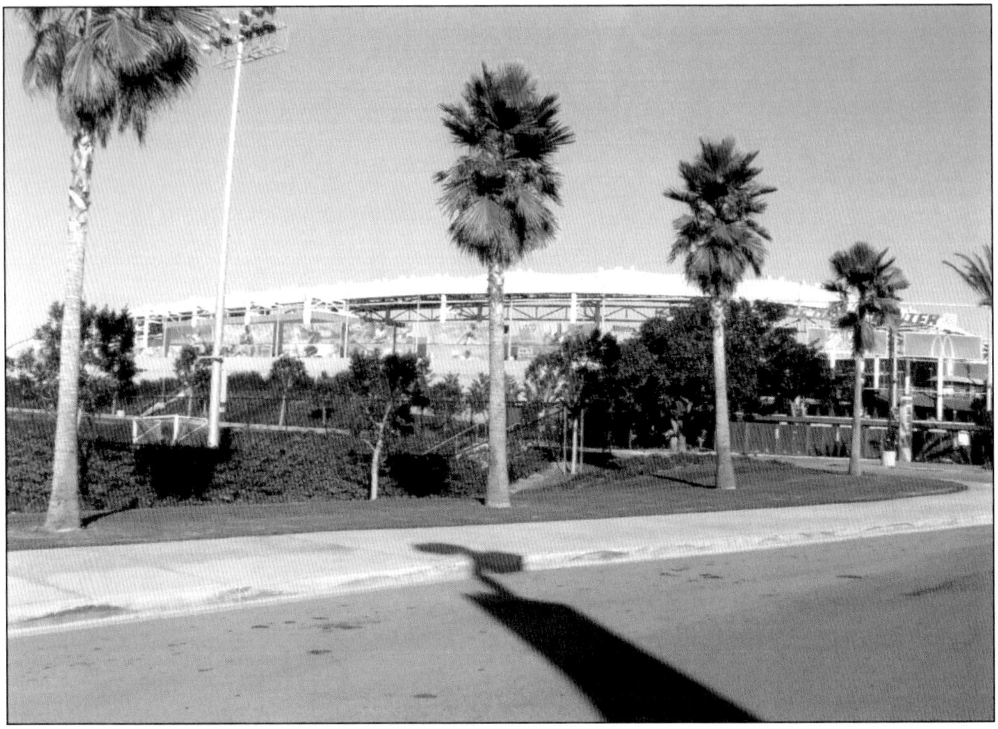

The Home Depot Center, on the southwest end of the CSUDH campus, was constructed amid considerable community debate and protest. It has brought world-class tennis and soccer to Carson and is a popular venue for concerts and community events.

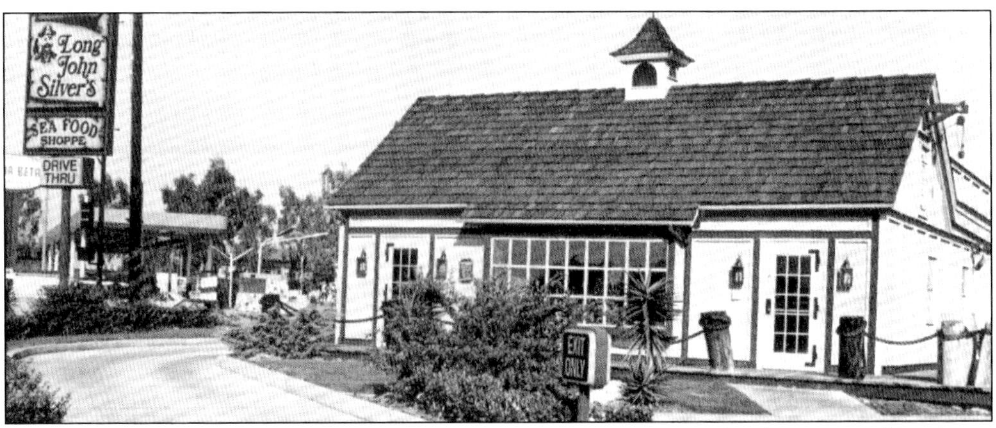

Long John Silver's, located at Carson and Main Streets, now the site of Yoshinoya Beef Bowl, was a winner in the commercial category of the Carson Beautiful Contest in 1983.

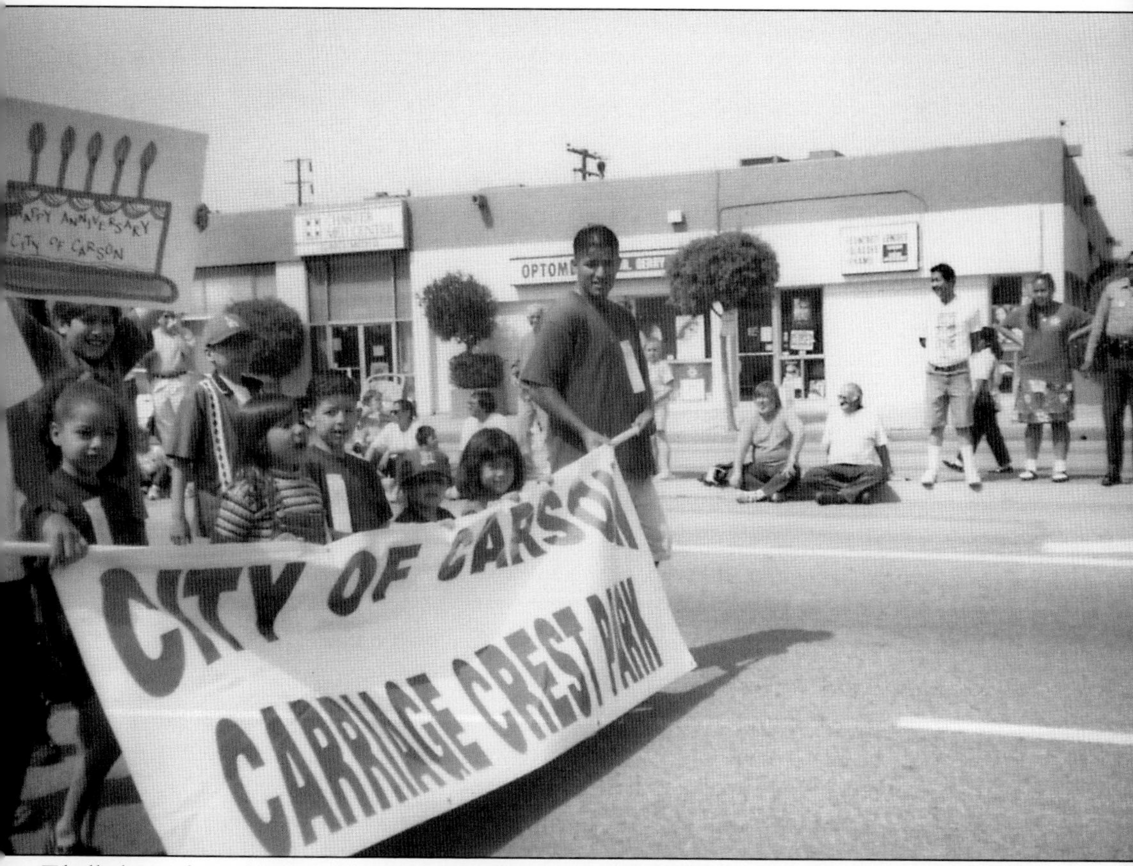

T-ball players from Carriage Crest Park march in Carson's 30th Anniversary Parade down Avalon Boulevard in 1998.

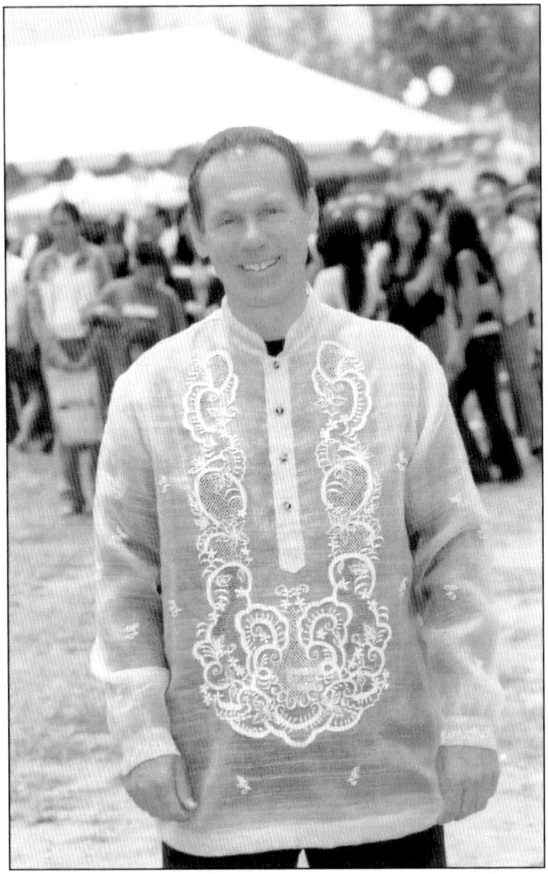

Mayor Jim Dear dons a traditional Filipino shirt for Philippine Independence Day in 2005. The event is held annually at Veteran's Park.

Some participants in the Philippine Independence Day Celebration in 2000 model uniforms representing the "katipuneros" who fought against the Spanish in the Spanish-American War of 1898, as well as one from the World War II era.

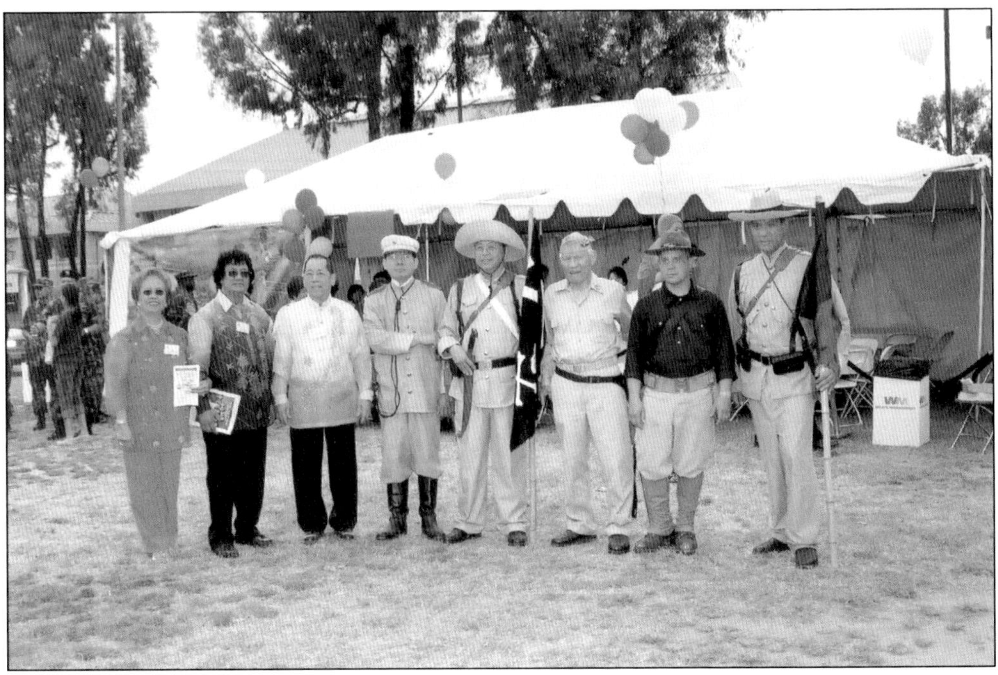

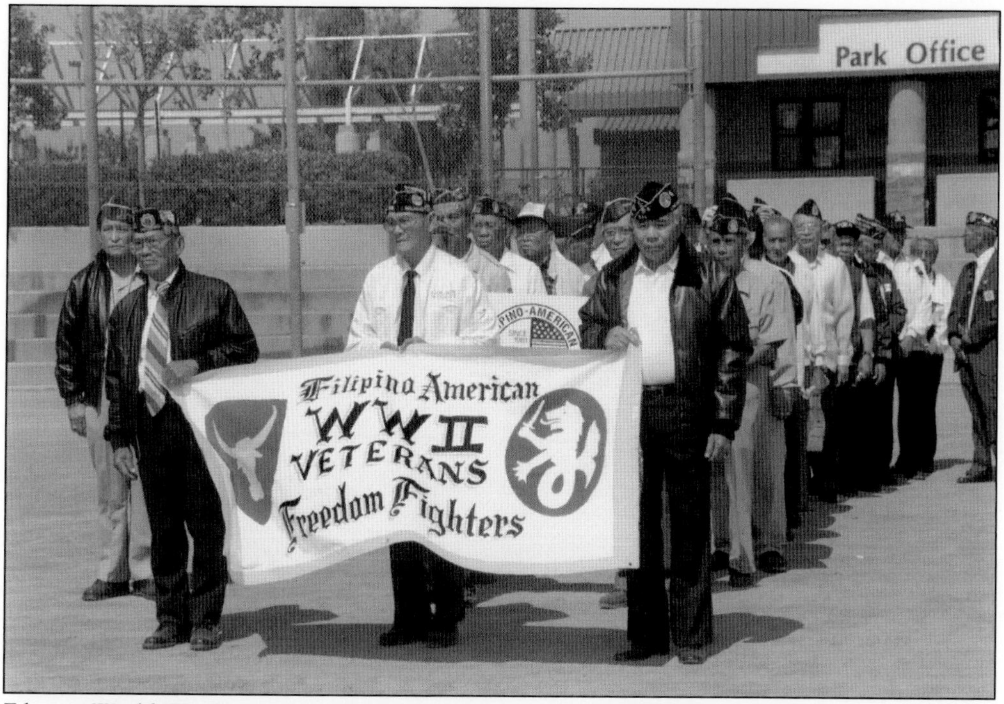

Filipino World War II veterans of the United States Armed Forces march during the Philippine Independence Day celebration in 1999.

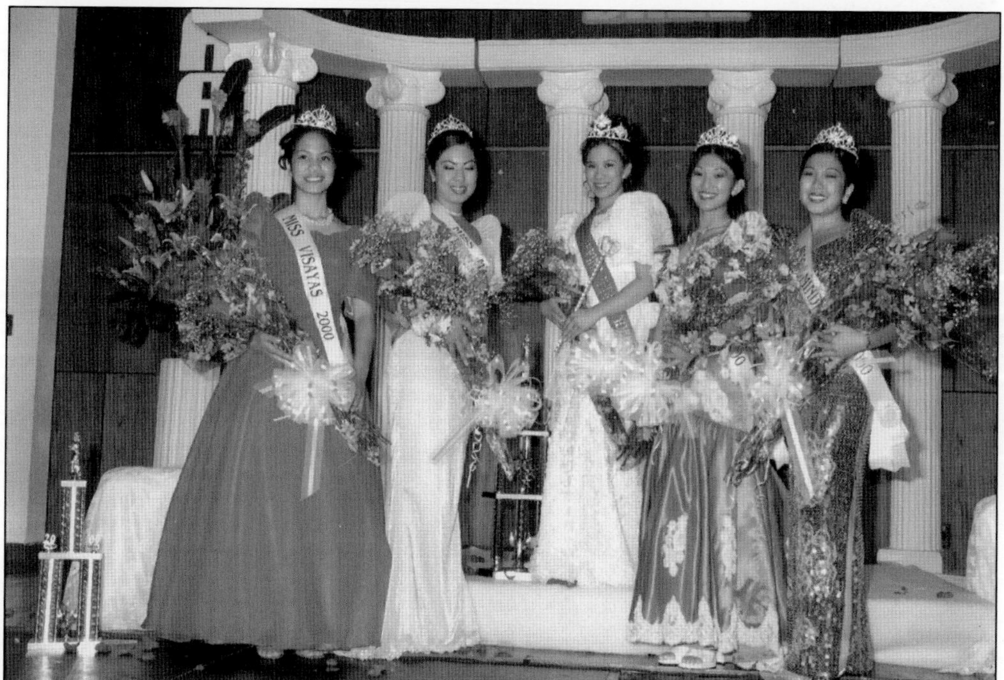

Philippine Independence Day beauty queens of 2000, from left to right, are Miss Philippine Independence Day, Desiree Acosta; Miss Manila, Aileen Mendoza; Miss Luzpin, Yvonne Rapanot; Miss Visaya, Christine Agaton; and Miss Mindanao, Charlene Ignacio.

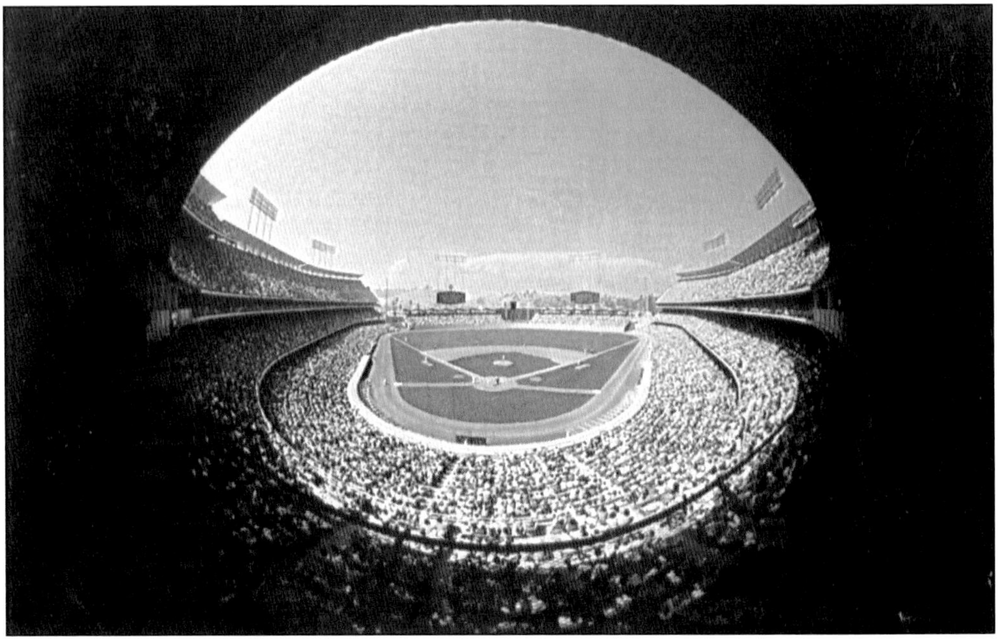

The city was the guest of honor at Dodger Stadium for Carson Night in 1974 to watch a Los Angeles team managed by Walter Alston that included Steve Garvey, Don Sutton, Bill Russell, Jimmy Wynn, and others. This was a souvenir photograph folder given away for the occasion.

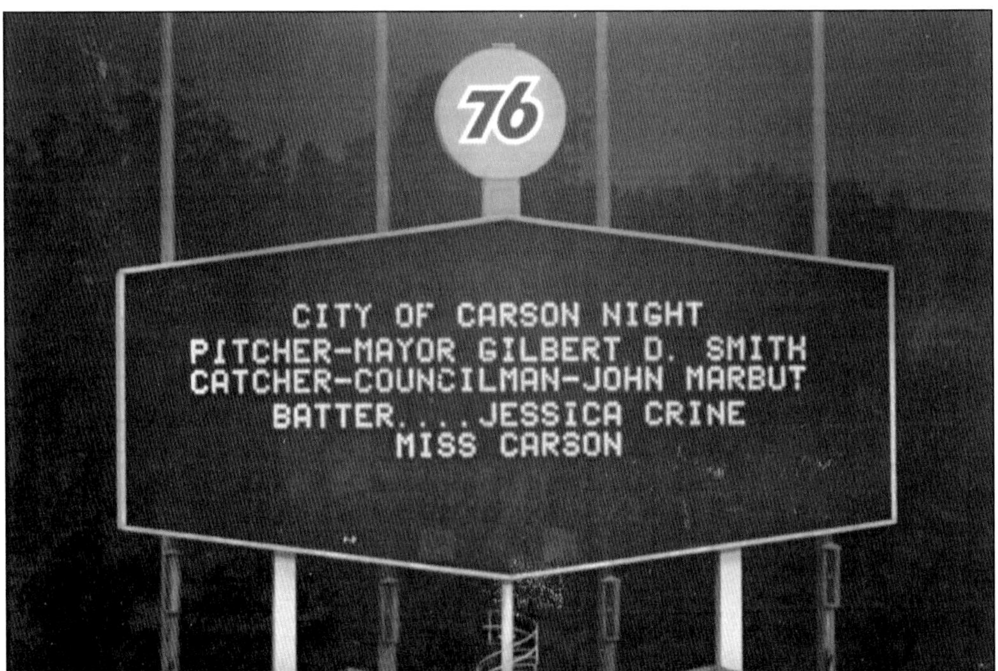

Preschool children trick or treat at Carson City Hall in 1986.

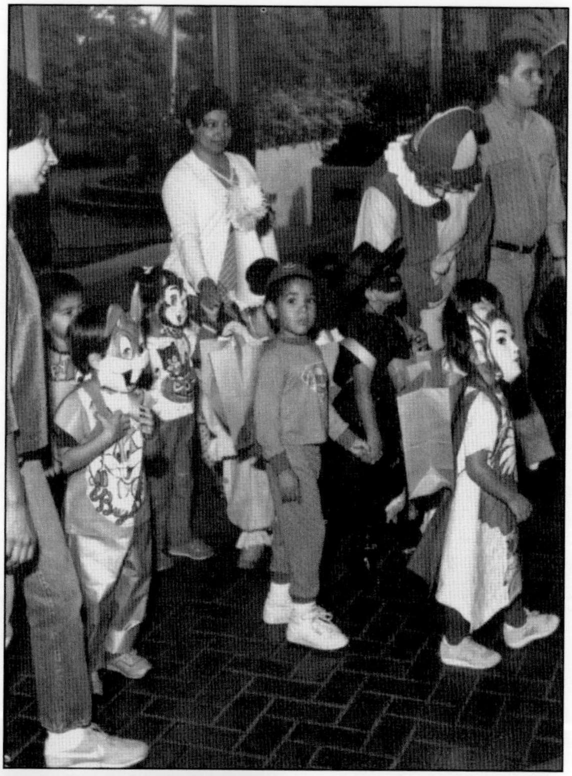

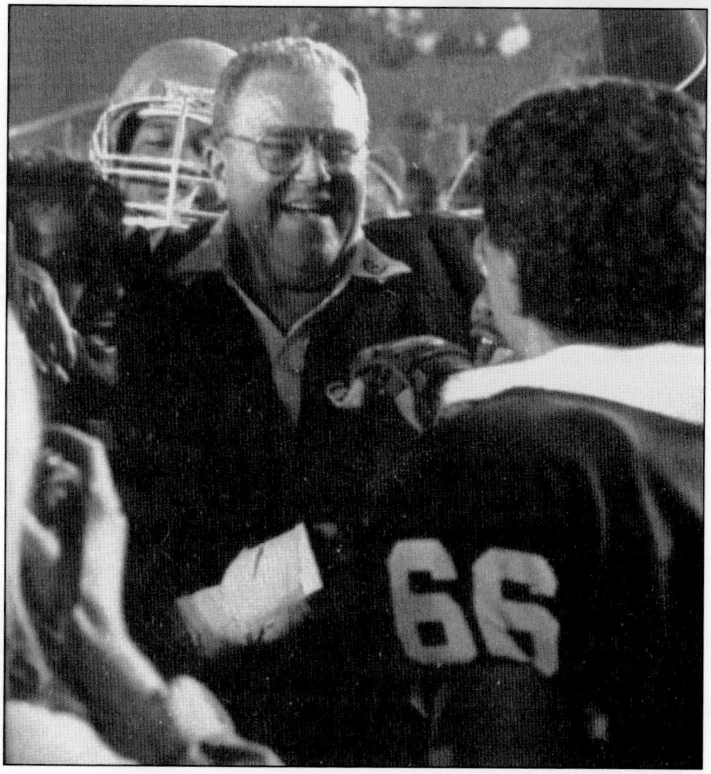

The Carson Colts, under Gene Vollnagle, were Los Angeles City High School Football Champions in 1966.

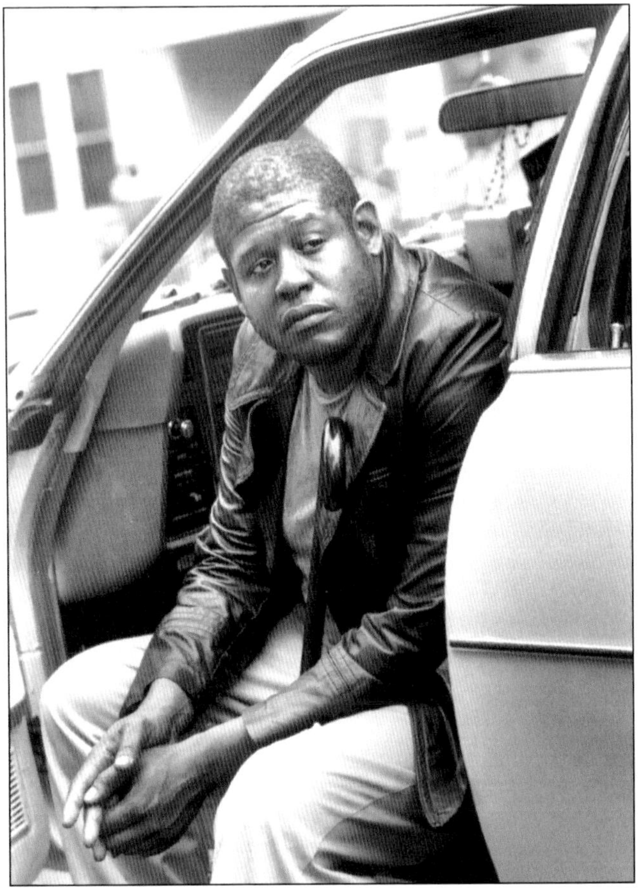

Forest Whitaker, who was born in Longview, Texas, became one of Hollywood's outstanding actors after growing up in Carson. He was named best actor at the Cannes Film Festival and received a Golden Globe nomination for his performance as jazzman Charlie Parker in Clint Eastwood's *Bird* (1988). He was twice nominated for Screen Actors Guild awards for his performances in *The Enemy Within* (1994) and *Deacons for Defense* (2003). He also won an Emmy award as a producer of the best TV movie, *Door to Door* (2002). He is at left in *Jason's Lyric* (1994) and below with Kiefer Sutherland (center) and Ray Liotta (right) in *Article 99* (1992). Whitaker's films include *Platoon* (1986), *The Color of Money* (1986), *Good Morning, Vietnam* (1987), and *Smoke* (1995). Whitaker directed the films *Waiting to Exhale* (1995) and *Hope Floats* (1998).

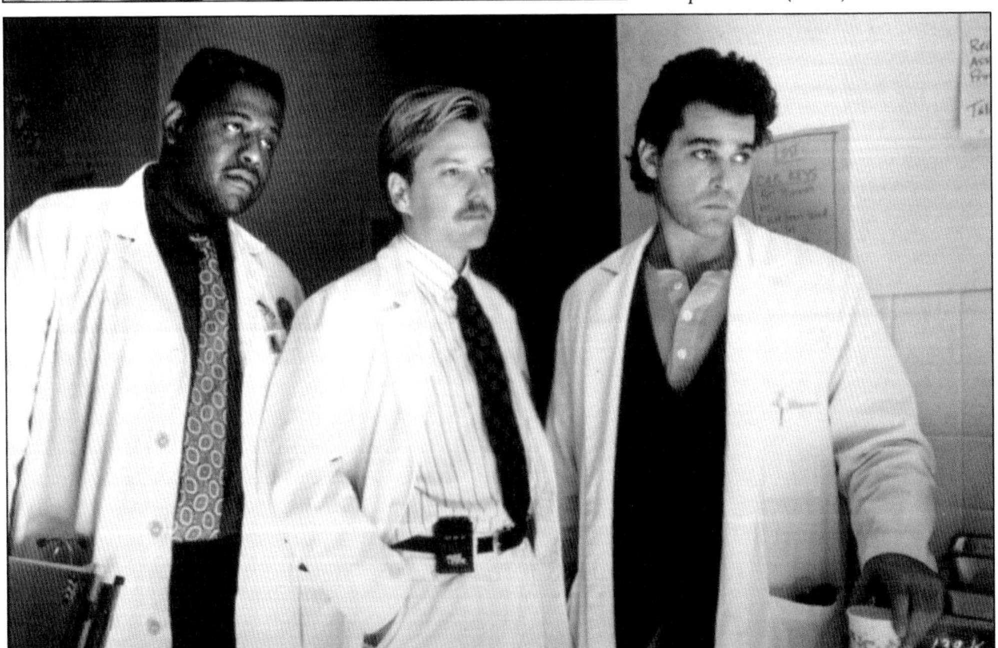

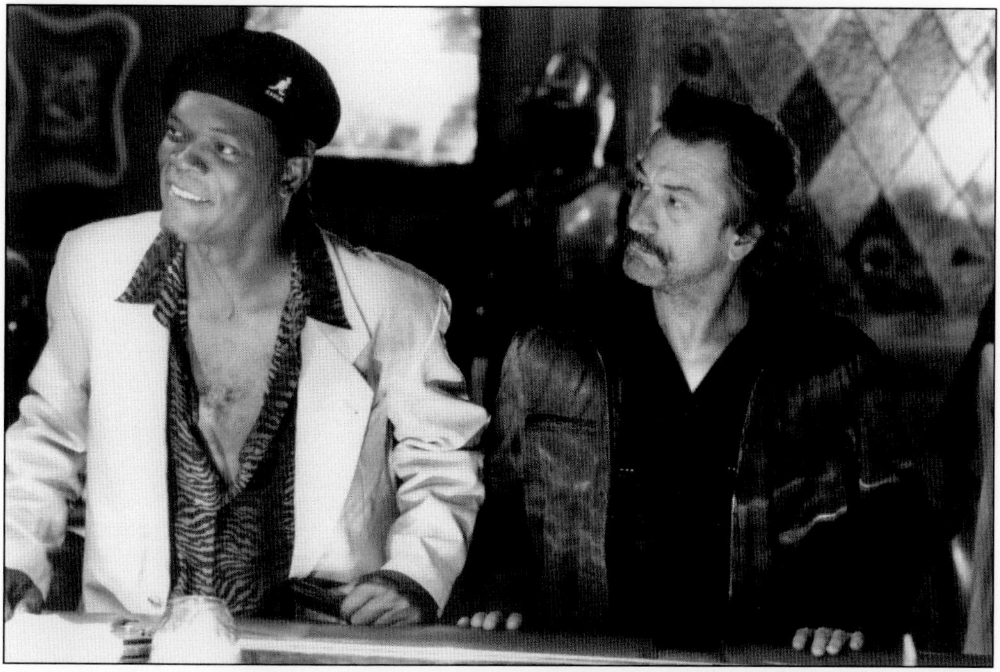

Writer/director Quentin Tarantino set his film *Jackie Brown* (1997) throughout Los Angeles County's South Bay communities, including Carson, where the bail bondsman played by Robert Forster (below) had his business. The film starred Samuel L. Jackson (top left) and Robert DeNiro (right) in the adaptation of Elmore Leonard's crime novel *Rum Punch*. Tarantino moved the story from Florida to his home stomping grounds, the South Bay, and cast former "blaxploitation" movie queen Pam Grier in the lead as a reluctant "go-fer" for Jackson's street thug. The film also starred Bridget Fonda, Michael Keaton, and Chris Tucker.

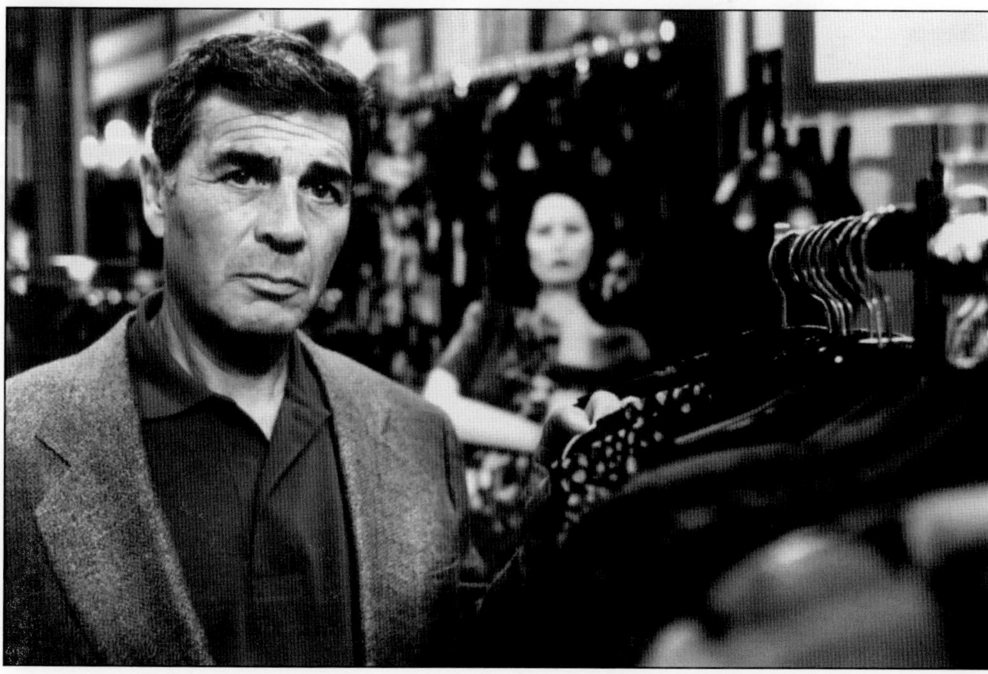

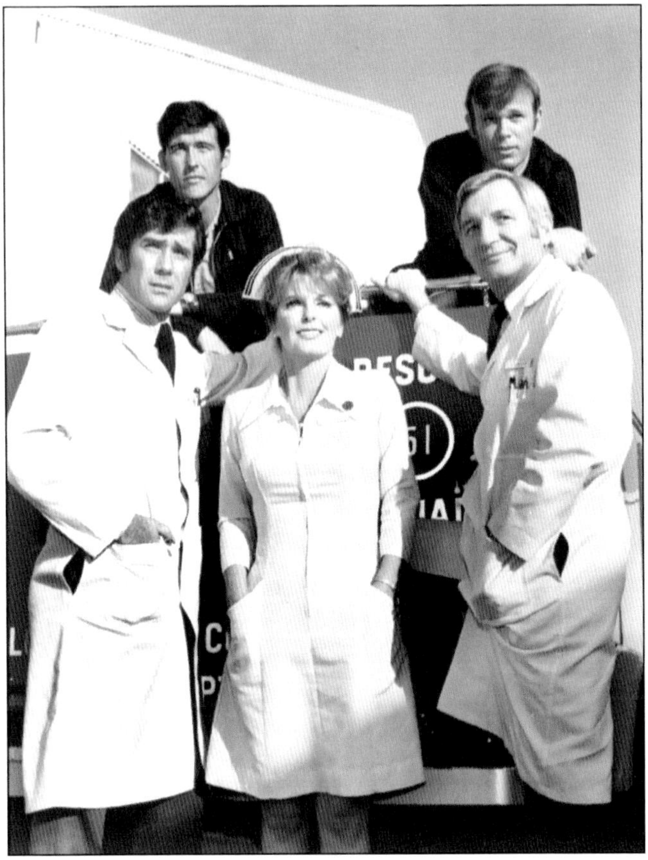

The garage doors that opened faithfully each week from 1972 to 1977 at the fire station on the hit NBC television show *Emergency* are located at Fire Station No. 127 on 223rd Street just east of Wilmington Avenue in Carson. In the left photograph is the cast of the show, which was produced by Jack Webb's Mark VII Productions. In the front row, from left to right, are Robert Fuller, Julie London, and Bobby Troupe; (second row) Randolph Mantooth and Kevin Tighe. The lettering on the front of the station house, below, reads "Robert A. Cinader Memorial Fire Station, City of Carson, Los Angeles County, Fire Station 127." Cinader was the executive producer for Mark VII and Webb's right-hand man for decades.

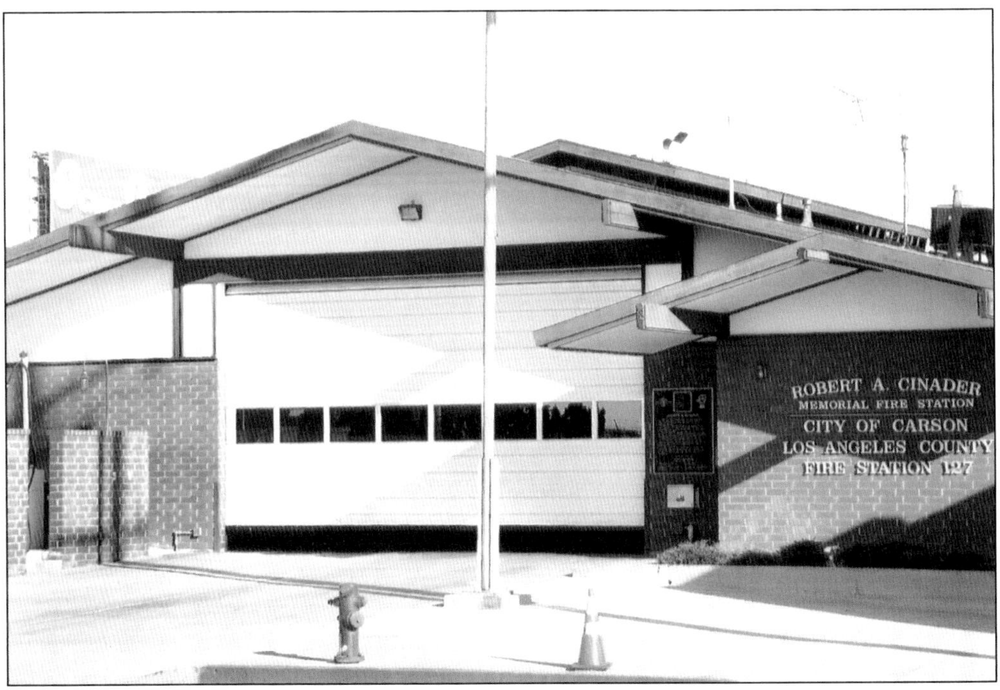

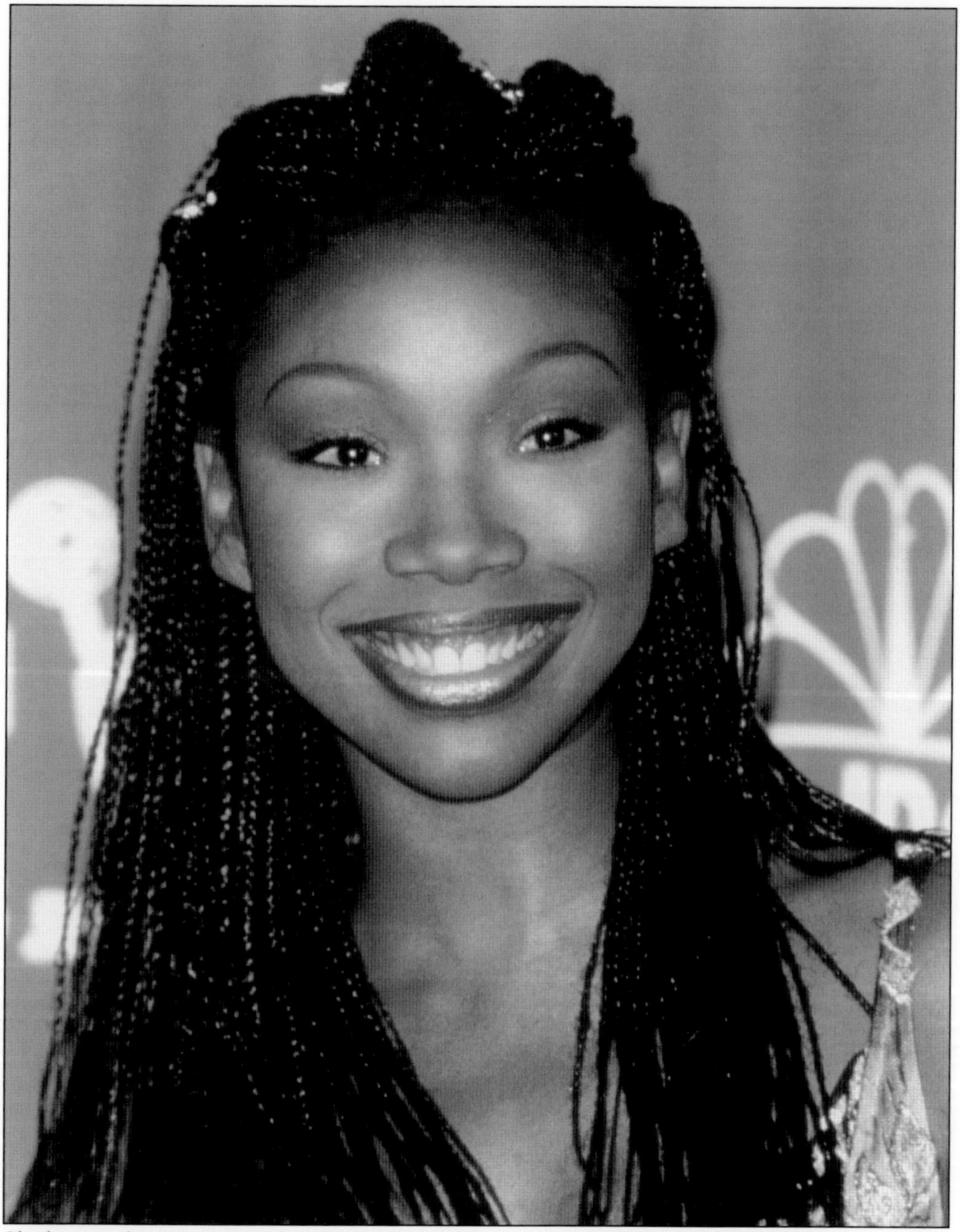

She became known in the music business, on television and radio, and in films simply as "Brandy." Brandy Norwood grew up in Carson and built a show-business career as the precocious star of the comedy series *Moesha*, which ran from 1996 to 2001. Her hits include "I Wanna Be Down," "Baby," Have You Ever," "The Boy Is Mine," "Brokenhearted," and "Sittin' Up in My Room," among others. Among her pan-showbiz accolades, Brandy was named one of the "50 most beautiful people" in 1996 by *People* magazine. She starred in a special presentation of Rodgers and Hammerstein's *Cinderella* (1997) with Whitney Houston, Whoopi Goldberg, and Bernadette Peters on television and in the feature film *I Still Know What You Did Last Summer* (1998).

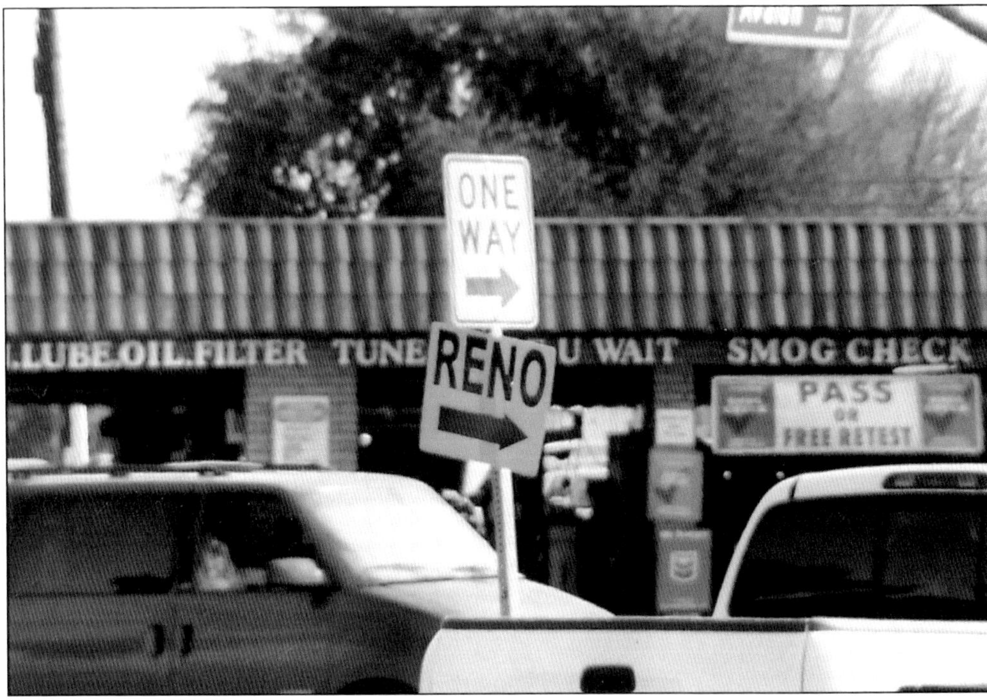

These photographs were taken on Avalon Boulevard in Carson of location shoots for the cast and crew of *Reno 911*, the Comedy Central drama that has been distributed by the cable channel since 2003. A satire of reality police shows, *Reno 911*, also pictured below, offers cop stereotypes in a supposed behind-the-scenes examination of actual police work. The advertising tagline is "They have what it takes to be cops: Badges." The Los Angeles County sheriff's station on Avalon Boulevard in Carson has served as the main visual for exterior shots of *Reno 911*, and the show is often shot in Carson.

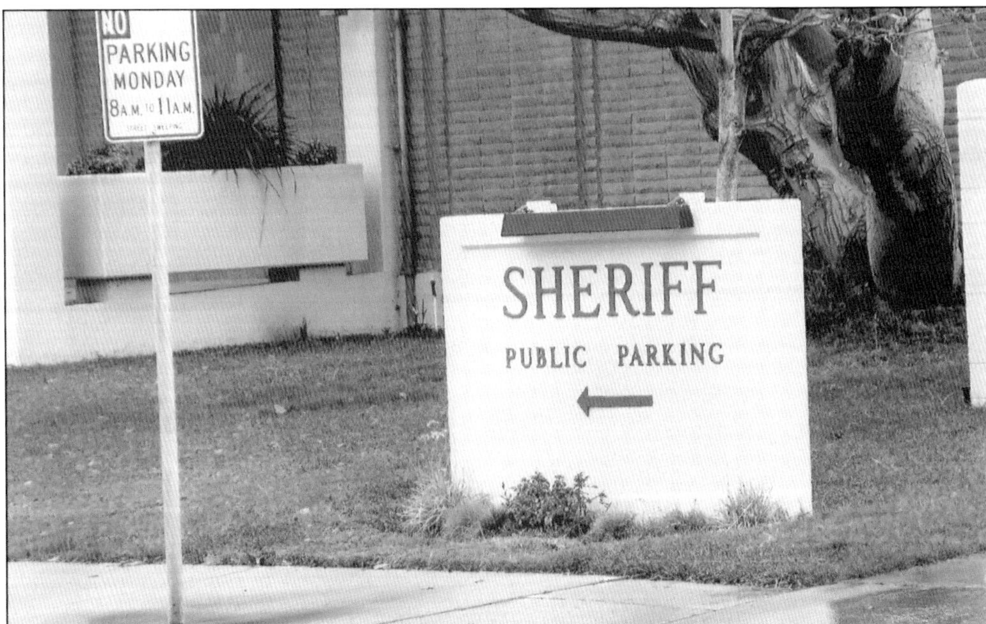

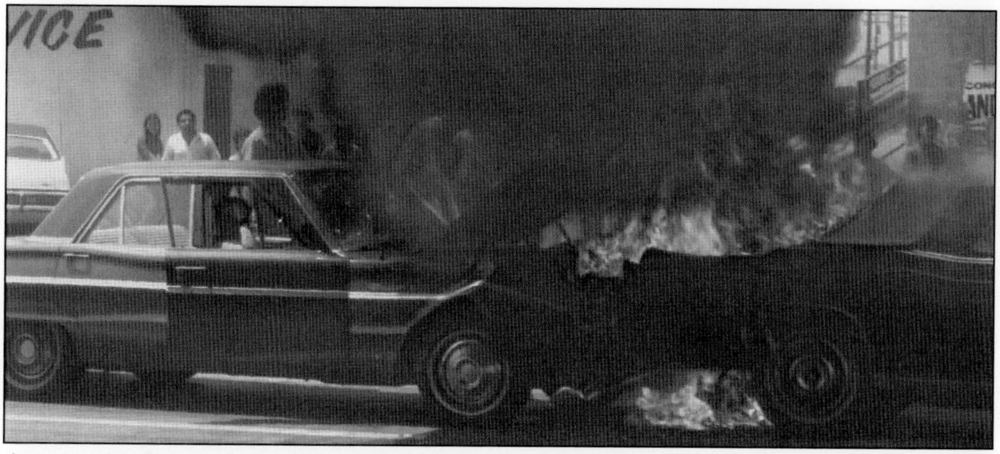

At one time, Carson claimed 88 junkyards. Among the creative projects to rise out of this mass of metal was *Gone in 60 Seconds* (1974), above, which was a low-budget, lowdown look at a larcenous art form of "boosting" cars and getting away with it quickly among the gear-head set. H. B. Halicki wrote, produced, directed, coordinated the stunts, wrote some of the music, and starred in the film, a cult classic that featured former Carson mayor Sak Yamamoto as himself, along with such car-industry names as Parnelli Jones, Christopher J. C. Agajanian, J. C. Agajanian Jr., and Gary Bettenhausen, among others. Part of the problem with taking other people's property is that sometimes a person can crash and burn. A retooling of *Gone in 60 Seconds* (2000) was given the Hollywood treatment once again with Nicolas Cage, Angelina Jolie, and Robert Duvall starring in the updated version. It was also filmed in Carson and various locations in the Ports of Los Angeles and Long Beach.

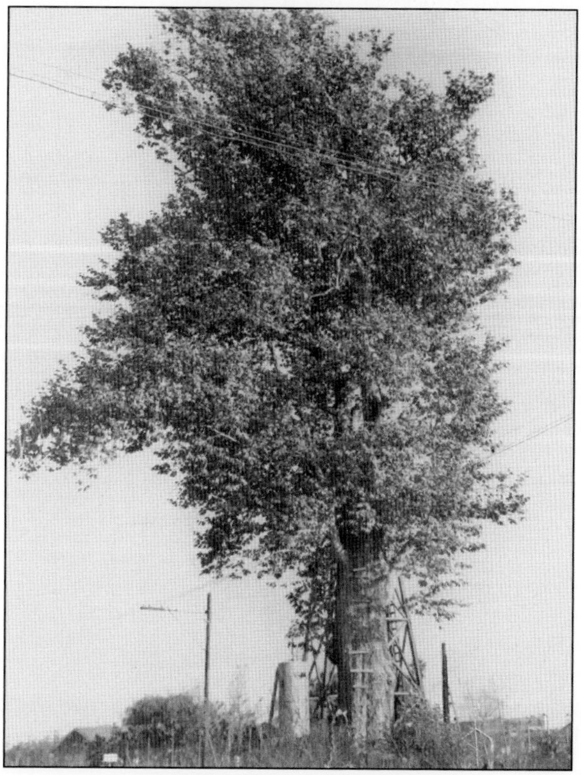

Pictured here in 1952 is the "Eagle Tree," an old sycamore located at Poppy and Short Streets (today's Compton). The tree still stands and was the northern boundary for the Rancho San Pedro. (Courtesy Special Collections and Archives, California State University, Dominguez Hills.)

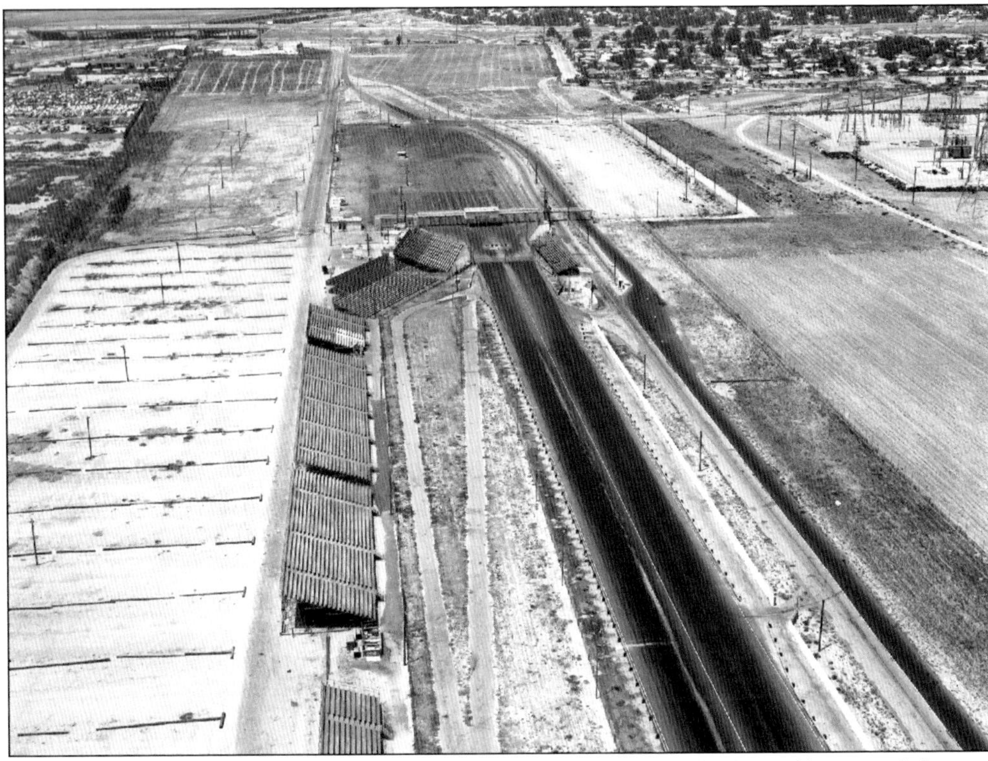

Lion's Dragstrip, located on Alameda and 223rd Streets, was originally formed by several chapters of local Lions Clubs in order to move auto racing off the streets and to a safer venue. Originally known as LADS (Lions Associated Dragstrip), it opened on October 9, 1955, and the last race was held on December 2, 1972.

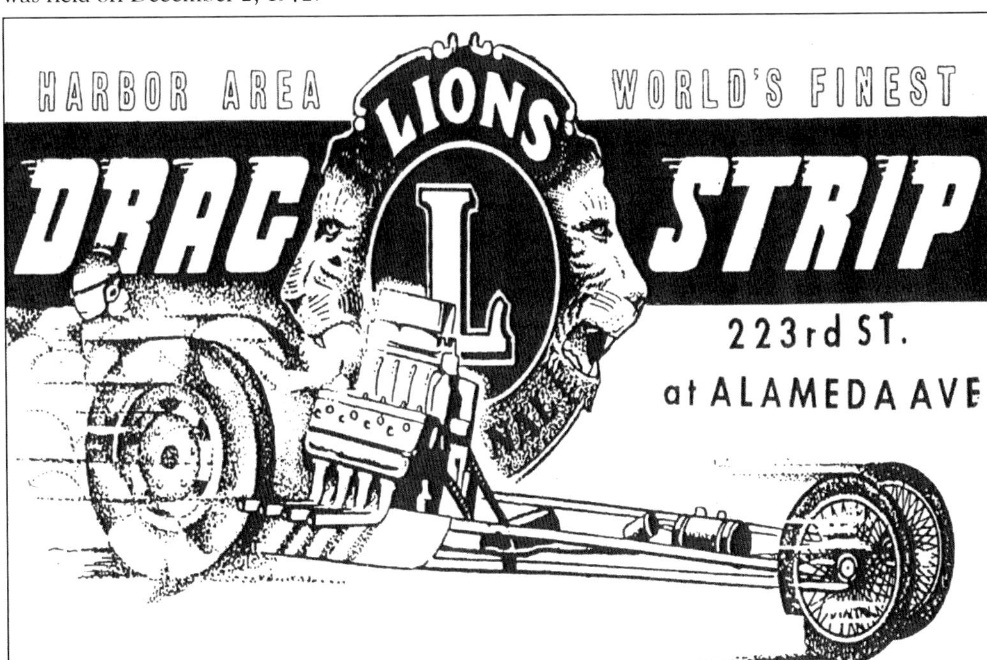

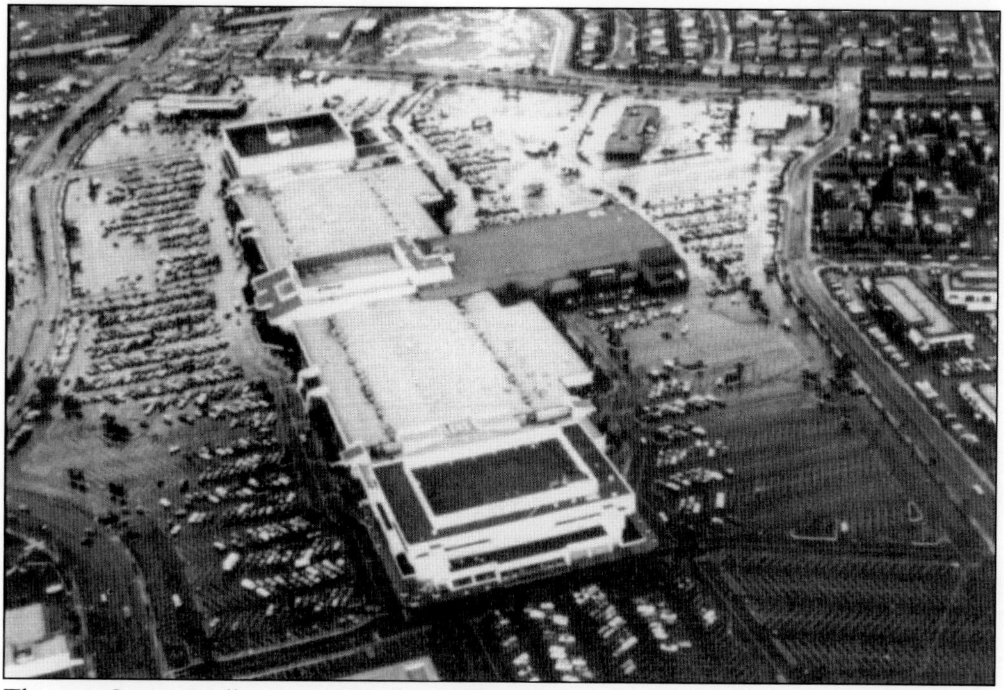

The new Carson Mall was completed in 1973, with Sears, J. C. Penney, and Broadway as the anchor stores.

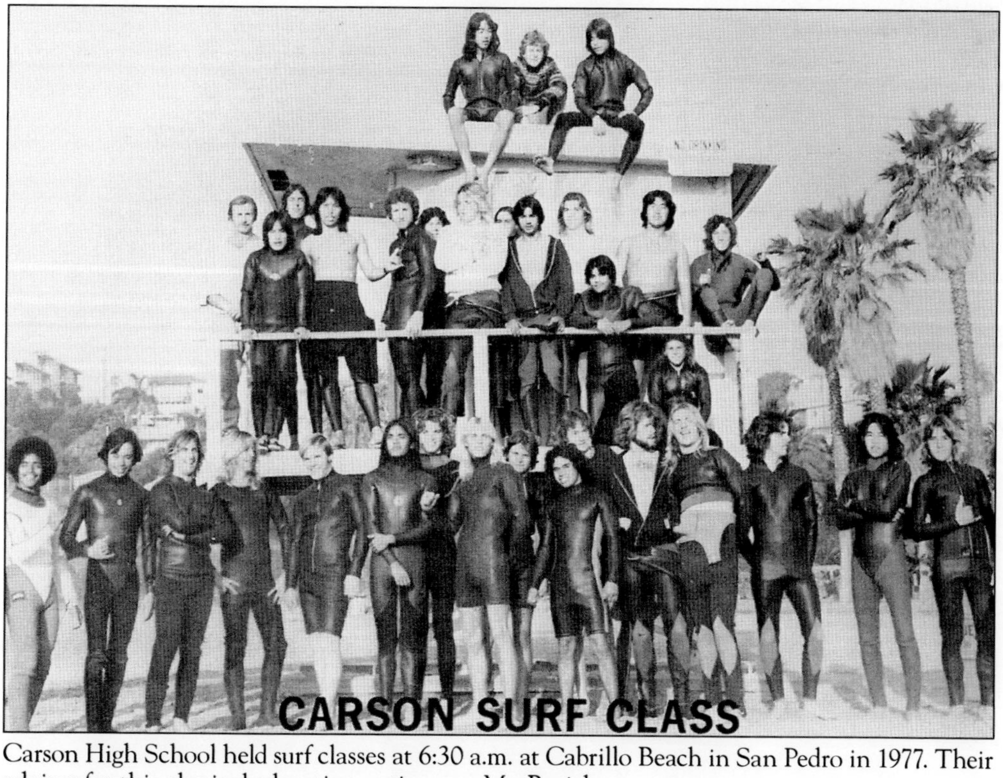

Carson High School held surf classes at 6:30 a.m. at Cabrillo Beach in San Pedro in 1977. Their advisor for this physical education option was Mr. Burich.

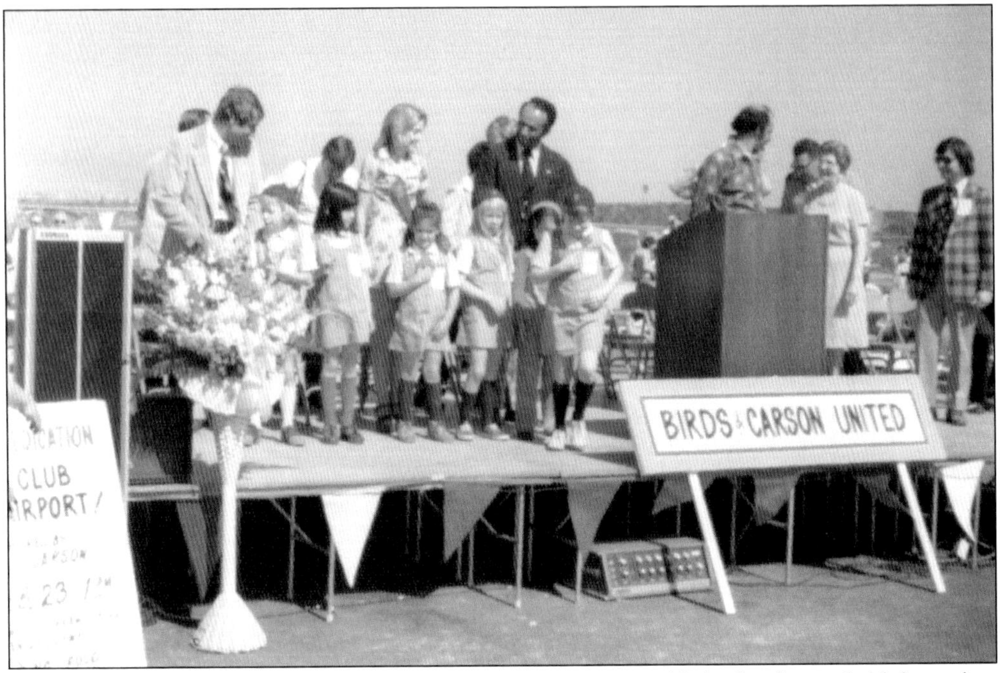

The BIRD (Beginners in Radio Drones) Club of Carson established a flying field for radio-controlled model aircraft in a large empty lot at the northwest corner of the California State University, Dominguez Hills, campus. Some BIRD members even represented the United States in worldwide competition. The field was dedicated on February 23, 1975, in an on-site ceremony. Here community dignitaries, including Mayor Gil Smith (center, in dark suit), pledge allegiance with Brownie Troop No. 1158. It is a pleasantly ironic twist that the 1910 Dominguez Air Meet was held only a stone's throw from this celebration of aviation in miniature, where even children could fly. On the site now is the Home Depot Center.

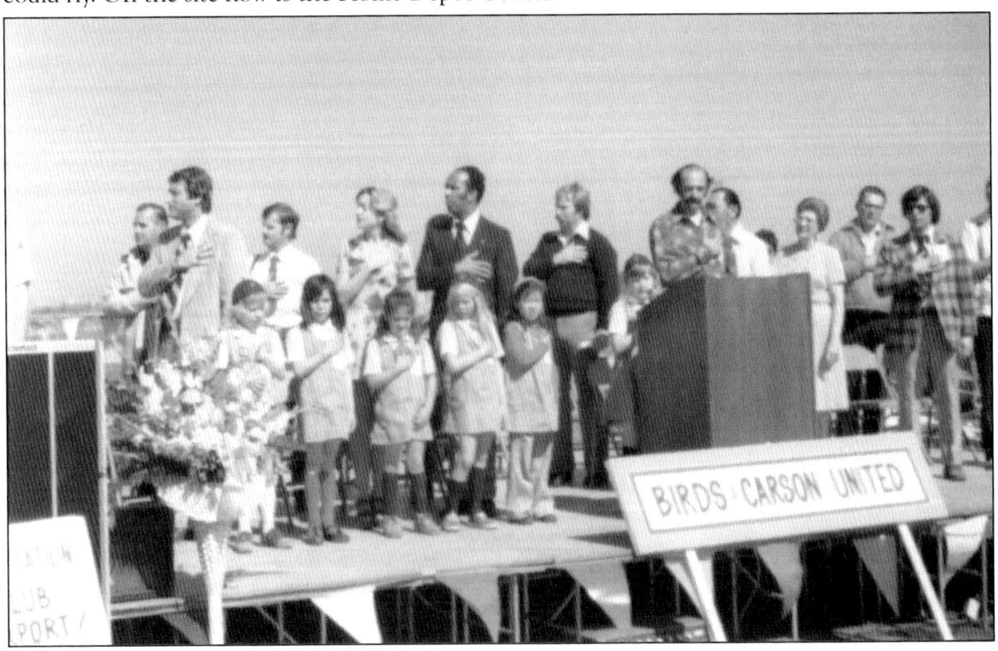

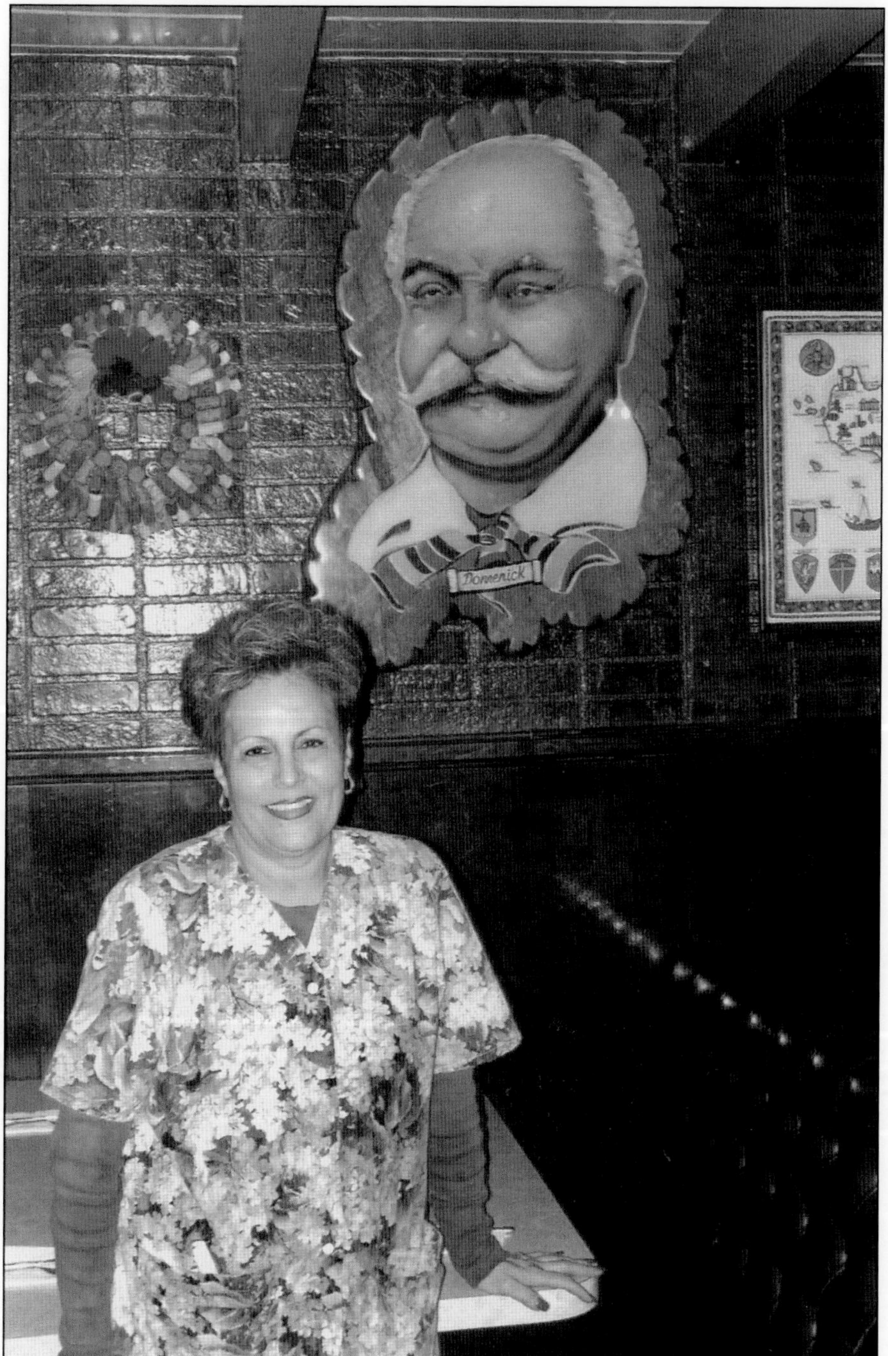

Domenick Sardisco opened his pizza house in 1956 at 24209 South Avalon Boulevard, which was then in the Wilmington section of Los Angeles but is now the city of Carson. Barbara Ruiz began waiting tables there in 1957 and remains one of the best-known faces in town. After Domenick passed away in 1978, his son Domenick Sardisco Jr. took over operations and remains there today. Here, after nearly 40 years, Barbara stands next to the familiar wooden plaque of Domenick Sr. in the restaurant.

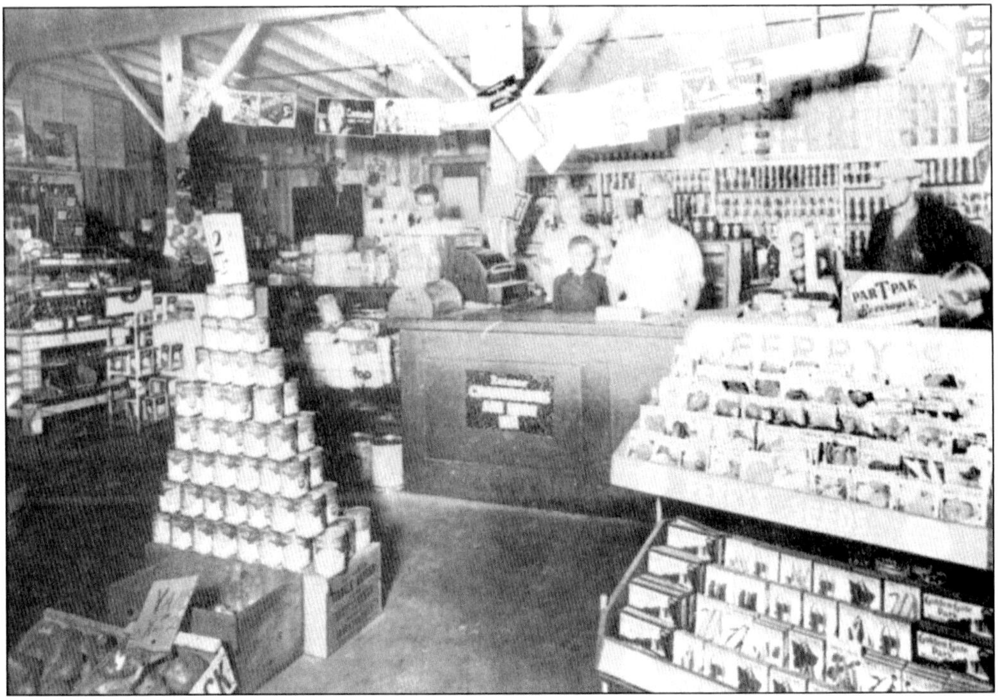

Around 1910, Hilpert's Store was located at the center of town, what was then 220th and Main Streets.

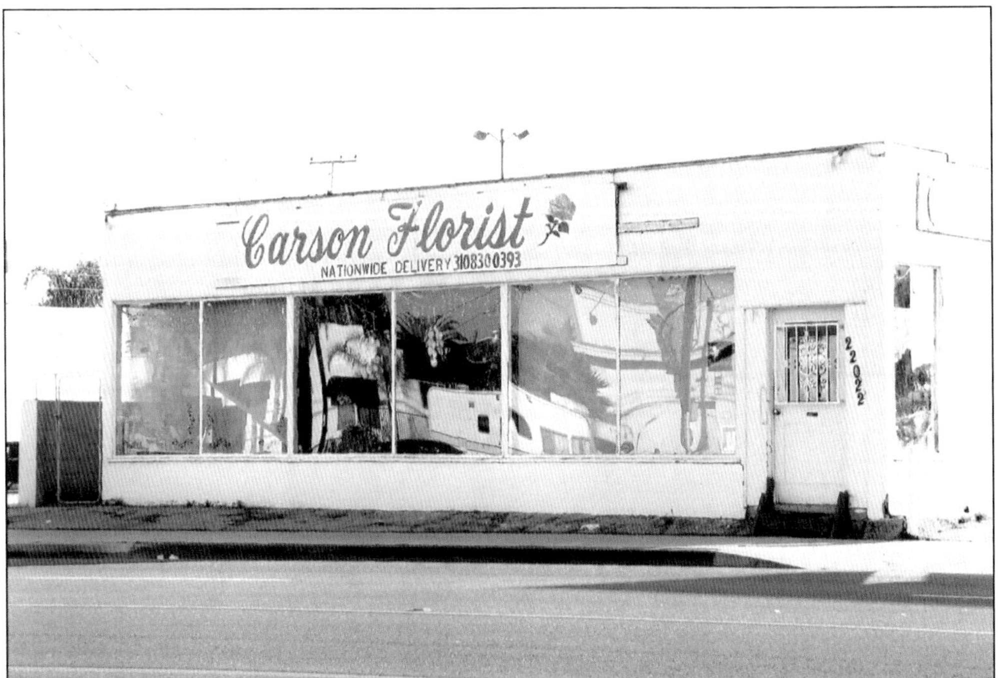

Today Carson Florists occupies the building at 22022 South Main Street.

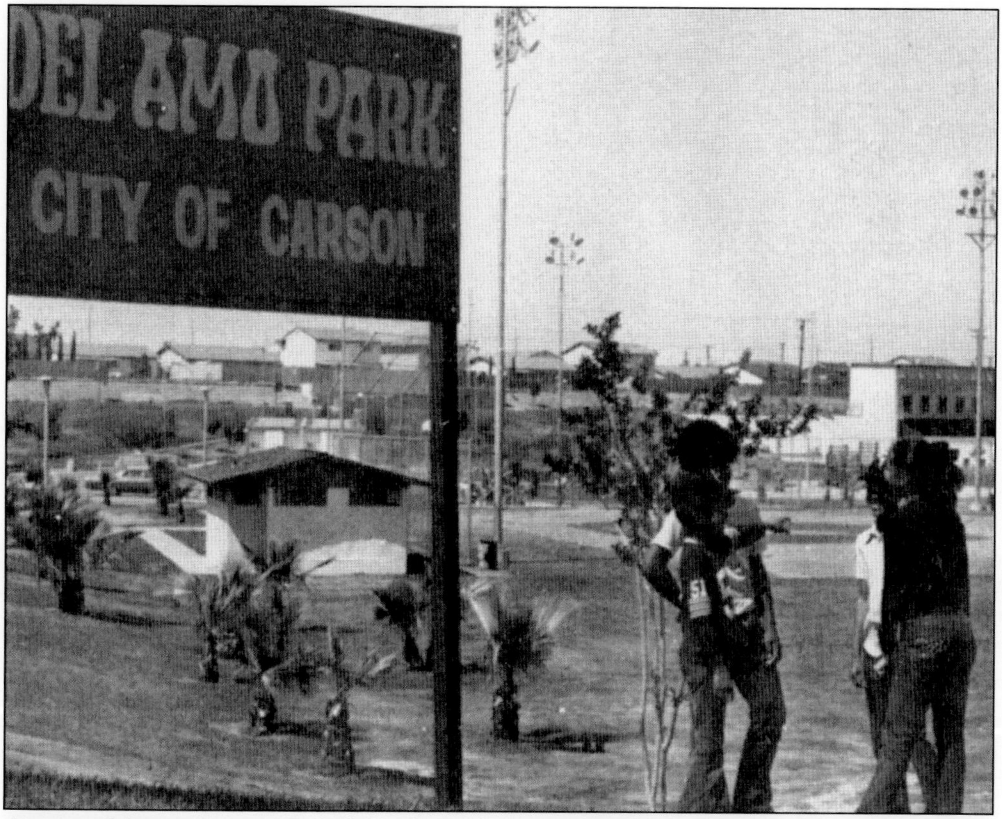

As part of Carson's ongoing parks and recreation development, Del Amo Park received new lights in 1973.

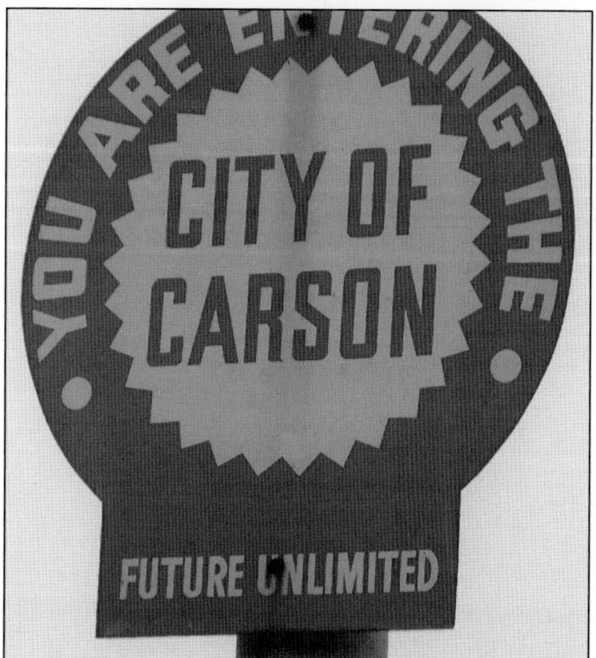

These small signs at Carson's borders have been continuously visible since 1968, when they were donated by the Lions Club and designed by Gil Smith. Originally they were a yellow sunburst on a blue background.

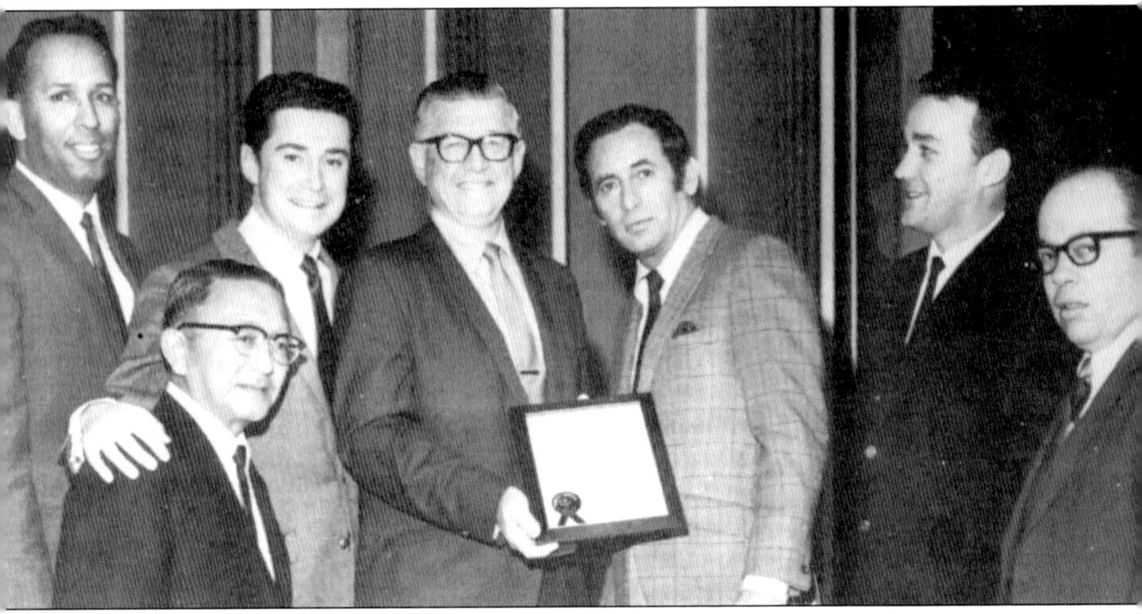

Carson's first anniversary was celebrated with a parade and fiesta on Saturday, February 22, 1969. The event was enthusiastically received, with the march attracting 2,000 participants and 45,000 spectators. The grand marshal was television's Regis Philbin, then emcee for *The Joey Bishop Show*. The date was celebrated Hollywood-style at the Channel 7 studio in January 1969 by proclaiming Joey Bishop as honorary mayor and "king of Carson." Pictured, from left to right, are councilmen Gil Smith and Sak Yamamoto, Regis Philbin, Mayor John Marbut, Joey Bishop, and councilmen John Junk and Rick Clark.

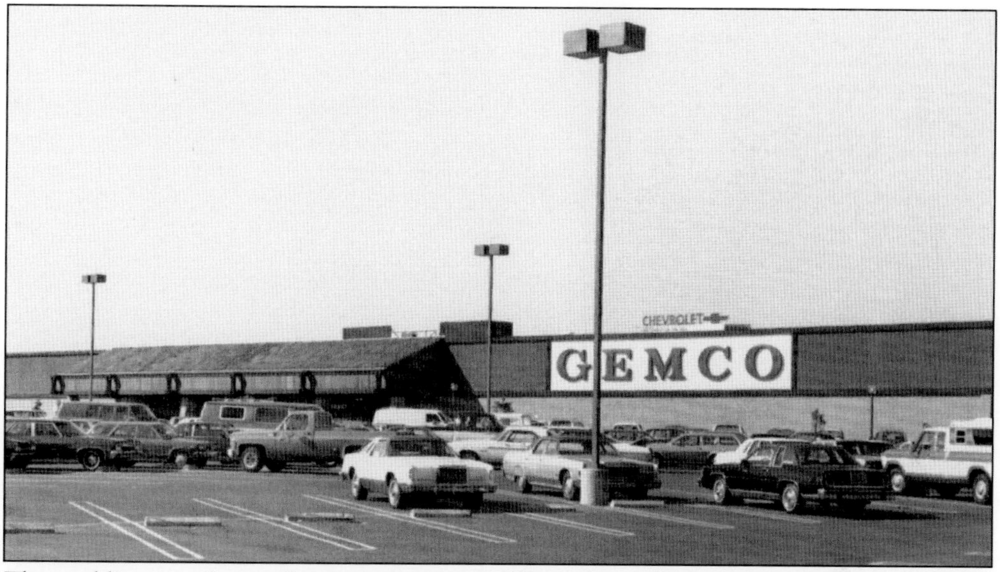

The sparkling new Gemco department store in 1978 was located at Sepulveda Boulevard and the Harbor Freeway. The site is now a Target store.

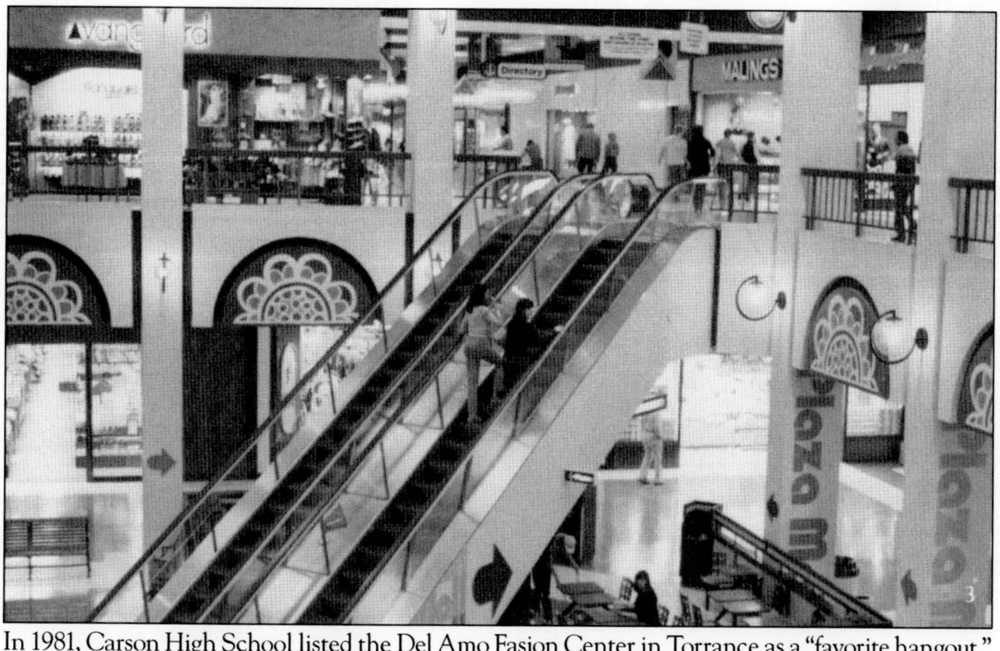

In 1981, Carson High School listed the Del Amo Fasion Center in Torrance as a "favorite hangout." It still is, but the decor has changed.

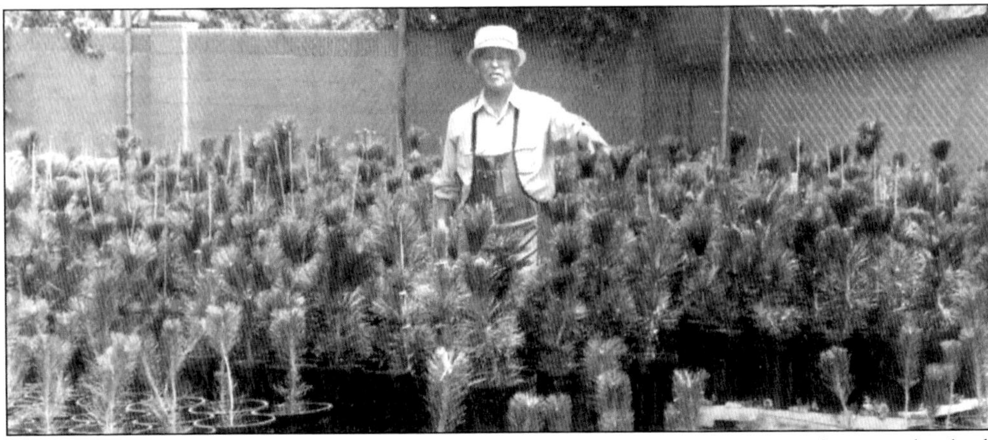

In 1987, Ototaro Yamamoto tends to 1,000 Japanese black pine trees grown from seed, which were donated by officials in Soka City, Japan, Carson's sister city.

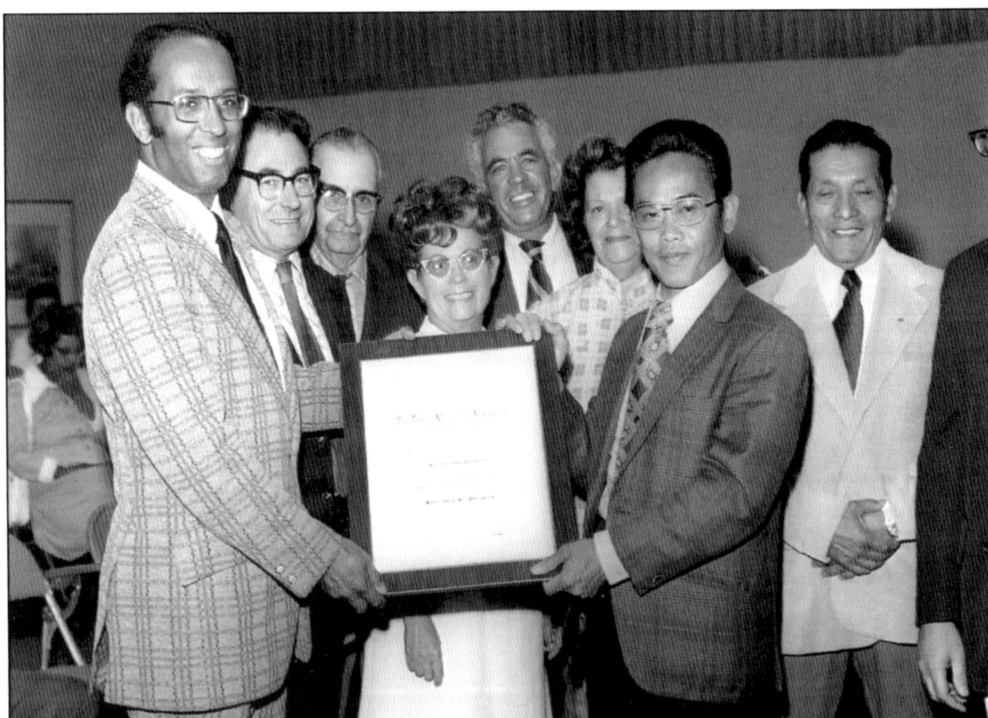

The City of Carson was recognized by the Town Affiliation Association of the United States for its Sister City program. Above, the Sister City Steering Committee celebrates the occasion in June 1974.

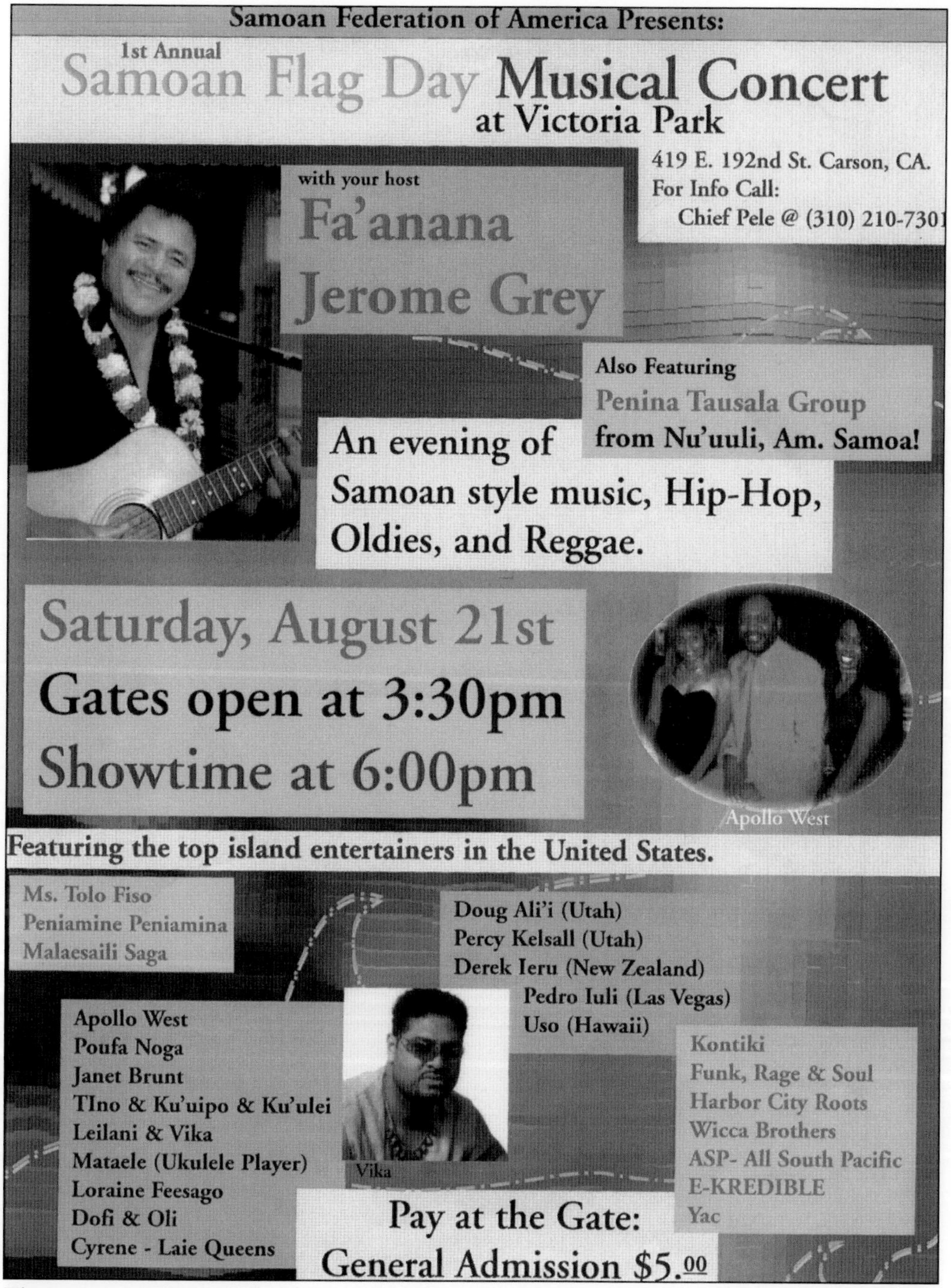

This poster commemorates the first-annual Samoan Flag Day Concert at Victoria Park in 2004.

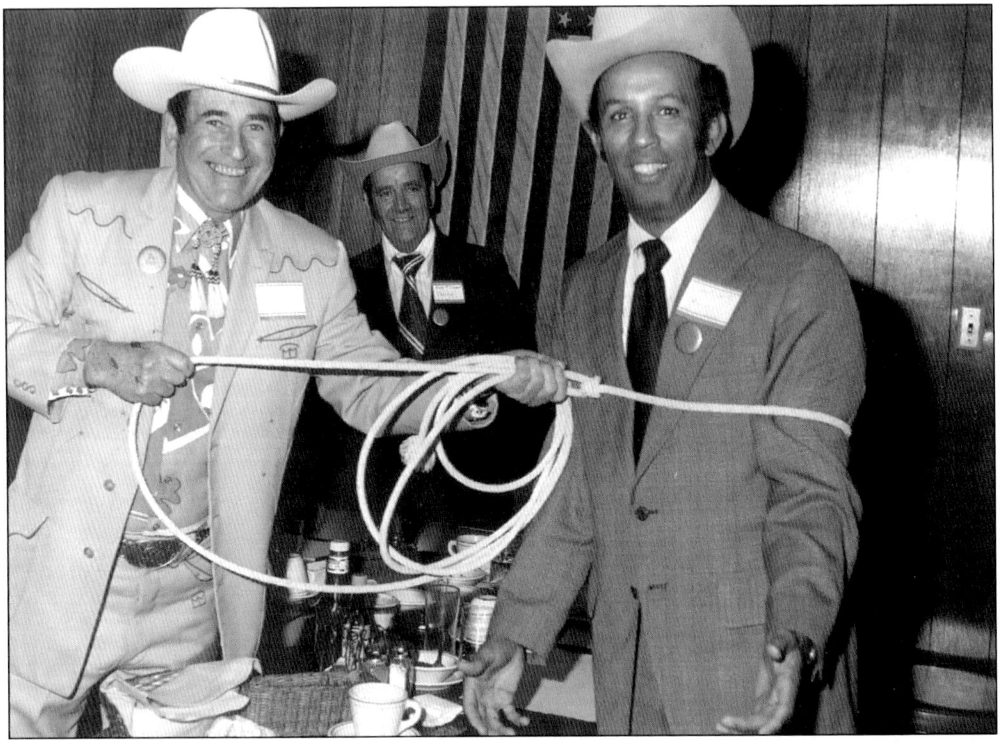

Montie Montana was a Hollywood actor in "B" westerns, a rodeo lariat-trick specialist, and a former stuntman in John Ford movies, including *The Man Who Shot Liberty Valance* (1962) and *Cheyenne Autumn* (1964). Montana made quite a career out of personal appearances on the chicken-dinner circuit throughout the Los Angeles area. Here in a staged publicity shot on the seventh anniversary of the City of Carson in 1975, Montana lassoes Mayor Gil Smith.

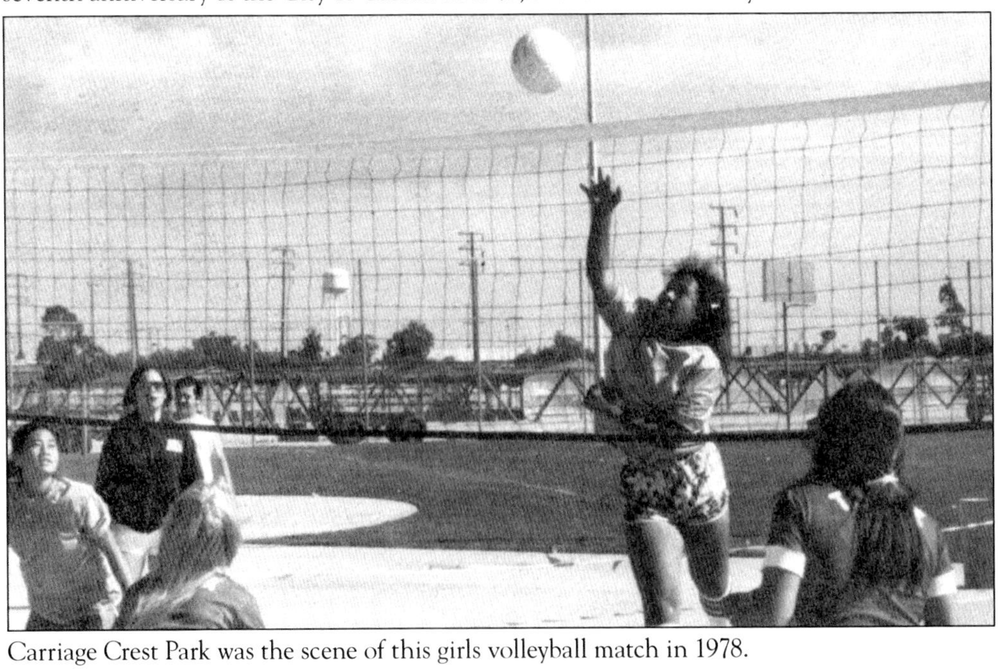

Carriage Crest Park was the scene of this girls volleyball match in 1978.

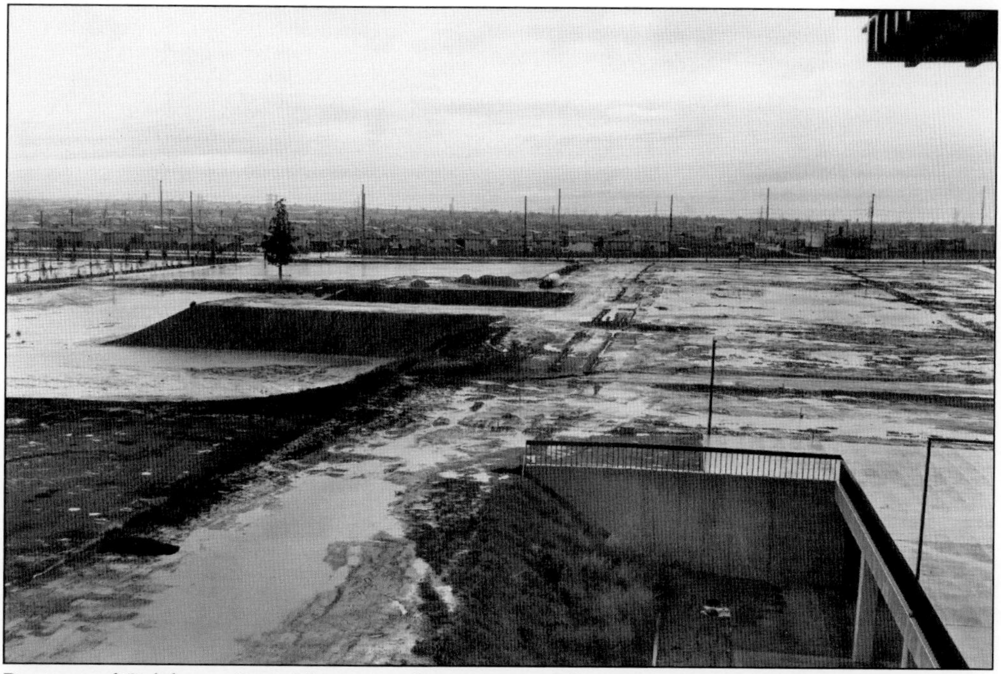

Portions of California State University, Dominguez Hills, were under construction in December 1971 when the site was flooded by heavy rains. (Courtesy Special Collections and Archives, California State University, Dominguez Hills.)

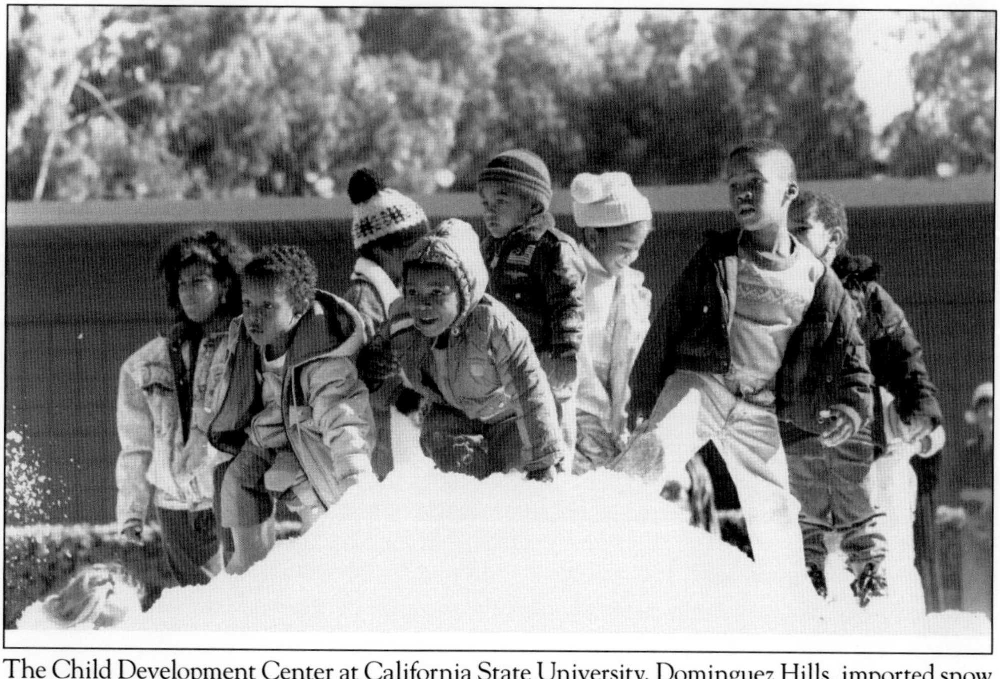

The Child Development Center at California State University, Dominguez Hills, imported snow for an unusual play day in 1982. (Courtesy Special Collections and Archives, California State University, Dominguez Hills.)

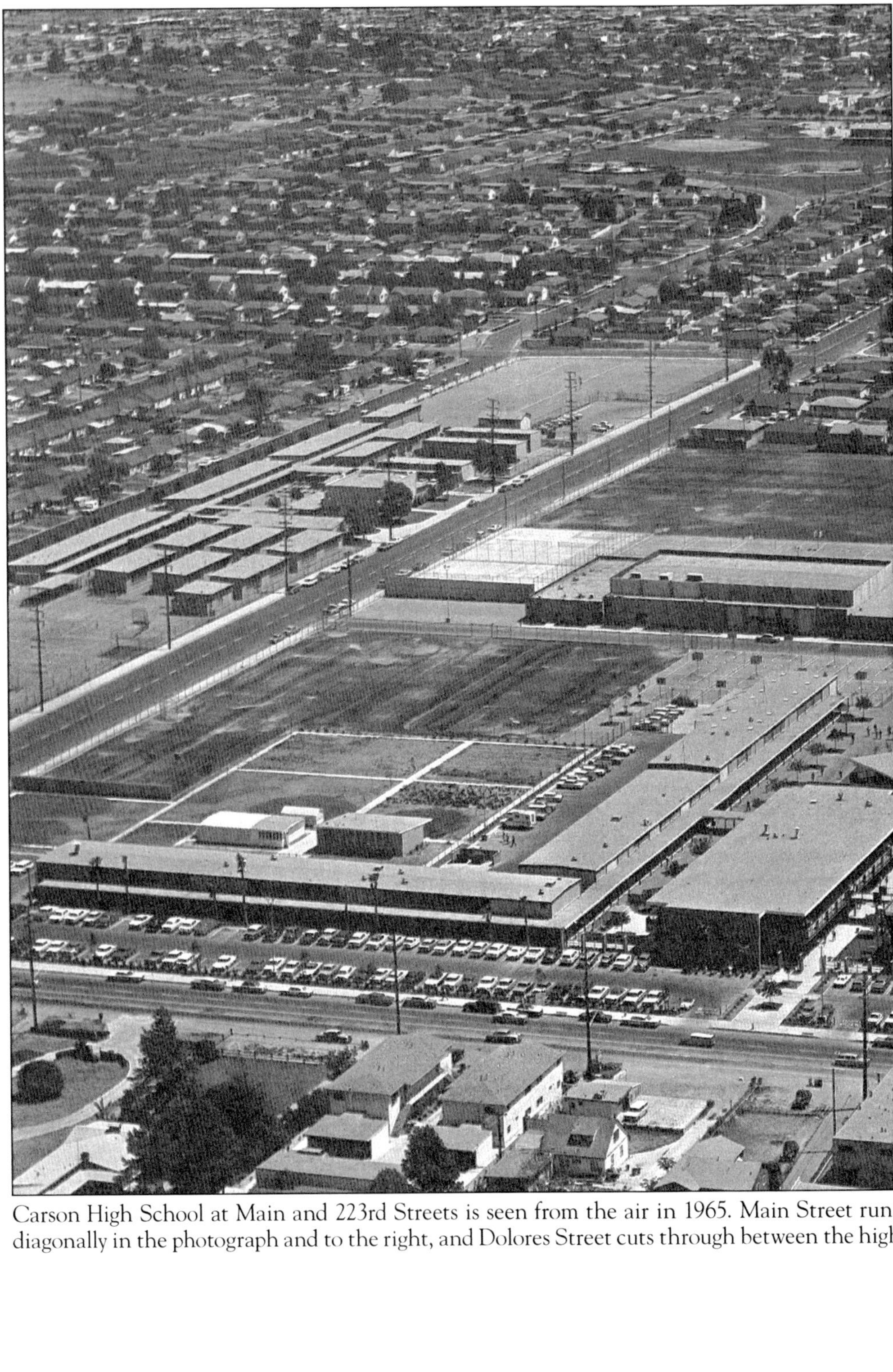

Carson High School at Main and 223rd Streets is seen from the air in 1965. Main Street runs diagonally in the photograph and to the right, and Dolores Street cuts through between the high

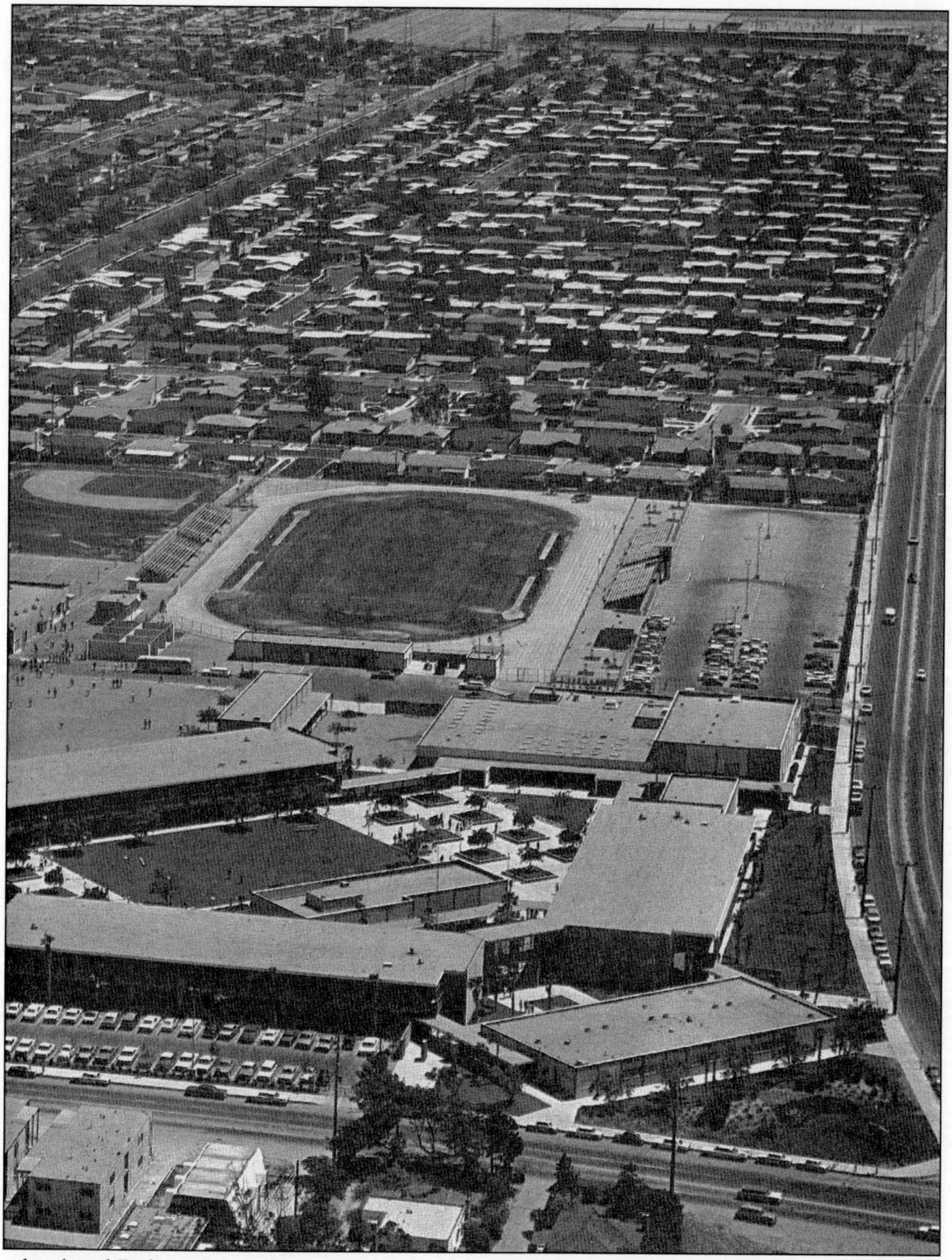

school and Dolores Street Elementary School. In the left image, facing a southerly direction, is Scott Park.

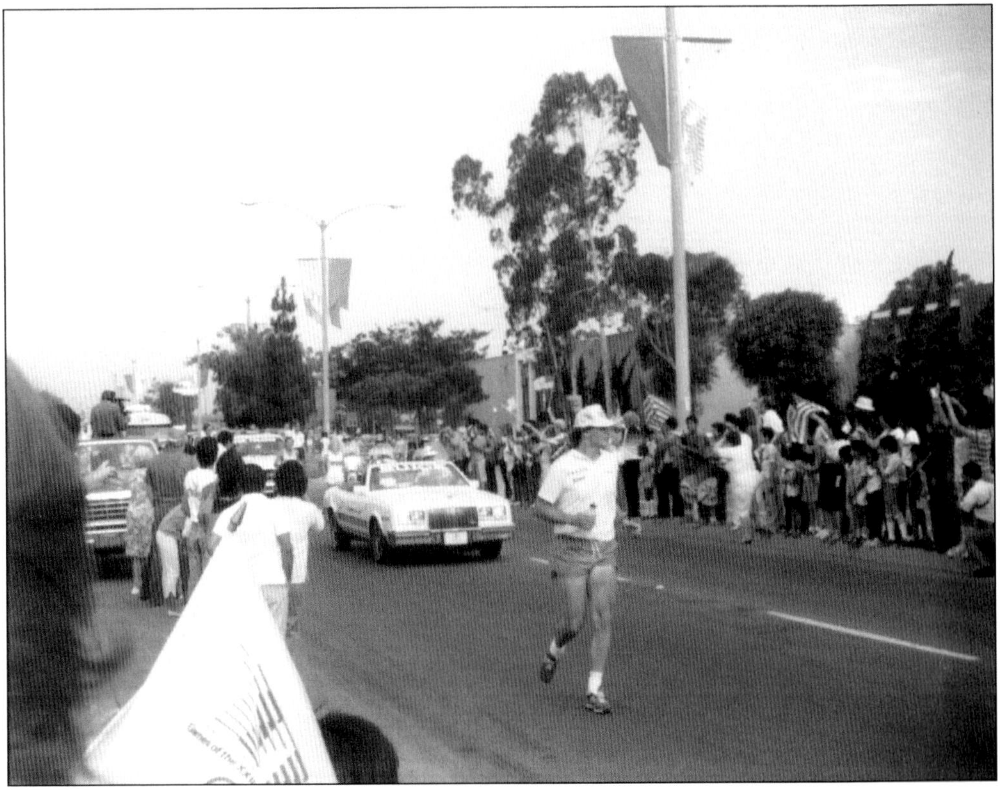

Above and below, the Veek family recorded the Olympic Torch as it passed through Carson in 1984 in front of Carson Street School at Foster's Freeze.

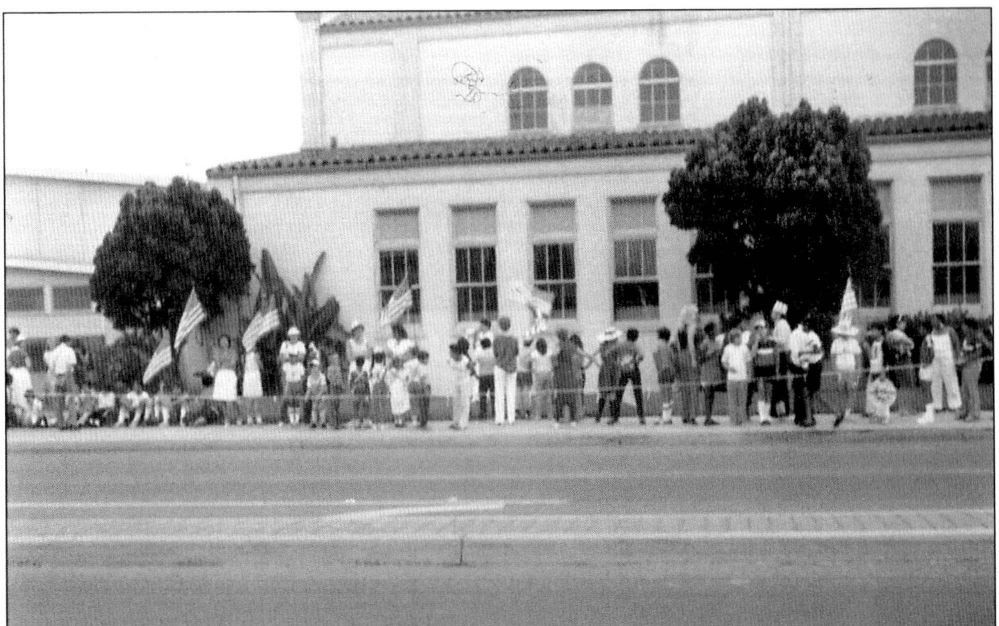

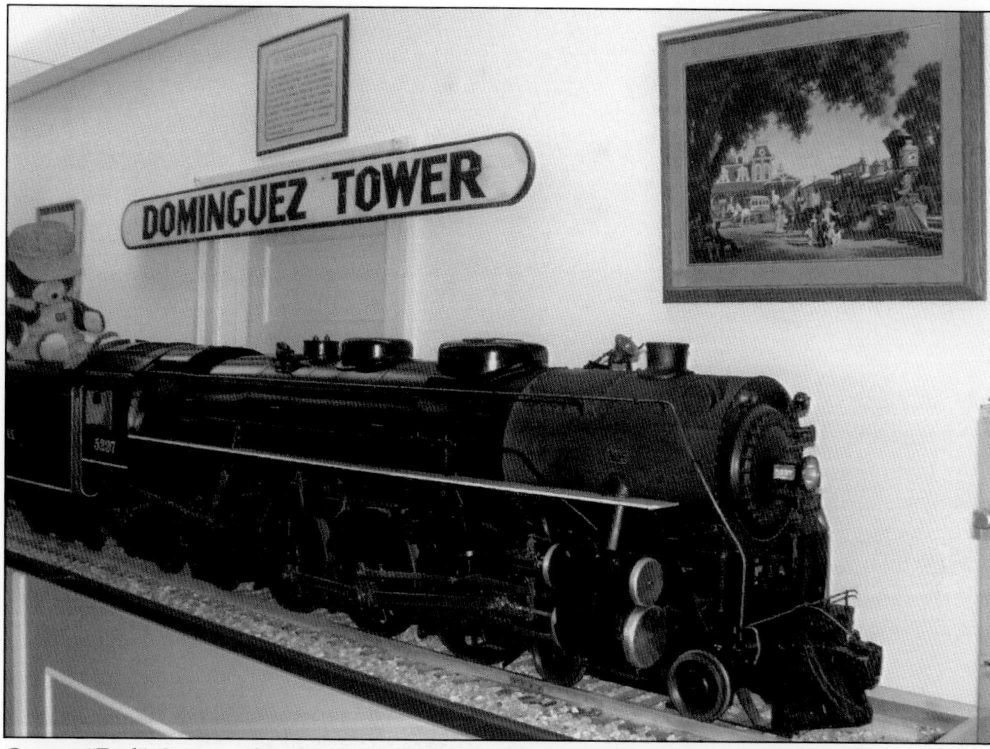

George "Earl" Carson, the grandson of Victoria Dominguez and George Henry Carson, took a keen interest in trains and built several scale-model engines. Some were used in Griffith Park in Los Angeles as children's rides with Earl himself in the engineer's coveralls. In 2005, a selection of his trains has been temporarily placed in the carriage house at the Dominguez Ranch adobe pending renovation of the museum exhibit.

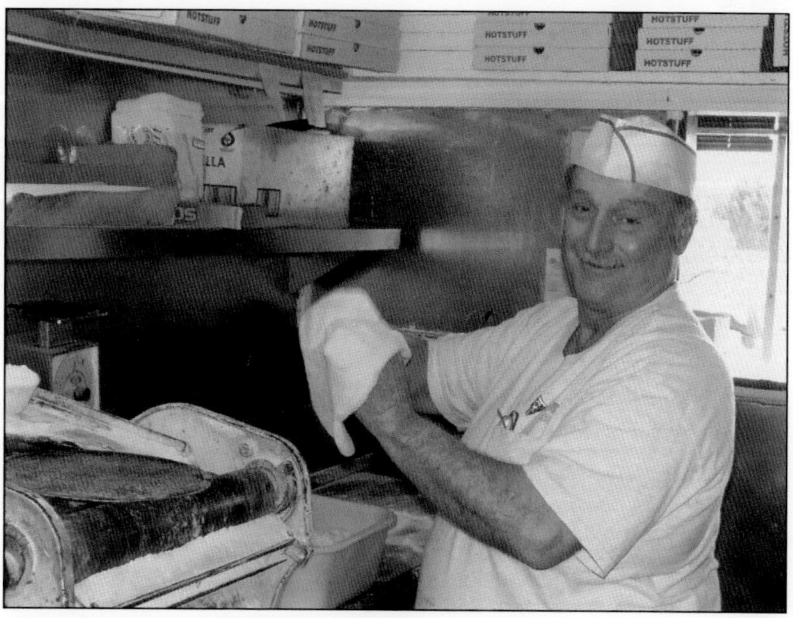

Jim Bono of Rosario's Pizza on Carson Street works on another masterpiece. The restaurant has been a Carson mainstay since the early 1970s.

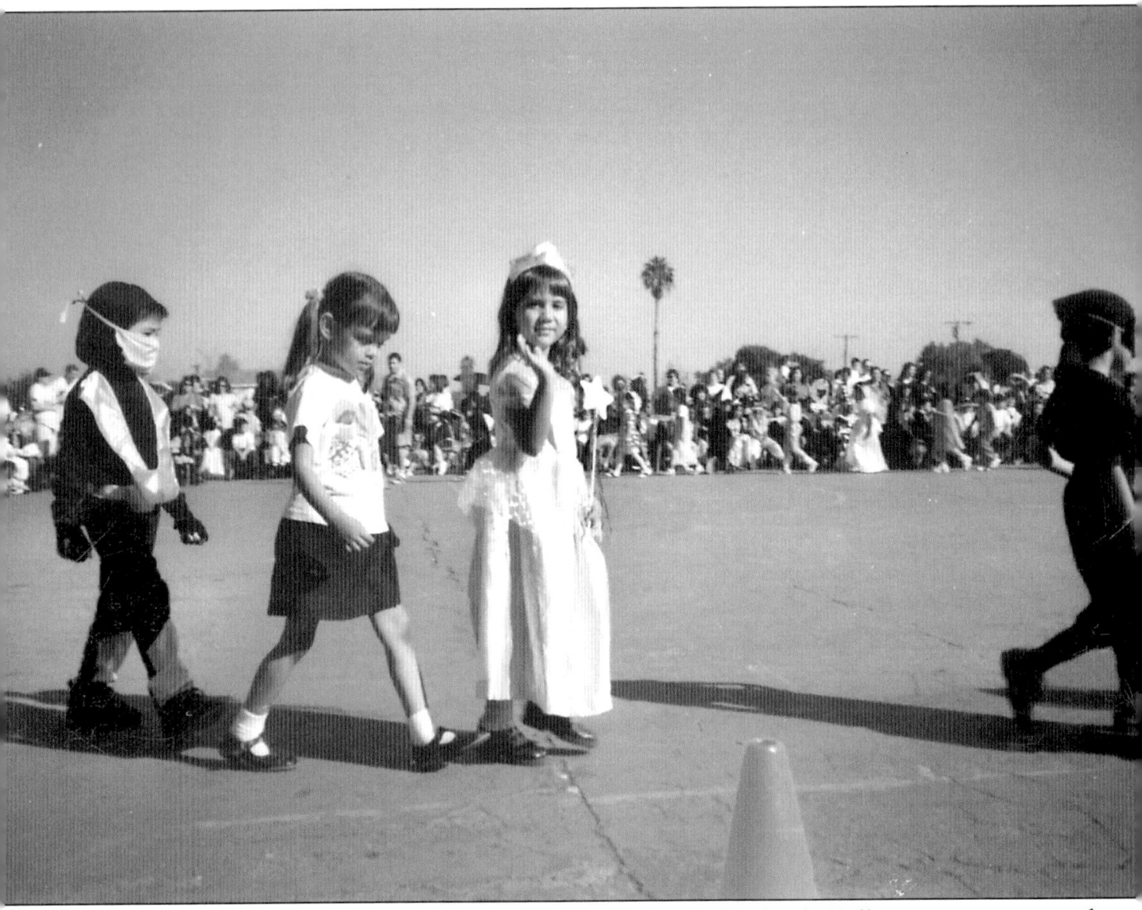

Of the events in Carson, the annual 232nd Place Elementary School's Halloween party is one of the dressier affairs. Here the 1998 edition is in full swing.

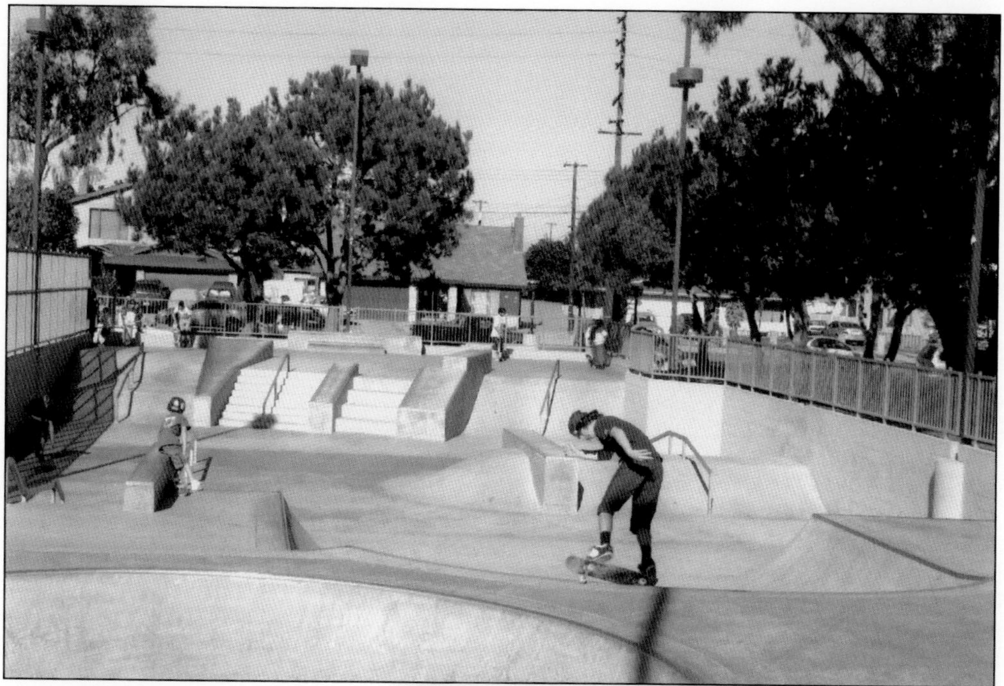

As would-be Tony Hawks have multiplied in Southern California, so have skate parks through the turn of the 21st century. Carson's skate park was installed in Veteran's Park in 2003.

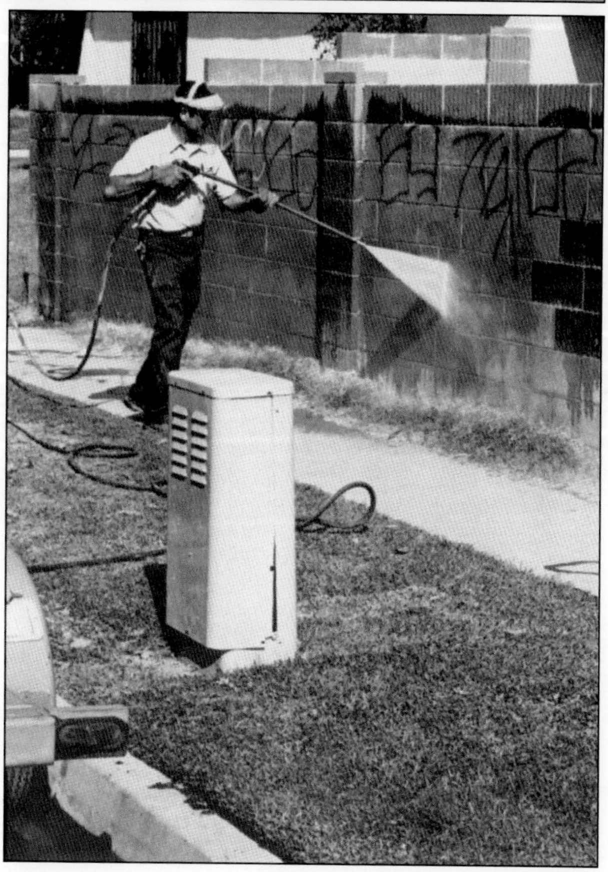

Painting over vandals' illegal signs, known by the city as "graffiti abatement," has been ongoing in Carson since 1982. Carson's graffiti hotline may be dialed by residents to have eyesores painted over. Despite frequent raids by "taggers," people who write graffiti, Carson has kept on top of the situation with strict enforcement.

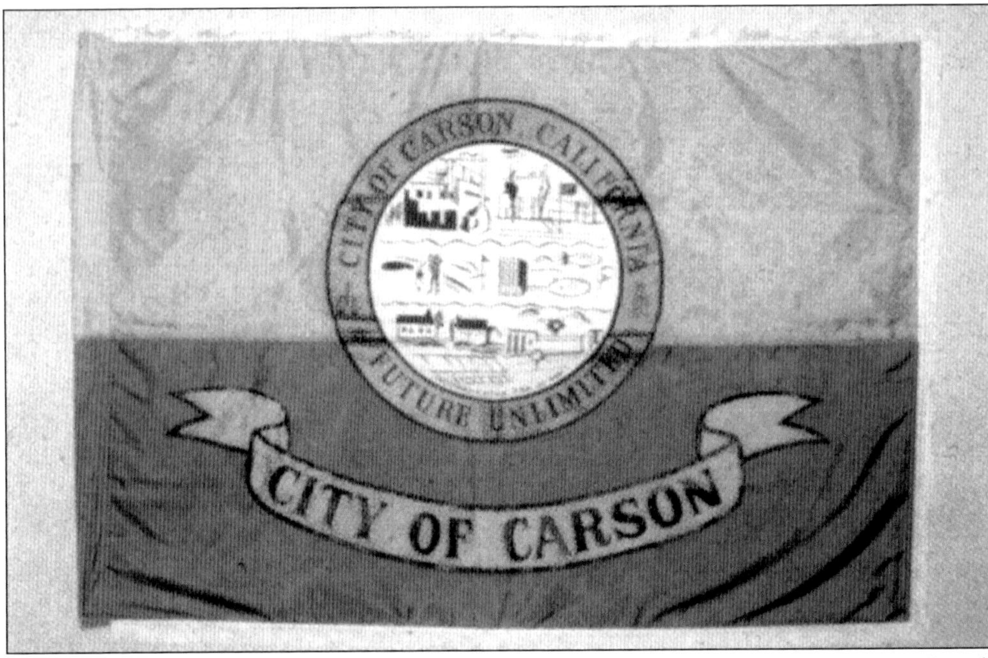

The City of Carson flies its own flag, which features iconic images such as the Dominguez Ranch adobe, the Goodyear blimp, and those representing golf and industry. The city seal was the work of local schoolchildren, submitted in a contest.

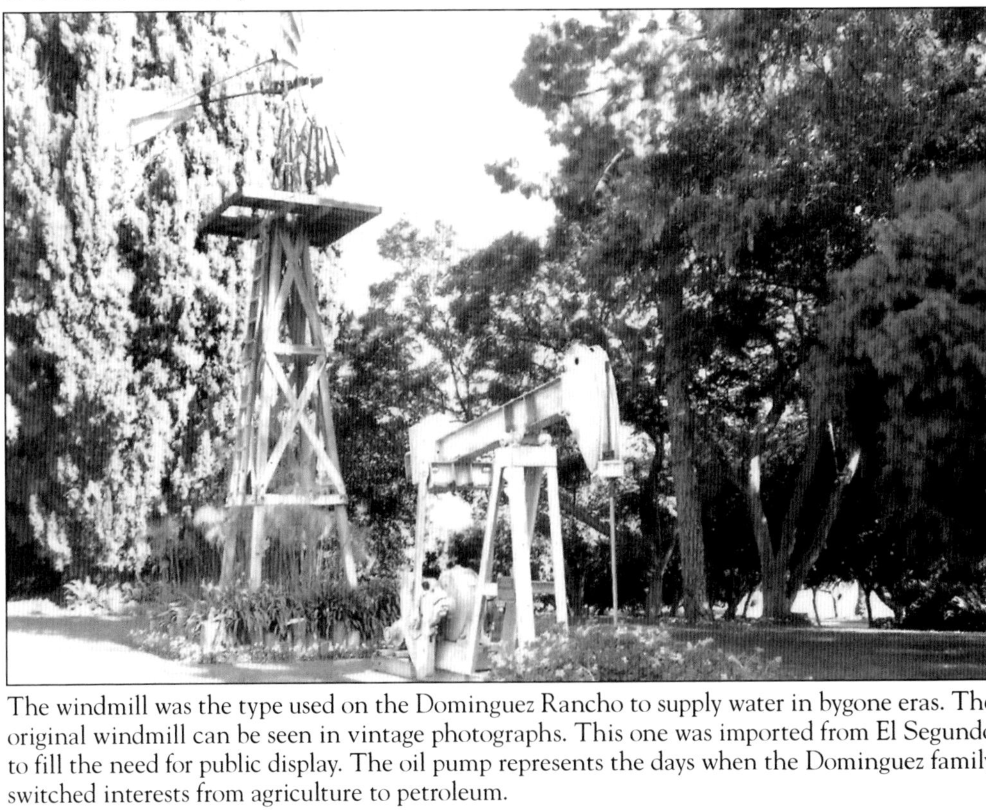

The windmill was the type used on the Dominguez Rancho to supply water in bygone eras. The original windmill can be seen in vintage photographs. This one was imported from El Segundo to fill the need for public display. The oil pump represents the days when the Dominguez family switched interests from agriculture to petroleum.

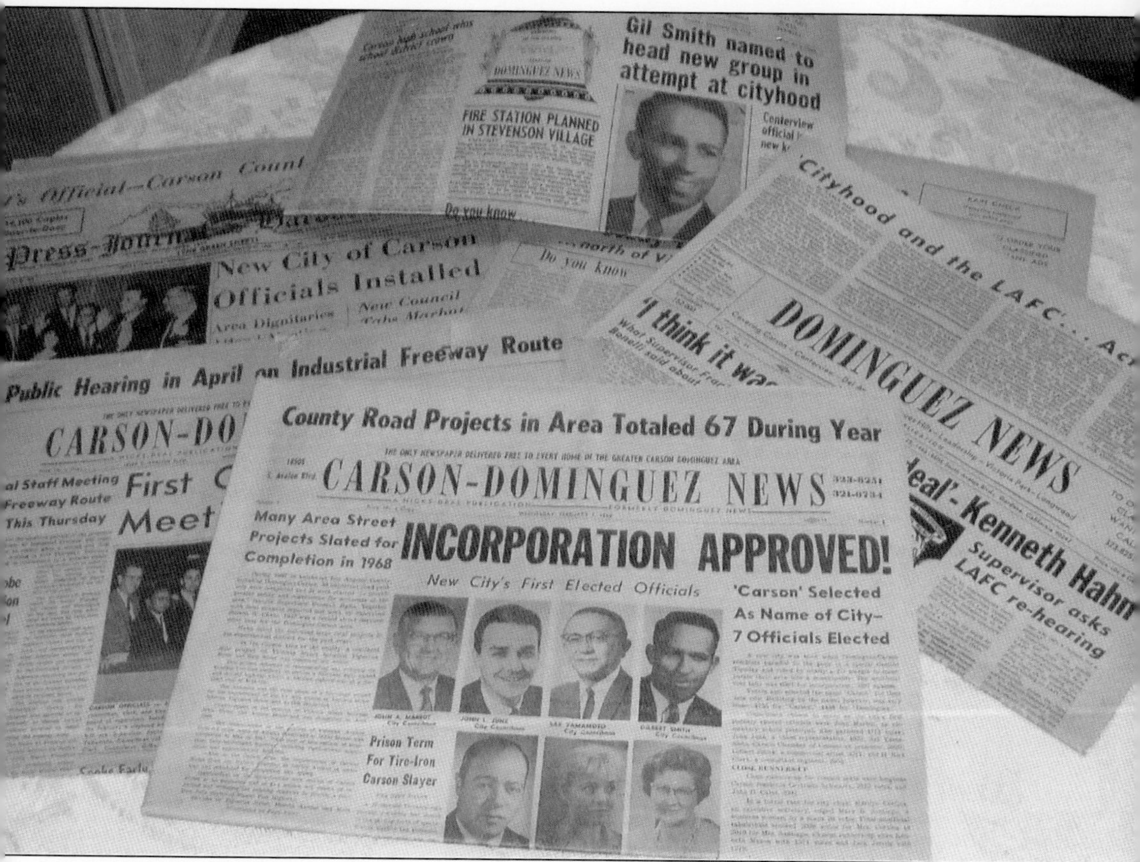

This collection of 1968 local newspapers discussed, debated, and finally heralded Carson's incorporation as a city.

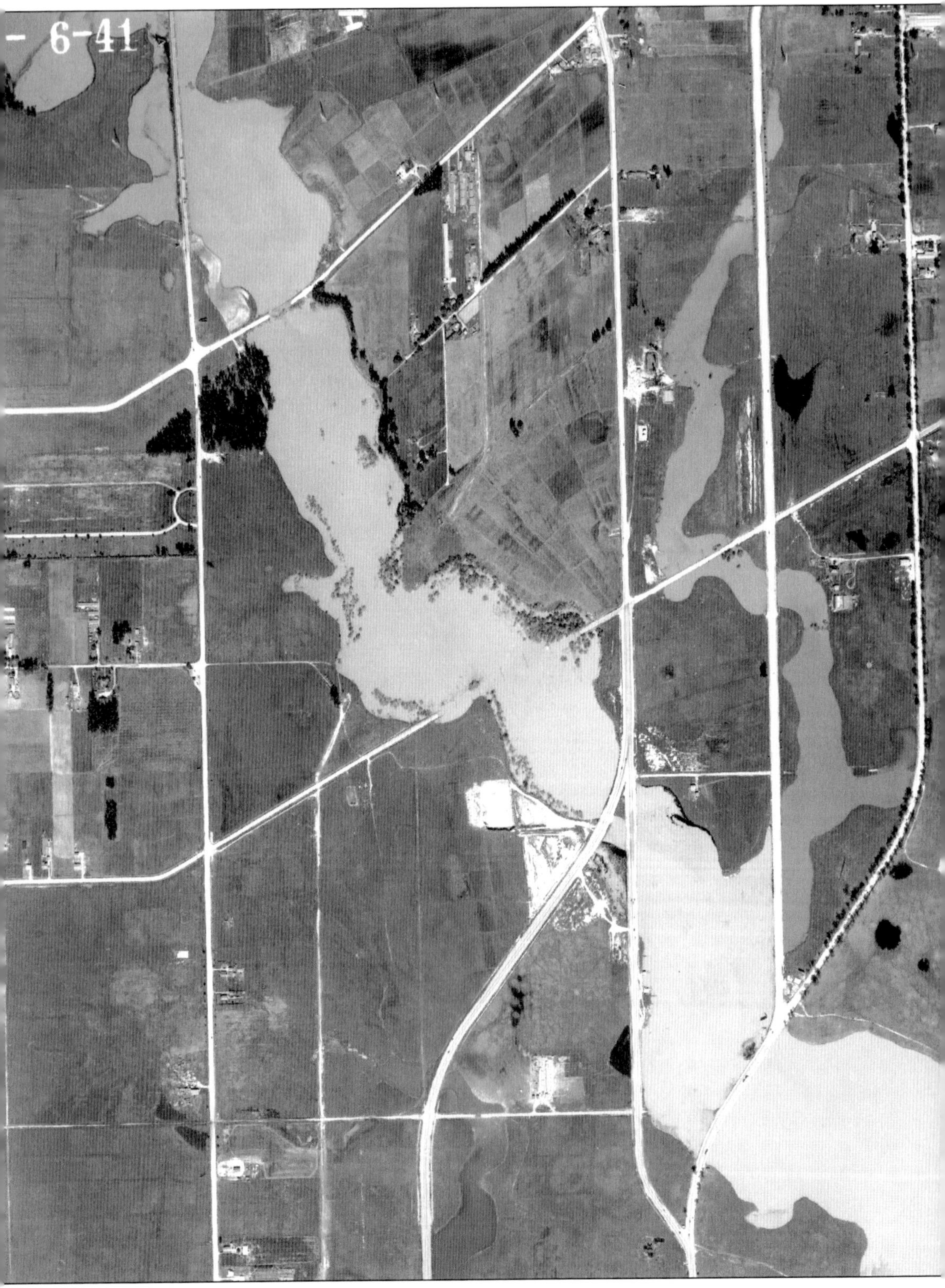
- 6-41

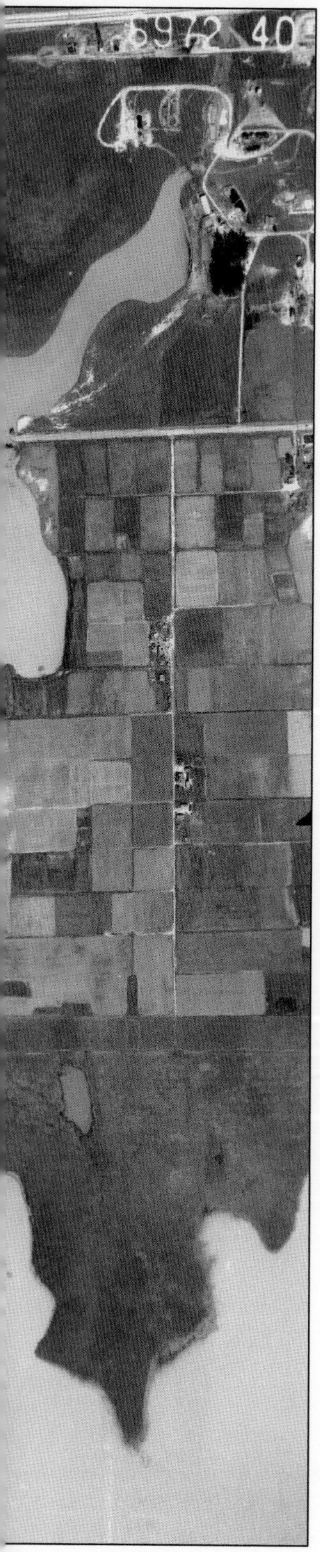

Flooding during winter rains was an annual hazard in many portions of Carson. Floods in 1914, 1916, and 1941 were particularly damaging. The 1941 edition, seen in this photograph of the Dominguez Slough, resulted in a 3,000-acre instant lake that extended from today's Goodyear airship site all the way to the Pacific Coast Highway. The Dominguez Channel was eventually built to control that sort of epic flooding. It crosses Avalon Boulevard diagonally at the South Bay Pavilion, otherwise known as the Carson Mall. The streets running north/south in the photograph are, from left to right, Vermont Avenue, Figueroa Street, Broadway, and Main Street that joins Broadway at the bottom of the photograph. The main east/west streets depicted are Albertoni, top, and Victoria Streets.

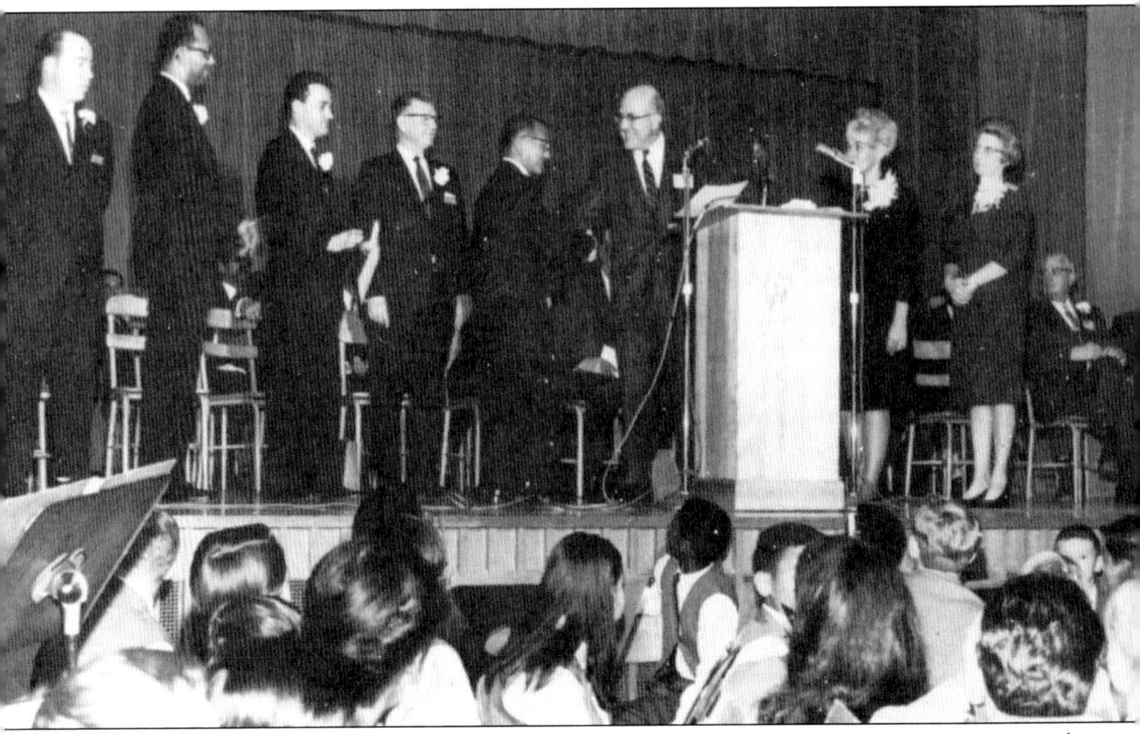

The defining moment in Carson's history as a city took place on February 20, 1968, in the Carson High School auditorium. Six hundred citizens gathered for the first city council meeting preceding incorporation. Here Los Angeles county clerk James Mize, at the podium, swears in the first Carson City Council at the inauguration ceremonies for the county's 77th city. The council, pictured from left to right, included H. Rick Clark, Gil Smith, John Junk, John Marbut, and Sak Yamamoto, newly appointed city clerk Marilyn Cortina, and city treasurer Dorothy Carter. Marbut was then selected as the first mayor.

BIBLIOGRAPHY

Cleland, Robert Glass. *Cattle on a Thousand Hills: Southern California, 1850–1880*. San Marino, CA: Huntington Library, 1941.

Decades '60s, '70s, '80s, '90s. Carson, CA: California State University, Dominguez Hills, 2000.

Deverell, William. *Whitewashed Adobe: The Rise of Los Angeles and the Remaking of Its Mexican Past*. Berkeley, CA: University of California Press, 2004.

Gillingham, Robert Cameron. *The Rancho San Pedro: The Story of a Famous Rancho in Los Angeles County and of Its Owners, the Dominguez Family*. San Pedro, CA: Museum Reproductions, 1983.

Grenier, Judson A., and Robert Cameron Gillingham. *California Legacy: The Jason Alexander Watson-Maria Dolores Dominguez De Watson Family, 1820–1980*. Los Angeles: Watson Land Company, 1987.

Hatfield, David D. *The Dominguez Air Meet*. Inglewood, CA: Northrup University Press, 1976.

Jerrills, Jack E. *History of a City . . . Carson*. Carson, CA: Jack E. Jerrills. 1972.

Mason, William. W. *Early Dominguez Families and Settlements of the Rancho San Pedro*. Carson, CA: California State University, Dominguez Hills, 1991.

Trejos, Charlotte M. My *Carson, Your Carson: A Picture Book of the Past and the Present*. Carson, CA: Trejos Literary Agency, 1987.

The Quality of Life: City of Carson Six Year Progress Report: Future Unlimited. Carson, CA: City of Carson Public Information Division, 1974.

Storied Past of the Rancho San Pedro. Carson, CA: Dominguez Estate Company, 1955.

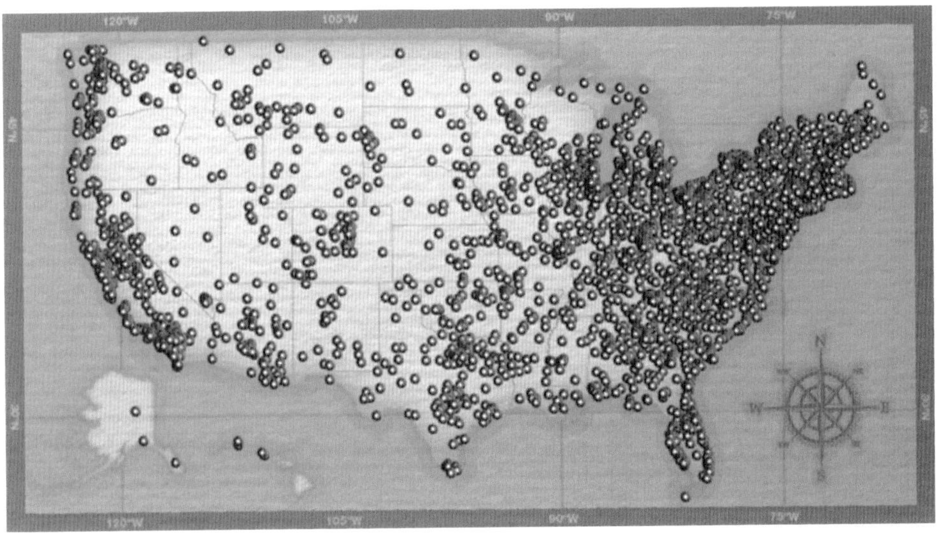

Consistent with our mission to preserve history on a local level, this book was printed in South Carolina on American-made paper and manufactured entirely in the United States. Products carrying the accredited Forest Stewardship Council (FSC) label are printed on 100 percent FSC-certified paper.

MADE IN THE USA